BIOTERRORISM
Threat of Massive Global Destruction

BIOTERRORISM
Threat of Massive Global Destruction

R C Mishra

AUTHORSPRESS
under the auspices of
International Institute of Bioinformatic Studies

Worldwide Circulation through Authorspress Global Network
First Published 2002
by Authorspress

E-35/103, Jawahar Park,
Laxmi Nagar, Delhi-110 092

e-mail: authorspress@yahoo.com
quantum_soul@mantramail.com

Typeset in NewCenturySchlbk by Chitra Computers

Bioterrorism: Threat of Massive Global Destruction
ISBN 81-7273-107-8

Printed in India at Tarun Offset Press, Delhi.

Preface

We are living in the age of the Big Biology. Biological sciences such as gene engineering, genetics, molecular biology and genomics promise to resolve problems that have plagued humankind for centuries, from the provision of enough food to the treatment of fatal diseases. But the achievements of biology can be used to protect life (vaccines and medicines) or to create new dangerous substances that can be used as biological weapons. Terrorists could sow unprecedented devastation by unleashing biological warfare agents. Many bacteria, fungi, viruses, rickettsial agents and toxins are used as bioweapons. Those mentioned most often include *Bacillus anthracis* (anthrax), *Yersinia pestis* (plague), Q fever, Tularemia, Smallpox, Botulinum toxin, Saxitoxin, Aflatoxin, Ricin, Staphylococcal enterotoxin B (SEB) *Venezuelan equine encephalitis* virus (VEE), hemorrhagic fevers and so on.

The potential of biological weapons to cause death and suffering is similar to that of nuclear weapons. A bioweapons attack could, like nuclear attack, push a nation beyond the "point of non-recovery." Reaction to a bioweapons attack could conceivably generate sufficient fear and urgency to threaten fundamental democratic principles and even confidence in government. Concern regarding the use of biological agents as tools of warfare or terrorism has led to measures to deter their use or, failing that, to deal with the consequences. Unlike chemical agents, which typically lead to violent disease syndromes within minutes at the site of exposure, diseases resulting from biological agents have incubation periods of days. Therefore, rather than a paramedic, it will likely be a physician who is first faced with evidence of the results of a biological attack.

The stressors associated with a biological terrorist attack could create high numbers of acute and potentially chronic psychiatric casualties who must be recognised, diagnosed, and treated to facilitate triage and medical care. Media communications, planning for quarantine and decontamination, and the role of community leaders are important to the mitigation of psychological consequences. Physicians will need to accurately diagnose anxiety, depression, bereavement, and organic brain syndromes to provide treatment, reassurance, and the relief of pain.

The Biological and Toxin Weapons Convention (BWC), which prohibits the acquisition of biological materials for hostile purposes and armed conflict, entered into force in 1975 and now has the participation of almost 140 nations. Yet international diplomatic efforts have not been entirely effective in preventing the enhancement and proliferation of offensive biological warfare programmes. The threats posed by biological weapons are likely to continue into the future. It is clear that we should revive the system of protection against them so as to quickly determine what agent was used, correctly diagnose the disease and provide proper treatment. We need a system of global protection. We should launch programmes of fundamental and applied research.

This book is a comprehensive attempt to provide authoritative information on bioterrorism—the threat of massive global destruction—that the contemporary world faces. It provides an indepth understanding of biological weapons, its past, present and future directions. It also deals with practical, scientific, precautionary methods to confront the escalated threat of bioterrorism. It will be a highly beneficial reference tool for all those concerned to live together.

R C Mishra

Contents

1
Introduction

Modern technologies that add efficiency, power and wonder to our lives inevitably deliver the same benefits to evildoers. Biotechnology is one among them, which holds the promise of a great future but like any other technological breakthrough, it is a double-edged sword. It could be panacea for eliminating hunger and disease from the globe but the same tools can be used in a deadly manner against mankind. The coming age of biotech will undoubtedly make programmable bacteria and viruses more accessible—to doctors, business and bioterrorists.

People all over the world are worried more about biological arms than about nuclear or chemical ones. Unlike either of the other two, biological weapons combine maximum destruction and easy availability. Nuclear arms have great killing capacity but are hard to get; chemical weapons are easy to get but lack such killing capacity; biological agents have both qualities.

A 1993 study by the Office of Technology Assessment of the US concluded that a single airplane delivering 100 kilograms of anthrax spores—a dormant phase of a bacillus that multiples rapidly in the body, producing toxins and rapid haemorrhaging—by aerosol on a clear, calm night over the Washington DC area could kill between one million and three million people, 300 times as many fatalities as if the plane had delivered sarin gas in inanities ten times larger.

The following are found to the major potential weapons of mass destruction in bioweapon category:

i) *Anthrax*: A staple of bioweapons arsenals for decades, the bacterium *Bacillus anthracis* might be engineered to resist antibiotics.

ii) *Plague*: In an famous episode in World War II, the Japanese army unleashed fleas infected with the *Yersinia pestic bacterium* on Chinese forces in Manchuria. The attack backfired, inflicting heavy tolls on both sides.

iii) *Q fever*: This disease is transmitted by the highly-infectious and heat-resistant *Coxiella burnetii rickettsia.* Not usually fatal, Q fever could be used primarily as an incapacitant.

iv) *Tularemia*: One of the most infectious bacteria, *Francisella tularensis* would kill one out of five people in a hypothetical scenario in which 50 kilogrammes of the weaponised agent were released 2 km upwind from a city.

v) *Smallpox*: Eradicated from the wild in 1980, *Variola major* is known to exist in only two restricted laboratories in Russia, and the United States.

vi) *Aflatoxin*: US intelligence reports in 1898 suggested, that Iraq was attempting to weaponise aflatoxin, a protein produced by a mould that grows on peanuts and other crops. Aflatoxin is highly toxic for human beings.

vii) *Ebola-influenza hybrid*: A flu strain equipped with the haemorrhagic proteins of *Ebola*, presumably still a fantasy, would be a fearsome weapon.

viii) *Botulinum toxin*: The most poisonous substance known, a single gram of this crystalline toxin from the *bacterium clostridium botulinum*, evenly dispersed and inhaled, would kill more than one million people.

ix) *Ricin*: In 1978, Soviet agents used ricin, a lethal toxin extracted from the castor bean, to murder Bulgarian defector Georgi Markov in London.

x) *RNAi*: Double-standard interference-RNA might be tailored to latch onto specific messenger RNA sequences, thus virtually silencing any gene.

xi) *Saxitoxin*: Eating shellfish contaminated by this alkaloid neurotoxin, produced by dinoflagellates, can lead to paralysis and death.

xii) *Substance P*: An aerosolised version of this neurotransmitter could be far more toxic than the potent chemical weapons sarin and VX.

Innovations in biotechnology have obviated many of the old problems in handling and preserving biological agents, and many have been freely available for scientific research. Terrorists are really proving to be great innovators. They require huge investments and targetable infrastructure, and are subject to credible threats. An aggrieved, decides to kill huge numbers of people will find the mission easier to accomplish with anthrax than with a nuclear explosion.

Although biological agents have been used in warfare for centuries, several events in the past decade have raised concerns that they could be used for terrorism. Revelations about the sophisticated biological-weapons programmes of the former Soviet Union and Iraq have heightened concerns that countries with offensive-research programmes, including those that sponsor international terrorism, might assist in the proliferation of agents, culturing capability and dissemination techniques, and might benefit in these undertakings from the availability of skilled laboratory technicians.

Chemical weapons were noticed more in the past decade, especially since they were used by Iraq against Iranian troops in the 1980-1988 Iran-Iraq war and against Kurdish civilians in 1988. Chemicals are far more widely available than nuclear weapons because the technology required to produce them is simpler, and large numbers of countries have undertaken chemical weapons programmes. But chemical weapons are not really in the same class as other weapons of mass destruction, in the sense of ability to inflict a huge number of civilian casualties in a single strike. The ballistic missile defence system will roughly cost about $60 billions.

Release of sarin nerve agent in Tokyo subway system in 1995 by the Aum Shinrikyo cult demonstrated that in the future terrorists might select unconventional weapons. Certain properties of biological pathogens may make them the ideal terrorist weapons, including (i) ease of procurement, (ii) ease of dissemination with low technology, and (iii) potential to overwhelm the medical system with large numbers of casualties.

Dissemination of a biological agent would be silent, and the incubation period allows a perpetrator to escape to great distances from the area of release before the first ill persons seek medical care. Countermeasures include intelligence gathering, physical protection, and detection systems. Medical countermeasures include laboratory diagnostics, vaccines, and mediations for prophylaxis and treatment. Public health, medical and environmental health personnel need to have a heightened awareness through education about the threat from biological agents.

The intentional use of biological pathogens to kill or incapacitate one's enemies has occurred sporadically for centuries. One of the earliest documented cases occurred at the Crimean port city of Kaffa in 1856. Besieging Tatar armies were striken with bubonic plague and decided to turn this unfortunate incident to their advantage by catapulting plague-ridden corpses into the city. Genoese defenders within the city walls subsequently contracted plague and fled to Italy, thus, carrying the disease to Europe. The resulting epidemics culminated in what we now know as the 'Black Death', which wiped out nearly one-third of the European populations in the Middle Ages. Until recently, concern over biological weapons focused mainly on their use by an adversary on the battlefield. Several events, however, have heightened concerns that these agents could be employed by terrorists.

As many as 18 countries currently are suspected of having biological-weapons research and development programmes. Of the seven countries listed by the state department as sponsors of international terrorism, at least five are known or suspected to have bioweapons programmes. Most notably, before the Gulf War, intelligence sources suspected that Iraq is admitted to having weaponised anthrax, botulinum toxin, and aflatoxin. With Iraqi officials grudgingly cooperating from 1991 to 1995, the United Nations Special Commission (UNSCOM) team found loads of circumstantial evidence—facilities with a high capacity for fermentation inconsistent with peaceful purposes as well as irreconcilable records—all pointing to a broad, clandestine programme aimed at "weaponising" bacteria, viruses, and toxins.

In 1992 the then Russian President Boris Yeltsin admitted that the Soviet had run this vast enterprise called Biopreparat. It establishes the point that the Soviets had clearly ignored the ban on offensive weapons in the Biological and Toxin Biological Weapons Convention (BWC), which the Soviets had ratified two decades earlier. Revolutions by defectors from the biological weapons programme of the former Soviet Union revealed the massive extent of that programme, including the industrial capacity to produce tons of biological agents, such as anthrax and smallpox each year. The Soviets used the signing of the Biological Weapons Convention in 1972 as a launching point for accelerating their programme. Moreover, they also saw the global eradication of smallpox and the subsequent discontinuation of vaccination against the disease as an opportunity to exploit smallpox as a weapon. Since the break-up of the Soviet Union, there has been concern that many of the scientists put out of work by the deteriorating economies of former Soviet States could take their expertise to a country developing biological warfare programmes.

There are several reasons for why terrorist organisations are using bioagents. First, the agents themselves are relatively easy to procure. Organisms such as *Clostridium botulinum*, *Bacillus anthraces*, *Yersinia pestis*, etc., could be collected from areas around the globe where the diseases are endemic—either from the soil or from diseased animals. Moreover, humorous legitimate laboratory supply houses around the world sell many agents that might be adapted for use as weapons. A terrorist conceivably could obtain pathogens by illegitimate means from these supply houses or from research laboratories. To produce biological weapons, one might employ the same fermentation technology that is commonly used in the production of legitimate products such as antibiotics, vaccines, wine and beer. This circumstance makes biological weapons production relatively easy to conceal and makes compliance with existing weapons conventions difficult to verify.

Many of the biological pathogens can have great downwind spread and high morbidity and mortality. To disseminate such agents as aerosols, a terrorist could fairly easily modify common spray devices, such as those used in the agriculture industry, to produce particles in the proper size for infecting humans. An important feature distinguishing bioweapons from other weapons is the incubation period characteristic of each biological agent. This period ranges from hours to weeks, but is generally on the order of days. A perpetrator could thus release an agent and be out of the country by the time the effects are recognised.

There are three general routes by which bioweapons may produce infection:

i) cutaneous,
ii) oral, and
iii) inhalation.

An intact skin provides an impermeable barrier to most biological weapons, with the exception of T2 mycotoxins. Therefore, to infect someone, a microorganism must enter through a break in the skin. This is what happened in 1978, when Bulgarian exile and BBC announcer Georgi Markov was assassinated by the Bulgarian secret service in London. A spring-loaded device was placed inside an umbrella, which injected a tiny metal pellet into Markov's leg. The pellet was through-bored, filled with ricin, and sealed with wax. The ricin, a toxin derived from the common castor bean, then leaked out of the pellet as the wax melted at body temperature.

A second route of infection involves oral intake of contaminated food or water. This route was demonstrated in 1984 when the Rajneesh cult inflected local salad bars in Dalles, Oregon, with *Salmonella typhimurium* in an attempt to influence the outcome of local elections. At least 751 cases of salmonelloisis resulted. Today, our society is perhaps more vulnerable to such foodborne contamination because more of our food sources are centralised. If an agent is used to successfully contaminate food at a central production or processing facility, persons across the country could be affected. Fortunately, it would be rather difficult to contaminate a large reservoir successfully with biological weapons for several reasons. First the dilution effect of a large reservoir would require that extremely large quantities of agent be used, which would be beyond the scope of a less-sophisticated terrorist and would make detection of the perpetrator at the time of attempted containation easier. Second, common disinfection with chlorination and filtering would render many—although not all—agents ineffective.

The third possible route of exposure is through inhalation. This route has the greatest potential to cause mass casualties. For exposure to occur through inhalation, inhaled particles must circumvent the respiratory muco-ciliary apparatus. Practices in the range of one to five micrometres (mum) are best able to do this. Particles greater than five to 10 mum would be captured and expelled by the muco-ciliary apparatus, and particles of less than one mum would likely be inhaled and subsequently exhaled.

The numerous smaller-scale biocrimes add to the fascination of criminal elements with biological weapons. Unfortunately, use, threat of use, interest in use, interest in acquisition, and actual acquisition have all increased notably during the decade of the 1990s. Several factors likely account for this, including the widespread knowledge provided in lay publication and on the internet, and the attention that this issue has garnered in the media. Although most cases of use have involved small-scale biocrimes, the ability clearly exists to acquire and produce these agents.

There are, after all, risks not only in underestimating the chemical and biological terrorist threat, but in overestimating it as well; so far, such downside risks have received scant attention. The most prominent of these include:

i) Raising public consciousness about the possible threat in a manner that emboldens and empowers criminals and terrorists to attempt precisely what the government and public want to avoid.

ii) Reassuring the public about the preparedness of government such that any government shortcoming is likely to be magnified to politically fatal levels.

iii) Pre-emptively undermining significant civil liberties in the name of enhanced homeland defence by encouraging over-reaction on the part of law enforcement agencies

iv) Expanding the role of the military into the realms of law enforcement by making the response to chemical and biological attacks a core military mission.

v) Distracting the military from chemical, biological, and conventional threats to country bases and embassies overseas.

Ultimately, the downside risks listed are at least as likely as the biological and chemical terrorism threats that might generate them. Either set of threats, if realised, could jeopardise our way of life. If we are serious about one, then we need to be serious about the other. Part of the difficulty in balancing these concerns is that it is easier to speculate on what terrorists may be able to do and design a programme to mitigate such threats than it is to know when and why to stop speculating and designing. Focusing on two broad considerations, however, should help. The first of these is determining just how practical current chemical and biological agents are for military and terrorists use. The second is identifying what defensive strengths the country can exploit to mitigate these threats.

The technical challenges of terrorists using traditional biological agents to produce massive fatalities are no less daunting. Effectively disseminating these agents is particularly difficult since traditional agents are lethal only if inhaled, and particles larger than 10 microns are likely to be blocked before they reach the lungs. On the other hand, agent particles approaching one micron are likely to be exhaled and so will not remain in the lungs. Operationally, particles sized between five and 10 microns are optional.

Spreading biological agent in particles of that precise size, however, is difficult. Indeed, the Federal Bureau of Investigation has yet to find a terror organisation that has built an effective mass-casualty biological agent delivery system. The only organisations that have done so are states. But dispersal of correctly sized biological particles still does not guarantee an effective attack. Sunlight kills or denatures most biological agents, and wind patterns and humidity matter. An anthrax attack under optimal conditions, for example, would be at least a thousand times more lethal than one made during a sunny day in light winds.

For soldiers and terrorists alike, these facts have operational consequences. First, biological and chemical agents would be most attractive to desperate nations and military commanders anxious to threaten opposing expeditionary forces and their use of local ports or airfields, or to test an invading nation's political will to continue operations. Secondly, while traditional biological agents would be potentially most effective in killing enemy forces, their delayed effect would not be anywhere near as telling as chemical agents in disrupting ongoing military operations. Thirdly, given the volatility of many chemical agents and the uncertainties associated with biological agent dissemination and their delayed and varied inoculation periods, a military decision to use such agents would be complicated. At a minimum, it might turn as much on an assessment of these agents likely physical impact as their impact on the enemy's will to continue to fight or to escalate the conflict.

There are hundreds of bioagents who can cause disease in humans. For most of these agents, whose potential for large-scale infection or intoxication is limited, local care providers and health departments can deal adequately with the consequences of a small-scale natural, accidental, or intentional release. In USA working groups form the Johns Hopkins Centre for Civilian Biodefence and the Centres for Disease that might cause a maximum credible event and for which specific and intense planning are needed to handle the consequences of a release on a large population. Such agents include smallpox, anthrax, plague, tularemia, botulinum toxin, and viral hero-marragic fevers. Recent laws passed by US Congress impose criminal penalties for the possession, manufacture, or use of biological weapons and give law enforcement agencies the right to seize potential agents or delivery devices.

Intelligence agencies and law enforcement personnel are developing sophisticated systems to monitor potential terrorists and to learn what they might use, and when they might use it. In the case of an unannounced biological attack, the first sign of the attack would likely be ill individuals seeking care. Surveillance systems are being developed that will identify an event rapidly, thus allowing medical counter-measures to be instituted in a timely fashion. Depending on when information or identification of a bioterrorist incident occurs, health care providers and their public health counter-parts could institute measures ranging from prophylaxis to treatment. There are only two licensed vaccines against high-threat agents: the anthrax and smallpox vaccines. Pre-exposure vaccination against anthrax in an unannounced bioterrorism incident would be likely, but because of concerns that some spores may lie dormant in the lungs for extended periods after exposure, the treating physician might use the vaccine as part of a post-exposure prophylaxis regimen, along with antibiotics, for those not yet clinically ill. The vaccine smallpox could be used to halt the propagation of an outbreak. The current supply of both anthrax and smallpox vaccines, however, is limited.

Many bacterial diseases have licensed treatments, although one must be somewhat concerned than an organisation with the sophistication to deploy an agent effectively might also be capable of developing antibiotics-resistant strains. For viral agents, treatment is more problematic since no effective antivirus are licensed for treatment of bioterrorism threat agents. In the case of smallpox, if an attack were to occur today, the best prevention would be immediate vaccination and isolation of those exposed, although research into effective antivirus is ongoing. Ribavirin has been shown to increase survival rates in patents with Lassa fever and has shown promise in the treatment of the viral haemorrhage fevers.

Physical protection affords an additional countermeasure. The gas masks provided by the military are effective against both chemical and biological agents. A HEPA-filtered mask would be expected to be effective in a biological weapon attack if one has no other means of protection. Unlike chemical agents, most biological agents can be effectively removed from human skin with soap and water. Therefore, there is no need, except, perhaps, in the case of highly contaminated individuals, to use bleach or other decontaminating agents. Also, by the time the incubation period has passed and the victims become ill, they may have changed and bathed, making decontamination of little utility.

Biological agents are non-volatile and relatively difficult to re-aerosols, so even without specific decontamination secondary exposure would be unlikely. This is in contrast to the circumstances associated with chemical agents, in which victims generally present immediately after an attack and may still have volatile agent on their bodies or clothes, putting the care provider and hospital environment at risk of contamination of secondary exposure. With biological agents, detection is more difficult than with chemical agents.

Various organisations are currently developing technologies to improve the speed and accuracy of methods for detecting and diagnosing biological agents. Several different response teams are being fielded or planned. In the case of a large-scale event, it is planned that civil personnel would have the lead role in mitigating the consequences with the military providing support when requested.

It is important for health care providers to become more aware of the threat of bioterrorism and how they will manage should a release occur. Education is one of the cornerstones of our defence. Through different forums and programmes against biological weapons, and military and non-military educational efforts, health care agencies can provide heightened awareness among the mass.

2

Historical Background of Biological Warfare

While turning the pages of history, we can regrettably realise that human race has always used all available technologies for destructive as well as for beneficial purposes. The modern development of biological agents as weapons has paralleled advances in basic and applied microbiology. These include the identification of virulent pathogens suitable for aerosol delivery and industrial-scale fermentation processes to produce large quantities of pathogens and toxins.

The history of biological warfare is difficult to assess because of a number of confounding factors. These include difficulties in verification of alleged or attempted biological attacks, the use of allegations of biological attacks for propaganda purposes, the paucity of pertinent microbiological or epidemiologic data, and the incidence of naturally occurring endemic or epidemic diseases during hostilities.

Biological warfare has evolved from the crude use of cadavers to contaminate water supplies to the development of specialised munitions for battlefield and covert use. Recognition of the potential impact of infectious diseases on armies resulted in the crudeuse of filth, cadavers, animal carcasses, and contagion as weapons. These have been used to contaminate wells, reservoirs, and other water sources of armies and civilian populations under attack since antiquity, through the Napoleonic era, and into the twentieth century.

Modern attempts to weaponise biological toxins such as botulinum and ricin were anticipated by the use of curare and amphibian-derived toxins as arrow poisons by aboriginal South Americans using neolithic technology. Fomites have been used to deliberately transmit infectious diseases since antiquity. The use of fomites directly against humans has continued, as evidenced by the smearing of pungi sticks with excrement by the Viet Cong in the early 1960s. One of the earliest recorded attempts of using fomites against a population illustrates the complex epidemiologic issues raised by biological warfare.

During the 14th century siege of Kaffa, the attacking Tatar force experienced an epidemic of plague. The Tatars attempted to convert their misfortune into an opportunity by catapulting the cadavers of their deceased into the city to initiate a plague epidemic. An outbreak of plague was followed by the retreat of defending forces and the conquest of Kaffa. Ships carrying plague-infected refugees (and possibly rats) sailed to Constantinople, Genoa, Venice, and other Mediterranean ports and are thought to have contributed to the second plague pandemic. However, given the complex ecology and epidemiology of plague, it may be an oversimplification to implicate the biological attack as the sole cause of the plague epidemic in Kaffa. Plague may have been imported into Kaffa by a natural cycle involving sylvatic and urban rodents and their fleas, and the population under siege may have been at increased risk of epidemics because of deteriorating sanitation and hygiene.

In the eighteenth century, during the French and Indian War, Sir Jeffrey Amherst, commander of British forces in North America, suggested the deliberate use of smallpox to "reduce" Native American tribes hostile to the British. An outbreak of smallpox at Fort Pitt resulted in the generation of fomites and an opportunity to execute Amherst's plan. On June 24, 1763, Captain Ecuyer, one of Amherst's subordinates, gave blankets and a handkerchief from the smallpox hospital to the Native Americans and recorded in his journal, "I hope it will have the desired effect." While this adaptation of the Trojan horse ruse was followed by epidemic smallpox among Native American tribes in the Ohio River valley, other contacts between colonists and Native Americans may have contributed to these epidemics. Smallpox epidemics among immunologically naive tribes of Native Americans following initial contacts with Europeans had been occurring for more than 200 years.

The 19th century witnessed the development of modern microbiology with the formulation of Koch's postulates and afforded the capability to isolate and produce stocks of specific pathogens. Substantial evidence suggests that Germany developed an ambitious biological warfare programme during World War I, featuring covert operations in neutral trading partners of the Allies to infect livestock and contaminate animal feed to be exported to the Allied forces. *Bacillus anthracis* and *Burkholderia (Pseudomonas) mallei*, the etiologic agents of anthrax and glanders, were to be used to infect Romanian sheep for export to Russia.

Cultures confiscated from the German Legation in Romania in 1916 were identified as *B. anthracis* and *B. mallei* at the Bucharest Institute of Bacteriology and Pathology. *Burkholderia mallei* was allegedly used by German saboteurs operating in Mesopotamia to inoculate 4,500 mules and in Franceto infect horses of the French cavalry. Argentinian livestock intended for export to Allied forces were infected with *B. anthracis* and *B. mallei*, resulting in the deaths of more than 200 mules from 1917 to 1918.

Operations in the United States included attempts to contaminate animal feed and to infect horses intended for export during World War I. In response to the horror of chemical warfare during World War I, international diplomatic efforts were directed toward limiting the proliferation and use of weapons of mass destruction. The first diplomatic attempt at limiting biological warfare was the 1925 Geneva Protocol for the Prohibition of the Use in War of Asphyxiating, Poisonous or Other Gases, and of Bacteriological Methods of Warfare. This treaty prohibited the use of biological weapons.

However, the treaty did not proscribe basic research, production, or possession of biological weapons, and many countries ratified the protocol while stipulating a right of retaliation. There were no provisions for inspection. Parties to the Geneva Protocol that began basic research programmes to develop biological weapons after World War I included Belgium, Canada, France, Great Britain, Italy, the Netherlands, Poland, and the Soviet Union. The United States did not ratify the Geneva Protocol until 1975.

Japan conducted biological weapons research in occupied Manchuria from 1932 until the end of World War II under the direction of Shiro Ishii and Kitano Misaji. Unit 731, a biological warfare research facility located near the town of Pingfan, was the centre of the Japanese biological weapons development programme and contained 150 buildings, five satellite camps, and a staff of more than 3,000 scientists and technicians. Additional units were located at Mukden, Changchun, and Nanking. Prisoners were infected with pathogens including *B. anthraces*, *Neisseria meningitidis*, *Shigella spp*, *Vibrio cholerae*, and *Yersinia pestis*. At least 10,000 prisoners died as a result of experimental infection or execution following experimentation during the Japanese programme between 1932 and 1945. As many as 15 million fleas were released per attack to initiate epidemics of plague.

Participants in the Japanese programme who had been captured by the Soviet Union during World War II admitted to 12 large-scale field trials of biological weapons in testimony obtained during war crimes prosecution. At least 11 Chinese cities were attacked with biological agents. Attacks featured contaminating water supplies and food items with pure cultures of *B. anthracis*, *V. cholerae*, *Shigella spp*, *Salmonella spp*, and *Y. pestis*. Cultures were also tossed directly into homes and sprayed from aircraft.

Plague was allegedly developed as a biological weapon by allowing laboratory-bred fleas to feed on plague-infected rats. These potentially infected fleas were then harvested and released from aircraft over Chinese cities. As many as 15 million fleas were released per attack to initiate epidemics of plague. Dr P.Z. King, Director General of the Chinese National Health Administration, attributed epidemic plague to these attacks; however, rigorous epidemiologic and bacteriologic data are not available.

The Japanese had not adequately prepared, trained, or equipped their own troops for the hazards of biological weapons. An attack on Changteh in 1941 reportedly led to approximately 10,000 biological casualties and 1,700 deaths among Japanese troops, with most cases due to cholera.

In Germany, with the support of high-ranking Nazi party officials, scientists began biological weapons research, although their results lagged far behind those of other countries. A German offensive biological weapons threat never materialised. Prisoners in Nazi concentration camps were forcibly infected with *Rickettsia prowazekii*, *Rickettsia mooseri*, *Hepatitis A virus*, and *Plasmodia spp* and treated with investigational vaccines and drugs. These inhumane experiments were done to study pathogenesis, to develop vaccines against *Rickettsiae*, and to develop sulphonamides rather than to develop biological weapons.

The only known German tactical use of biological warfare was the pollution of a large reservoir in north-western Bohemia with sewage in May 1945. Ironically, the combination of a vaccine and a serologic test was used as a biological defence against the Nazis. The German army avoided areas with epidemic typhus by using the Weil-Felix reaction for diagnosis. Consequently, physicians used Proteus OX-19 as a vaccine to induce biological false-positive tests for typhus in an area of occupied Poland, and residents were protected from deportation to concentration camps. The Allies developed biological weapons for potential retaliatory use in response to German biological attack. Bomb experiments of weaponised spores of *B. anthracis* were conducted on Gruinard Island near the coast of Scotland and resulted in heavy contamination.

The offensive biological programme of United States began in 1942 under the direction of a civilian agency, the War Reserve Service. The programme included a research and development facility at Camp Detrick, Md, testing sites in Mississippi and Utah, and a production facility in Terre Haute, Ind. Experiments were conducted using pathogens, including *B. anthracis* and *B. rucellasuis*. However, the production facility lacked adequate engineering safety measures. These findings precluded large-scale production of biological weapons during World War II, although 5,000 bombs filled with *Banthracis* spores were produced at a pilot plant at Camp Detrick. After the war, the production facility was leased and converted to commercial pharmaceutical production. Basic research and development activities were continued at Camp Detrick. Ishii, Misaji, and other Japanese scientists in American custody who had participated in the Unit 731 programme were granted immunity from war crimes prosecution on the condition that they would disclose information obtained during their programme.

During the Korean War, the programme was expanded and a new production facility incorporating adequate biosafety measures was constructed at Pine Bluff, Ark. Technical advances allowed large-scale fermentation, concentration, storage, and weaponisation of microorganisms; production was begun in 1954. In addition, a programme to develop countermeasures, including vaccines, antisera, and therapeutic agents to protect troops from possible biological attack, was begun in 1953. Animal studies were performed at Fort Detrick, at remote desert sites, and on barges in the Pacific Ocean. Human experimentation using military and civilian volunteers was initiated in 1955. Biological munitions were detonated inside a one million litre, hollow, metallic, spherical aerosolisation chamber at Fort Detrick known as the "eight ball". Volunteers inside the chamber were exposed to *Francisella tularensis* and *Coxiella burnetii*. These and other challenge studies were done to determine vulnerability to aerosolised pathogens and the efficacy of vaccines, prophylaxis, and therapies under development.

Additional studies were done using simulants. *Aspergillus fumigatus*, *B. subtilis var globigii*, and *Serratia marcescens* were selected for use as simulants; these organisms were thought to be non-pathogenic and were used to study production and storage techniques as well as aerosolisation methods, the behaviour of aerosols over large geographic areas, and the effects of solar irradiation and climatic conditions on the viability of aerosolised organisms.

Cities were surreptitiously used as laboratories to test aerosolisation and dispersal methods when simulants were released during covert experiments in New York City, San Francisco, and other sites between 1949 and 1968. Concerns regarding potential public health hazards of simulant studies were raised after an outbreak of urinary tract infections caused by nosocomial *S. marcescens* occurred at Stanford University Hospital between September 1950 and February 1951. The outbreak followed covert experiments using *S. marcescens* as a simulant in San Francisco. The outbreak involved 11 cases, resulting in one transient bacteremia and one death from endocarditis. All patients had undergone urinary tract catheterisation, and five had undergone cystoscopy for urologic indications.

Exposure to multiple antibiotics was cited as a contributing factor to the outbreak. No similar outbreaks were reported by other hospitals in the San Francisco area. This outbreak is thought to represent an early example of nosocomial epidemics caused by opportunists of low virulence, related to antibiotic use, new medical devices, and surgical procedures. In view of the temporal relationship of the outbreak with the simulant studies, the army convened an investigative panel in 1952, including members from the Communicable Disease Centre, the National Institutes of Health, the City of New York Health Department, and Ohio State University. The panel did not comment directly on the possible association of the nosocomial outbreak and the simulant studies. The panel recommended continued use of *S. marcescens* in view of its low virulence, but added that a search for better simulants to replace *S. marcescens* should be pursued.

However, simulant studies using *S. marcescens* continued until 1968. Public interest in these covert experiments was aroused in 1976 when *Washington Post* reported them and implied that the endocarditis death was a direct result of the simulant testing. It was further implied that sudden increases in the incidence of pneumonia in Calhoun County, Alabama, and Key West, Fla, were related to simulant studies at those locales.

As a result of the ensuing public outcry, Senate hearings were held in 1977, and the army was severely criticised for the continued use of *S. marcescens* following awareness of the Stanford outbreak. None the less, several facts cast doubt on an etiologic relationship between military use of *S. marcescens* and outbreaks of human disease. The Centres for Disease Control reported that in 100 outbreaks of *S. marcescens* infection, none was caused by the 8UK strain used by the army.

Numerous reports during the 1970s postulated a link between the army experiments and cases of *S. marcescens* endocarditis, septic arthritis, and osteomyelitis in California heroin addicts; where strains were available for testing, they were likewise shown to differ antigenically from the army test strain. A review of the role of *S. marcescens* in the army biological programme was published in 1979. There were 456 cases of occupational infections acquired at Fort Detrick during the offensive biological programme, at a rate of less than 10 infections per one million hours worked. The rate of occupational infection was well within the contemporary standards of the National Safety Council and below the rates reported from other laboratories. There were three fatalities due to occupationally acquired infections—two cases of anthrax in 1951 and 1958 and a case of viral encephalitis in 1964. The mortality rate was lower than those of other contemporary surveys of laboratory-acquired infections. There were 48 occupational infections and no fatalities reported from production and testing sites. The safety programme included the development and use of new vaccines as well as engineering safety measures. By the late 1960s, the US military had developed a biological arsenal that included numerous bacterial pathogens, toxins, and fungal plant pathogens that could be directed against crops to induce crop failure and famine.

The United States was accused by Soviet Union, China, and North Korea of using biological warfare in the Korean War. These accusations were supported by a series of investigations conducted by the International Scientific Commission, a group of scientists, and other organisations, not part of the commission. Although these investigations were described as impartial, they were carefully controlled by the North Korean and Chinese governments. The United States admitted to having biological warfare capabilities, but denied using biological weapons.

The United States requested impartial investigations. The International Committee of the Red Cross suggested the formation of a special commission to investigate, and the World Health Organisation offered to intervene. Neither China nor North Korea responded to the International Committee of the Red Cross, and the World Health Organisation's offer was rebuffed as a disguised attempt at espionage. Consequently, the United States and 15 other nations submitted a resolution to the United Nations (UN) requesting the formation of a neutral commission to investigate the allegations; however, implementation of the resolution was prevented by the Soviet Union.

The credibility of the United States was undermined by its failure to ratify the 1925 Geneva Protocol, by knowledge of its offensive biological warfare programme, and the suspected covert collaboration with the Unit 731 scientists. Although unsubstantiated, the accusations of US use of biological weapons attracted wide attention and resulted in a loss of international goodwill toward the United States.

During the cold war era, numerous unsubstantiated allegations were made. These included Soviet accusations of US biological weapons testing against Canadian Eskimos resulting in a plague epidemic and of a US and Columbian biological attack on Columbian and Bolivian peasants. The United States also was accused of planning to initiate an epidemic of cholera in south-eastern China and of the covert release of dengue in Cuba.

Similarly, the US allegations that Soviet armed forces and their proxies had used aerosolised trichothecene mycotoxins, potent inhibitors of DNA and protein synthesis derived from the fungi of the genus *Fusarium*, in Laos, Kampuchea and Afghanistan are widely regarded as erroneous. The remote locations of the alleged attacks made intelligence investigations extremely difficult. Attacks were never witnessed by Western intelligence operatives, and samples of the aerosols were not recovered. Confounding factors included the following:

i) contradictory testimonies from survivors of the alleged attack,
ii) discrepancies in reported symptoms,
iii) low disease rates in the allegedly exposed populations,
iv) the recovery of mycotoxin in less than 10 per cent of the clinical and environmental samples submitted,
v) the presence of *Fusarium* organisms as environmental commensals,
vi) the possible decay of toxin under prevailing environmental conditions,
vii) conflicting results of toxin assays from different laboratories,
viii) the similarity of alleged yellow rain deposits recovered from environmental surfaces to bee faeces in ultra-structural appearance and pollen and mould content, and

ix) the natural occurrence of showers of bee faeces from swarms of honeybees in the rain forests of South-east Asia.

During the late 1960s, there was increasing international concern regarding the indiscriminate nature, unpredictability, epidemiologic risks, and lack of epidemiologic control measures for biological weapons, as well as the ineffectiveness of the 1925 Geneva Protocol for preventing biological weapons proliferation. In July 1969, Great Britain submitted a proposal to the Committee on Disarmament of the UN prohibiting the development, production, and stockpiling of biological weapons and providing for inspections in response to alleged violations. During the following September, the Warsaw Pact nations submitted a biological disarmament proposal similar to the British proposal, but without provisions for inspections. Two months later, the World Health Organisation issued a report regarding the potential consequences of biological warfare. Subsequently, the 1972 Convention on the Prohibition of the Development, Production, and Stockpiling of Bacteriological (Biological) and Toxin Weapons and on Their Destruction (BWC) was developed.

The BWC prohibits the development, possession, and stockpiling of pathogens or toxins in "quantities that have no justification for prophylactic, protective or other peaceful purposes." The BWC also prohibits the development of delivery systems intended to disperse biological agents and requires parties to destroy stocks of biological agents, delivery systems, and equipment within nine months of ratifying the treaty. Transferring biological warfare technology or expertise to other countries is also prohibited. Signatories that have not yet ratified the BWC are obliged to refrain from activities that would defeat the purpose of the treaty until they explicitly communicate their intention not to ratify. However, there are unresolved controversies regarding the quantities of pathogens required for benevolent research and the definition of "defensive" research.

Allegations of infractions may be lodged with the UN Security Council, which may in turn initiate inspections of accused parties; however, this provision is undermined by the right of Security Council members to veto proposed inspections. The treaty was ratified in April 1972 and went into effect in March 1975. There were more than 100 signatory nations, including Iraq and the members of the Security Council. Review conferences were held in 1981, 1986, 1991, and 1996, and 2001.

In 1970, President Nixon terminated the US offensive biological weapons programme by executive order. The United States adopted a policy never to use biological weapons, including toxins, under any circumstances whatsoever. National Security Decisions issued during November 1969 (microorganisms) and February 1970 (toxins), mandated the cessation of offensive biological research and production and the destruction of the biological arsenal. Research efforts were directed exclusively to the development of defensive measures such as diagnostic tests, vaccines, and therapies for potential biological weapons threats.

Stocks of pathogens and the entire biological arsenal were destroyed between May 1971 and February 1973 under the auspices of the US Department of Agriculture, the US Department of Health, Education and Welfare, and the Departments of Natural Resources of Arkansas, Colorado, and Maryland. Small quantities of pathogens were retained at Fort Detrick to test the efficacy of investigational preventive measures and therapies.

The Central Intelligence Agency was admonished during a 1975 congressional hearing for illegally retaining samples of toxins after presidential orders mandating their destruction. After the termination of the offensive biological programme, the US Army Medical Research Institute of Infectious Diseases (USAMRIID) was established to continue the development of medical defences for the US military against potential biological attack. The mission of USAMRIID is to conduct research to develop strategies, products, information, and training programmes for medical defence against potential biological weapons. Endemic or epidemic infectious diseases due to highly virulent pathogens requiring high-level containment for laboratory safety are also studied. The USAMRIID is an open research institution; no research is classified.

Many signatory nations of the 1972 BWC, including Iraq and the former Soviet Union, have participated in activities outlawed by the convention. These events demonstrate the ineffectiveness of the convention as the sole means for eradicating biological weapons and preventing further proliferation. Biological weapons were used for covert assassination during the 1970s. Ricin, a lethal toxin derived from castor beans, was weaponised by the secret service of the Soviet Union and deployed by the Bulgarian secret service. Metallic pellets that were 1.7 mm in diameter were cross-drilled, filled with ricin, and sealed with wax intended to melt at body temperature. The pellets were discharged from spring-powered weapons disguised as umbrellas. These weapons were used to assassinate Georgi Markov, a Bulgarian defector living in London, and during an unsuccessful assassination attempt against another defector, Vladamir Kostov, in 1978.

During April 1979, an epidemic of anthrax occurred among people who lived or worked within a distance of four km in a narrow zone downwind of a Soviet military microbiology facility in Sverdlovsk. In addition, livestock died of anthrax along the extended axis of the epidemic zone out to a distance of 50 km. The facility was suspected by Western intelligence of being a biological warfare research facility, and the epidemic was attributed by Western analysts to the accidental airborne release of anthrax spores. The Soviets maintained that the epidemic was caused by ingestion of contaminated meat purchased on the black market.

In 1992, Boris Yeltsin, the then president of Russia, admitted that the facility had been part of an offensive biological weapons programme and that the epidemic had been caused by a non-intentional release of anthrax spores. It was determined that air filters had not been activated early on the morning of April 3. Inhalation anthrax was identified at autopsy as the cause of death in victims. At least 77 cases and 66 deaths occurred, constituting the largest documented epidemic of inhalation anthrax in history.

The Soviets continued an offensive biological warfare programme after the BWC of 1972 under the aegis of Biopreparat, an organisation under the Ministry of Defence. During the 1970s and 1980s, Biopreparat operated at least six research laboratories and five production facilities and employed up to 55,000 scientists and technicians. The extensive programme of the former Soviet Union is now controlled largely by Russia. Yeltsin stated in 1992 that he would end further offensive biological research and production; however, the degree to which the programme has been reduced is not known.

A 1995 report estimated that the Russian programme continues to employ 25,000 to 30,000 people. Before the Persian Gulf War, intelligence reports suggested that the Iraqi regime had sponsored an ambitious biological warfare programme. Coalition forces prepared for potential biological warfare by training in protective masks and equipment, reviewing decontamination procedures, and immunising troops against potential biological warfare threats. Approximately 150,000 US troops received a Food and Drug Administration—licensed toxoid vaccine against anthrax, and 8,000 received a botulinum toxoid vaccine approved by the Food and Drug Administration as an Investigational New Drug.

Information about the Iraqi offensive biological programme was obtained after the Persian Gulf War during UN weapons inspections. Iraqi officials admitted to having had an offensive biological weapons programme that included basic research on *B. anthracis*, *Rotavirus*, *Camel pox virus*, aflatoxin, botulinum toxins, mycotoxins, and an anticrop agent. Fortunately, biological weapons were not used during the Persian Gulf War. The Iraqi government claims to have destroyed its biological arsenal after the war. Research and production facilities that had escaped destruction during the war were demolished by the UN Special Commission on Iraq (UNSCOM) in 1996. The Persian Gulf War and post-war findings have lead to a recent decision by the US military to develop a plan to immunise troops against anthrax.

After initial explorations in the late 1970s, Iraq's biological warfare programme commenced in earnest in 1985. By the time Operation Desert Storm ended with a ceasefire in April 1991, Iraqi scientists had investigated the biological warfare potential of five bacterial strains, one fungal strain, five viruses, and four toxins. In addition, two bacterial species, *Bacillus subtilis* and *Bacillus thuringiensis*, were developed for use as simulants. Two pathogenic bacteria were studied—*Bacillus anthraces* (the cause of anthrax) and *Clostridium perfringens* (the cause of gas gangrene).

Research on anthrax was initiated in 1985 at Muthanna State Establishment, the principal Iraqi chemical weapons facility, but was transferred in 1987 to Salman Pak just south of Baghdad, which became the centre for biological warfare research and development. Some anthrax strains were imported from culture collections in France and the United States; others were local isolates. At Salman Pak, four strains were characterised, their media and storage requirements were established, and their pathogenicity was evaluated in animal models.

Research findings were applied at the Al Hakam Single Cell Protein Production Plant, Iraq's major production facility for biological warfare agents, to begin mass production of anthrax in 1989. Eventually, approximately 8,000 L of solution with an anthrax spore and cell count of 109 /mL was produced. Of this, 6,000 L was used to fill weapons; the remainder was stored at Al Hakam. A reference strain of *C. perfringens* was imported from the United States in 1985.

Experimental work using mice commenced in 1988 to determine the infectivity of *Clostridium* spores, the ability of spores to initiate disease, and their degree of virulence. During 1990, 340 L of solution containing *Clostridium* was produced at Al Hakam. The Iraqis claim, however, that no attempt was made to develop *Clostridium* for weapons use. One fungal strain with crop destroying potential, wheat cover smut, was evaluated for use as a weapon. Research carried out at Salman Pak in 1985 demonstrated that wheat cover smut spores sprayed over immature wheat plants would be lethal to the crop.

In 1988, young wheat plants growing in large fields near the town of Mosul were infected with this agent; the infected wheat subsequently was harvested and moved to Fudaliyah for storage. The Iraqis claim that no attempt was made to recover fungus from the harvest and that the infected crop was destroyed in 1990. The investigation of wheat smut implies that Iraqi leaders knew that biological weapons were more than antipersonnel weapons; they could also be used against crops as part of economic warfare. Beginning in early 1990, scientists at the Foot and Mouth Disease Centre at Al Manal investigated five viruses for their potential utility as biological weapons. Two agents, Congo-Crimean hemorrhagic virus and yellow fever virus, were found to be unsuitable since they required vectors for dispersal. The remainder, enterovirus 17, human rotavirus, and camelpox virus, were researched further, and a large egg incubator was obtained to mass produce the viruses. Reportedly, only certain growth characteristics of the viruses were elucidated before the programme was terminated in 1990. Enterovirus 17 and human rotavirus may have been investigated for use as incapacitating biological warfare agents, while camel pox might have been considered an ethnic weapon.

Iraqi research of organisms that produce aflatoxin, including *Aspergillus flavus* and *Aspergillus parasiticus*, led to the development of methods for growing aflatoxin producing organisms on wet rice. Individual types of aflatoxin were identified, and some aflatoxin containing solutions were tested in animal models.

Production of aflatoxin began in 1989 at Salman Pak, where approximately 2200 L of solution was eventually manufactured. An unknown quantity of this cache was used to fill weapons; the remainder was stored.

The Iraqis produced 20,000 L of solution containing botulinum toxin of unknown strength and type at Al Hakam and Al Manal during 1989 and 1990, using a *Clostridium botulinum* strain imported from the United States. Of this, 12,000 L was used in field testing or to fill warheads; unused toxin was stored at Al Hakam.

The castor bean plant (*Ricinus communis*), grown widely in Iraq, naturally produces ricin. During 1989, approximately 10 L of concentrated ricin solution was manufactured at Salman Pak. While some was tested in animal models and some used as payload in artillery shells, the fate of most is unknown. Ricin might have been researched because it is plentiful and known to be effective for assassination.

In 1990, Iraqi scientists investigated the ability of *Fusarium oxysporium* and *Fusarium granarium* to produce tricothecene mycotoxins. The fungi were grown on damp, supplemented rice; toxins were extracted by organic solvents and dried in a rotary evaporator. The Iraqis claim to have produced 20 mL of tricothecene-containing solution, some of which wastested in animal models. The fate of the remainder is unknown. Tricothecenes may have been investigated because some can penetrate skin or because of their alleged history as components of "yellow rain."

Iraq's chemical arsenal included 250 lb (LD-250) and 400-lb (R-400) bombs. Based on successful chemical warfare, some of these bombs were adapted to hold 60 L and 85 L of biological solution, respectively. When deemed necessary, the walls of the chambers containing the payload were coated with an inert epoxy paint to protect the biological agents from the toxic effects of contact with metal. Testing determined that the R-400 was the more suitable munition for biological warfare. In 1990, 200 R-400 biological bombs were produced; of these, 100 were filled with botulinum toxin, 50 with anthrax, and seven with aflatoxin. These biologically armed bombs were deployed at two sites, ready for immediate use. A few 155-mm calibre artillery shells were filled with ricin for field testing.

More than 800 SCUD missiles had procured by Iraq from Soviet bloc countries before 1991 and had manufactured about 80 itself. Some SCUDs, renamed Al Husseins, were enhanced to double their range. In 1990, the Muthanna State Establishment received a special shipment of 100 Al Husseins. Of these, 25 were fitted with biological warheads: 13 with botulinum toxin, 10 with aflatoxin, and two with anthrax. All reportedly were deployed: 10 in a deep railway tunnel and 15 in holes dug along the Tigris River. The warheads of an unknown number of SAKR-18 122-mm rockets were filled with botulinum toxin, aflatoxin, or the simulant *B. subtilis*, and field tested.

Iraqi munitions that depended on explosion for agent dispersal were of similar design—a tube filled with an explosive charge (burster)—was placed in the centre of a chamber containing the biological agent. At the moment of impact, the burster would explode, rupturing the outer wall of the munition and dispersing the payload. The Iraqis possessed several hundred modern Italian made pesticide dispersal systems that were fitted with sprayer nozzles capable of generating aerosols of the 1-μm to 5-μm size optimal for biological warfare. Some sprayers and appropriate holding tanks were installed on aircraft and land vehicles.

In 1990, the Iraqis modified a MIG-21 fighter plane to be a remotely piloted vehicle and equipped it with a 2200-L belly tank and a spray mechanism. In a field test carried out in January 1991, the remotely piloted vehicle sprayed a solution laden with a biological simulant over a practice target range. The results of this test are not known. Soon after, Iraq had accepted a ceasefire under United Nations Security Council Resolution 687. In April 1991, biological warfare programme personnel reportedly were ordered to destroy all biological warfare agents. A two-step process was used for this purpose:

i) stores of biological warfare agents were treated with formaldehyde and potassium permanganate;
ii) the residuum was poured onto bare ground near Al Hakam's perimeter.

Five years later, UNSCOM was unable to recover either residuum or its breakdown products from the claimed dump sites. What this means is not clear. Natural forces might have completely degraded the residuum over time, Iraqi authorities may be mistaken as to the location of dumps, or they may be lying about the purported destruction. Biological warfare munitions supposedly were destroyed at the same time as the agents. Bombs and warheads were opened and formaldehyde and potassium permanganate were added to the solution they contained. Later, munitions were crushed by bulldozers and burned in pits. Finally, the remains were concealed by detonating general purpose bombs among them. Many test munitions were simply thrown into the Tigris River.

While some whole and many fragmented R-400 shave been recovered by UNSCOM, it cannot certify that all biological bombs have been destroyed, nor does it have solid evidence on the fate of missile warheads. United Nations Security Council Resolution 687 specifies that facilities and equipment used in support of any of Iraq's weapons of mass destruction programmes are to be destroyed by UNSCOM or the IAEA.

A few days before the first UNSCOM biological inspection team arrived at Salman Pak on August 2, 1991, the Iraqis themselves blew up part of the facility and covered it with a thick layer of dirt. In addition, some implicative equipment, such as aerosol test chambers, were removed and crushed. However, other biological warfare facilities remained operational and the Iraqis tried to conceal their real purpose. Nevertheless, their true function was eventually discerned. In May and June 1996, Iraqi workers, overseen by UNSCOM inspectors, obliterated the Al Hakamplant and the equipment at Al Manal that had produced biological weapons.

Between 1985 and April 1991, Iraq developed anthrax, botulinum toxin, and aflatoxin for biological warfare; 200 bombs and 25 ballistic missiles laden with biological agents were deployed by the time Operation Desert Storm occurred. Although cause for concern, if used during the Persian Gulf War, Iraq's biological warfare arsenal probably would have been militarily ineffective for three reasons:

i) it was small;
ii) payload dispersal mechanisms were inefficient; and
iii) coalition forces dominated the theatre of war.

Despite the Gulf War defeat, the Iraqi biological warfare threat has not been extinguished. Saddam Hussein remains in power, and his desire to acquire weapons of mass destruction continues unabated.

A biological weapon is more than just a pathogenic microorganism or toxin. It is a system composed of four major components. They are:

i) payload (the biological agent),
ii) munition (a container that keeps the payload intact and virulent during delivery),
iii) delivery system (missile, artillery shell, aircraft, etc.), and
iv) dispersal mechanism (an explosive force or spray device to dispense the agent to the target population).

Iraq is said to have the following bioweapons in its possession.

i) *Anthrax*: Anthrax is one of the main bioweapons which Iraq is having. Anthrax spores are extremely hardy, and they retain virulence during storage. Anthrax cells and spores dispersed in aerosol can inflict heavy casualties on unprotected populations, and if treatment with appropriate antibiotics is not begun soon after exposure, a morbidity rate of 65 per cent to 80 per cent will result.

Anthrax slated for weapons may be produced as slurry or dry powder. Anthrax slurry, while easier to manufacture than powder, is less efficient for biological warfare purposes; agents in slurry lose virulence relatively quickly and, more importantly, slurry is troublesome to disperse as an aerosol with particles of optimal size. Yet, although Iraq possessed dryers and grinders that could have been used to produce dry anthrax, all of its deployed biological warfare munitions were filled with wet anthrax. The Iraqis may have been unable to overcome either the technical difficulties or the safety problems inherent in dry anthrax production.

ii) *Botulinum Toxin*: The botulinum toxin is very attractive to the Iraqis because of its characteristic properties. While most cases of botulinum intoxication are caused by ingested contaminated food, aerosolised toxin is deadly. For example, eight kilogrammes of the concentrated botulinum toxin dispersed over an area of 100 km would deliver a median lethal dose (LD50) dose to the entire unprotected population located therein, assuming optimal meteorological conditions. Given the extreme lethality of the agent, it is reasonable to assume that this solution would be deadly in small doses if delivered effectively to unprotected persons.

iii) *Aflatoxin*: Although well known to medical science as a powerful nephrotoxin and hepatotoxin, aflatoxin has no known property useful for biological warfare. Possible explanations for Iraq's interest in aflatoxin include:

a) Iraqi scientists may have discovered that aflatoxin possessed a previously unknown property useful for biological warfare applications;

b) Iraqi planners may have intended to use aflatoxin's long-term carcinogenic properties as a means of terrorising targeted civilian populations; or

c) Since aflatoxin is easier to manufacture than most other toxins, the Iraqi biological warfare programme's

> staff might have chosen to produce it to meet production goals set by higher authorities, rather than for its perceived biological warfare value.

Iraqi biological warfare munitions depended on impact detonation for primary dispersal of agents. This method is exceedingly inefficient because:

i) an explosion inevitably renders harmless much of the payload;
ii) impact detonation drives a substantial part of the payload into the ground;
iii) the small part of the payload aerosolised by explosion generally is not propelled beyond a few tens of metres; and
iv) the size of aerosolised particles varies widely, from large clumps to particles of smaller than 1 μm.

For these reasons, had Iraq's biological warfare munitions actually been used, their effect would have been limited to contaminating a relatively small area of ground surrounding the point of impact and exposing nearby individuals to aerosolised pathogens or toxins. Al Husseins lacked an inertial guidance system, which made them inaccurate. Biological agents delivered by aerosol would have presented a more credible threat to coalition forces, but such a system most probably was not in use during Operation Desert Storm.

The defensive capabilities of coalition forces also must be taken into account. First, coalition forces had overwhelming air superiority and unsurpassed ability to detect and destroy airborne aircraft. In addition, Iraq's meteorological stations and communications network had been destroyed by coalition bombings. Without accurate forecasts, airborne biological agents might have been blown onto friendly forces or been dispersed over empty desert. Second, coalition forces had been trained to expect chemical attacks by Iraq, and were well equipped to defend themselves. The standard antichemical defence methods and equipment would also have provided adequate protection against all known Iraqi biological weapons.

The military effectiveness of troops garbed in protective suits is decreased because the ability of soldiers to perform complex manual tasks is limited, their observational powers reduced, and they tire quickly, especially in hot weather. Therefore, just by making its opponents believe that a biological attack was imminent, the Iraqis would have forced them to garb themselves, which would have impaired the coalition forces' combat effectiveness and mobility.

Investigations of US forces taking part in the Persian Gulf War found several deficiencies with biological warfare defence preparedness, including shortfalls in defensive equipment, inadequate training, and shortages in medical support. However, the primary weakness of the coalition forces in regard to biological warfare was that they did not have "standoff" or "point detection" capabilities.

Therefore, the Iraqis had been able to mount a surprise attack using aerosol laden with anthrax or botulinum toxin and had wind conditions been such that the aerosol was carried into positions held by coalition forces, the attack probably would not have been detected. Thus, no warning would have been sounded for troops to protect themselves by garbing or seeking shelter. Since only approximately 150,000 troops received the first vaccination against anthrax and a smaller proportion of that 150, 000 received a second vaccination (6 vaccinations in 1 year are necessary for full protection), the first indication of the attack would have appeared three to six days later when soldiers began to present symptoms of pneumonic anthrax. Although anthrax is treatable by commonly available antibiotics, it is questionable whether sufficient supplies would have been on hand to adequately treat a large number of exposed individuals.

The Iraqis had been able to attack the coalition forces' rear positions, such as airfields, ports, and troop assembly areas, with anthrax or botulinum toxin aerosol, a similar situation would have ensued. Heavy casualties among troops and civilian workers, compounded by panic, would have caused serious disruptions. The coalition forces' ability to operate would have been severely compromised as the flow of vital supplies decreased to a trickle, communications were hindered, and medical facilities overwhelmed.

The Iraqi leadership is capable of ordering attacks on purely civilian targets. It began when the Iraqis launched missiles against helpless Iranian cities of no obvious military value, during the Iraq-Iran war of 1980 to 1986. The Iranians retaliated in kind. After an exchange of several hundred missiles, the episode ended with, apparently, neither side having gained militarily from the exchange. The cost to both, however, was immense—many thousand dead and wounded civilians, as well as incalculable misery for hundreds of thousands of city dwellers. Cities were also targeted during the Persian Gulf War but on a much smaller scale. The Iraqis launched SCUD missiles against Israeli cities, but the Israelis chose not to retaliate.

While the number of casualties caused directly by biological weapons probably would have been low, the targeted population's terrified reaction to these bombs or missiles may have caused more harm than the weapons themselves. The combination of direct casualties brought about by disease in combination with casualties caused by the resultant panic likely would have caused more injuries and death than were produced by high explosives.

If Operation Desert Storm not had intervened, the Iraq would have possessed a formidable suite of weapons of mass destruction by 1997. It could have deployed ballistic missiles with a range of about 2,000 km capable of delivering up to a 1-ton payload. Further, Iraqi commanders would have been able to select the type of warhead required for a particular mission. Thus, a nuclear or biological warhead might have been used to achieve a strategic objective; for example, to destroy the capital of a neighbour or to threaten more distant nations that might wish to intervene on the side of Iraq's opponent in any conflict. If, on the other hand, a tactical strike was to be undertaken, for example, the destruction of a smaller target such as a troop formation, a short-range missile fitted with a chemical warhead might have been appropriate. Thus, the ballistic missile component was the heart of Iraq's weapons of mass destruction programme.

UNSCOM's and the IAEA's ongoing monitoring and verification programme and the imposition of import and export controls had deterred a resurgent overt programme by Iraq to develop weapons of mass destruction. If these agencies were removed from Iraq, either by the United Nations Security Council deciding to terminate their missions or by the Iraqi government expelling them, Iraq might restart such a programme. If so, it probably would be reconstructed along lines familiar to Iraqi planners, beginning with the acquisition of a powerful ballistic missile capability. It appears that Iraq may already be on its way to realising such a capability. The main missile research station, Sa'ad 16 located at Al Kindi, which was demolished by bombs during the Persian Gulf War, has been completely rebuilt.

Iraq possesses hundreds of ballistic missiles with a range of 150 km or less allowed by the terms of the 1991 ceasefire. It may also possess HY-2, SS-N-2, and C-601 cruise missiles, although UNSCOM has seen no firm evidence of this. The United Nations Special Commission has dismantled or otherwise accounted for the destruction of most of the SCUD missiles that survived the Persian Gulf War, but commission members still believe some operational SCUD missiles remain undetected.

Iraqi rocket scientists are believed to be honing their skills while working for Libya's leader, Mu'ammar Qaddaffi. For these reasons, and despite limitations imposed by UN Security Council Resolution 647, Iraq might already possesses potent ballistic and, perhaps, cruise missile capabilities and the trained personnel to deploy and operate them.

Nuclear warheads cannot be acquired for at least five years because the IAEA has destroyed most if not all Iraqi nuclear weapons-related facilities. Similarly, UNSCOM has supervised the destruction of most, perhaps all, of Iraq's chemical warfare agents, as well as equipment and facilities used by the chemical warfare programme. Thus, no chemicals would be available immediately to arm ballistic missiles.

The workforce of more than 200 persons who staffed Iraq's biological warfare programme is intact. Iraq's civilian biotechnological infrastructure, comprising more than 80 research, development, and production facilities, is whole and well equipped. Since most biotechnological equipment is dual use, some of the currently operative facilities could be rapidly converted to biological warfare work.

The Iraqis retain hidden stores of freeze-dried organisms from its former biological warfare programme. Since Iraq maintains these human, biological, and industrial resources, it could reconstitute a biological warfare programme rapidly and be able to manufacture militarily significant quantities of biological warfare agents within six months.

Further, the armourers who adapted chemical munitions to hold biological agents before the Persian Gulf War are still available. With their assistance, stockpiled conventional munitions could be modified within the six-month timeframe and loaded with biological warfare agents Iraq could reconstitute a biological warfare programme rapidly and be able to manufacture militarily significant quantities of biological warfare agents within six months. Weapons produced immediately by a resurgent Iraqi biological warfare programme, even if unimproved over the weapons developed before 1991, could be deployed in support of aggressive moves.

Except for the coalition partner countries and Israel, the armed forces of the region's nations probably are inadequately prepared to defeat a biological attack. Further, all of the region's civilian populations are unprotected. Thus, if Iraq were able to maintain secrecy and deploy biological weapons to tactical sites, opponents would face a very difficult situation because most soldiers and all civilians would be vulnerable both to diseases brought about by biological warfare agents and to panic that these weapons would induce among threatened or attacked populations.

As to its geopolitical standing, distrustful relations exist between Iraq and its neighbours as before; in fact, Iraq's leader may perceive himself as even more beleaguered and as having additional scores to settle. In consideration of this unsettled situation, it is wise to prepare for the possibility of Iraq's trying once again to gain a dominant position in the Middle East. It is reasonable to assume that, as before, Iraq will attempt to overcome the numerical superiority of regional opponents by resorting to the use of weapons of mass destruction. Iraq's former ballistic and cruise missiles and biological warfare components would be the easiest and quickest to reassemble.

The key barrier to Iraq reacquiring weapons of mass destruction undoubtedly is the collective international will that sustains the several United Nations Security Council resolutions designed to ensure a subdued Iraq. A further reflection of that will is the support the council gives UNSCOM, especially with regard to biological warfare.

Before the Persian Gulf War, Iraq placed high priority on developing a strong biotechnological capability. This effort will probably be continued and expanded once the United Nations lifts economic sanctions. The Iraqi government may attempt to apply biotechnology for various legitimate enterprises, including enhancing the ability of crop plants to withstand abiotic and biotic stress, manufacturing biological fertilizers and pesticides, producing single-cell protein, and developing diagnostic methods for animal and human diseases.

Due to the dual use character of biotechnology, however, much of the expertise, equipment, supplies, and facilities devoted to civilian biotechnological pursuits could be redirected to biological warfare applications. The UN Commission's actions to closely and continuously monitor

Iraq's biological research, development, production, and testing facilities is the best guarantee that these facilities are unable to take up such work. Further, UNSCOM's awareness of the locations of Iraq's bioscientists and chemical engineers who staffed the former biological warfare programme makes it less likely that they could be used by secret facilities to perform illicit research and development.

The biological threat posed by non-state-sponsored terrorists was demonstrated by the intentional contamination of salad bars in Oregon restaurants with *Salmonella typhimurium* by the Rajneeshee cult during late September 1984. This incident resulted in 751 cases of enteritis and 45 hospitalisations. Although the Rajneeshees were suspected, and despite rigorous epidemiologic analyses by the Wasco-Sherman Public Health Department, the Oregon State Health Division, and the Centres for Disease Control, the origin of the epidemic as a deliberate biological attack was not confirmed until a cult member admitted to the attack in 1985. The threat of biological terrorism resurfaced following the Aum Shinrikyo sarin attack of the Tokyo subway system in March 1995. Police raids and investigations of the cult's facilities disclosed evidence of a rudimentary biological weapons programme. The cult was allegedly conducting research of *Banthracis, Clostridium botulinum*, and *C. burnetii*. The cult's arsenal seized by police allegedly contained botulinum toxin and drone aircraft equipped with spray tanks.

The history of biolcgical terrorism teaches two lessons. One, it is fairly easy to mount a biological attack with food-borne pathogens, which are not difficult to procure and propagate. This type of attack can certainly cause many people to become ill but is not likely to kill them. Local health providers usually are well equipped to deal with the consequences of such an attack. Second, special technical skill and knowledge are necessary to develop biological weapons capable of killing large numbers of people.

REFERENCES

Becket, B., *Weapons of Tomorrow*, New York, NY: Plenum Press, 1983.

Daplan, D.E., Marshall A., *The Cult at the End of the World*, New York, NY: Crown Publishing Group, 1996.

Derbes, V.J., *De Mussis and the Great Plague of 1348: A Forgotten Episode of Bacteriological War*, JAMA, 1966.

Fenner, F. Henderson D.A., Arita I, Jezek Z, Ladnyi, I.D., *Smallpox and Its Eradication*, Geneva, Switzerland: World Health Organisation, 1988.

Geissler E., *Biological and Toxin Weapons Today*, New York, NY: Oxford University Press Inc., 1986.

Goldstein, L., "Saddam's Biological Warfare Card" *Washington Post*, October 11, 1996.

Harris, S.H., *Factories of Death*, New York, NY: Routledge, 1994.

Harris, S., *Japanese Biological Warfare Research on Humans: A Case Study of Microbiology and Ethics*, Ann NY Acad Sci., 1992.

Parkman, F., *The Conspiracy of Pontiac and the Indian War after the Conquest of Canada*, Boston, Mass: Little Brown & Co Inc., 1901.

Robertson, A. G., Robertson, L. J., *From Asps to Allegations: Biological Warfare in History*, Mil Med., 1995.

Rolicka, M., *New Studies Disputing Allegations of Bacteriological Warfare during the Korean War*, Mil Med., 1995.

Schaap, B., *US Biological Warfare: The 1981 Cuban Dengue Epidemic, Covert Action*, 1982.

Sims, N.A., *The Diplomacy of Biological Disarmament*, New York, NY: Plenum Press, 1983.

Stearn, E.W., Stearn, A.E., *The Effect of Smallpox on the Destiny of the Amerindian*, Boston, Mass: Bruce Humphries, 1945.

Stockholm International Peace Research Institute (SPIRI), *The Rise of CB Weapons: The Problem of Chemical and Biological Warfare*, New York, NY: Humanities Press, 1971, 1.

Stubbs, M., *Has the West an Achilles Heel: Possibilities of Biological Weapons*, NATO's Fifteen Nations, June/July 1962.

Tomlin, V.V., Berezhnai R.V., *Exposure of Criminal Activity of the Japanese Military Authorities Regarding Preparation for Biological Warfare*, Voen Med Zh., 1985.

US Congress, *Biological Testing Involving Human Subjects by the Department of Defense*, 1977.

US Dept of the Army, *US Army Activity in the US Biological Warfare Programs*, Washington DC: US Dept of the Army, February 24, 1977.

WHO Group of Consultants, *Health Aspects of Chemical and Biological Weapons*, Geneva, Switzerland: World Health Organisation, 1970.

Yu, V.L., *Serratia marcescens: Historical Perspective and Clinical Review*, N Engl J Med., 1979.

Zilinskas, R.A., *Iraq's Biological Weapons: The Past as Future?*, JAMA, 1997, 278:418-424.

3

Nature of Bioweapons

Terrorists could sow unprecedented devastation by unleashing biological warfare agents. Many bacteria, fungi, viruses, rickettsial agents and toxins are used as bioweapons. Those mentioned most often include *Bacillus anthraces* (anthrax), botulinum toxin, *Yersinia pestis* (plague), ricin, staphylococcal enterotoxin B (SEB), and *Venezuelan equine encephalitis* virus (VEE).

Viruses, and toxins, used as biological weapons share some common characteristics. They can be dispersed in aerosols of particle size one to five micrometres, which may remain suspended for hours and if inhaled will penetrate into distal bronchioles and terminal alveoli of victims. Particles larger than five microns would tend to be filtered out in the upper airway. The aerosols may be delivered by simple technology, including industrial sprayers with nozzles modified to generate the smaller particle size. The aerosol could be delivered from a line source such as an airplane or boat travelling upwind of the intended target, or from a point source such as a stationary sprayer or missile dispensing agent-containing bomblets in an area upwind of the target.

The weather in the target areas is very important in the employment of biological agents as aerosols, as higher wind speeds tend to break up the aerosol cloud, and stable wind direction is obviously important. Inversion conditions and lower wind speeds, five to 10 miles per hour, conditions which occur more often during night-time and early morning hours, would be ideal for dispensing such aerosols. Other possible routes of exposure for biological agents include percutaneous, oral, intentional contamination of food and water, etc.

Diseases produced by the offensive use of biological agents could be lethal and/or disabling. Some major lethal agents include *Bacillus anthraces*, botulinum toxin, and *Francisella tularensis*, while incapacitating agents include SEB and *Coxiella burnetii*. Agents, such as *Yersinia pestis* and *C. burnetii*, would produce pulmonary syndromes characteristic of the endemic disease they produce in nature. Others, such as botulinum toxin, although delivered by a different route of exposure than usual with endemic disease, would produce a similar clinical picture to that commonly seen with oral exposure. Person-to-person spread could be important for some agents, such as smallpox and pneumonic plague, and local disease cycles might occur if a competent vector for a bacterium or virus is present in the environment.

Scientists have estimated that 50 kilograms of aerosolised *B. anthraces* spores dispensed by a line source two kilometres upwind of a population centre of 500,000 unprotected people in ideal meteorological conditions, would travel greater than 20 kilometres, downwind, and kill/incapacitate up to 125,000 people in the path of the biological cloud. If *F. tularensis* was dispensed, the number of dead/incapacitated was estimated to be about 125,000. Thus, certain biological organisms could truly be weapons of mass destruction, if they are properly employed as offensive weapons under ideal meteorological conditions.

Unlike chemical agents, which typically lead to violent disease syndromes within minutes at the site of exposure, diseases resulting from biological agents have incubation periods of days. Therefore, rather than a paramedic, it will likely be a physician who is first faced with evidence of the results of a biological attack. We provide here a primer on 10 classic biological warfare agents to increase the likelihood of their being considered in a differential diagnosis. Although the resultant diseases are rarely seen in many countries today, accepted diagnostic and epidemiologic principles apply; if the cause is identified quickly, appropriate therapy can be initiated and the impact of a terrorist attack greatly reduced.

The potential impact of biological weapons is well illustrated by a 1970 World Health Organisation (WHO) publication. It is estimated that 50 kg of aerosolised *Bacillus anthraces* spores, for example, dispensed by an airplane two km upwind of a population centre of 500,000 unprotected people in ideal meteorological conditions would travel more than 20 km and kill or incapacitate up to 220,000 people, nearly half of those in the path of the biological cloud. If *Francisella tularensis* were dispensed, the number of dead or incapacitated would be about 155,000. Thus, if properly used as offensive weapons under ideal meteorological conditions, certain biological agents could cause mass casualties. In addition to their detrimental health effects on the targeted population, the hostile use of BW agents would be likely to cause significant impacts on the health care system. Patients would present in unprecedented numbers, and demands for intensive care might overwhelm medical resources. Special medications or vaccines not generally available in standard pharmaceutical stocks potentially would be required. Health care professionals and laboratory personnel might need added physical protection, and autopsy and interment of remains could present unusual hazards.

The medical response to the threat or use of biological weapons differs depending on whether medical measures are used before exposure or after exposure and whether symptoms are present. If provided before exposure, active immunisation or prophylaxis with antibiotics may prevent illness. Active immunisation is probably the best modality for future protection of military forces against a wide variety of biological threats. For civilian populations, pre-exposure medical countermeasures would likely not be used. After exposure, but before symptoms arise, active or passive immunisation, as well as pre-treatment with therapeutic antibiotics or antiviral drugs, may ameliorate disease symptoms. After onset of illness, only diagnosis of the disease and general supportive care plus specific medical treatment are left to health-care providers.

Bacteria, viruses, or toxins (of microbial, plant, or animal origin) may be used as BW agents. Examples of microbial agents and toxins that could be used as BW agents include *B. anthraces* (anthrax), botulinum toxin, *Yersinia pestis* (plague), staphylococcal enterotoxin B (SEB), and *Venezuelan equine encephalitis* (VEE) virus. Despite the very different characteristics of these organisms and toxins, these agents used as weapons share some common characteristics. They can be dispersed in aerosols of particle size approximately 1 to 10 μm, which may remain suspended (in certain weather conditions) for hours and, if inhaled, can penetrate into distal bronchioles and terminal alveoli of the exposed.

The aerosols may be delivered by simple technology, including industrial sprayers with nozzle and energy source modified to generate the smaller particle size. The aerosol could be delivered from a line source, such as an airplane or boat, travelling upwind of the intended target or from a point source, such as a stationary sprayer or missile bomblets, containing an agent in an area upwind of the target. The meteorological conditions in the target area are very important in the use of BW agents as aerosols because higher wind speeds and turbulence tend to break up the aerosol cloud. Other possible routes of exposure for BW agents include oral, by intentional contamination of food and water, and percutaneous. These other routes of exposure are considered less important than the respiratory route in the context of strategic use of BW agents.

Since biological agents, incapacitating or lethal, produce a more prolonged period of illness than chemical agents, the impact on the health care infrastructure could be enormous. Person-to-person spread could be important for some agents, and local disease cycles might occur if a competent vector for a bacterium or virus is present in the environment.

Table 1
BW agents: Information on diagnostics, medical management, and vaccines

Agent	*Infective dose*	*Diagnostic samples(BSL)*	*Diagnostic assay*	*Patient precautions*	*Vaccine availability*
Anthrax	8000 to 50,000 spores	Blood (BSL-2)	Gram stain Ag-ELISA, Serology:ELISA	Standard precautions	Michigan Biological Products Institute vaccine (licensed): 0.5 mL SC at 0, 2, 4 wk and 6, 12, 18 mo, then annual boosters
Brucellosis	10-100 organisms	Blood, bone marrow, acute and convale scent sera (BSL-3)	Serology: agglutination Culture	Standard precautions Contact isolation if draining lesions present	No vaccine available for human use
Plague	100-500 organisms	Blood, sputum, lymph node aspirate (BSL-2/3)	Gram or Wright-Giemsa Stain Ag-ELISA, Culture, Serology: ELISA, IFA	Pneumonic: droplet precautions until patient treated for 3 days	Greer inactivated vaccine (licensed): 1.0 mL, then 0.2 mL boost at 1-3 and 3-6 mo

(Contd...)

(Contd...)

Q fever	1-10 organisms	Serum (BSL-2/3)	Serology: ELISA, IFA	Standard precautions	IND 610-inactivated whole cell vaccine given as single 0.5 mL SC
Tularemia	10-50 organisms	Blood, sputum, serum EM of tissue (BSL-2/3)	Culture Serology: agglutination	Standard precautions	Live attenuated vaccine (IND): scarification
Smallpox	Assumed low (10-100 organisms)	Pharyngeal swab, scab material (BSL-4)	ELISA, PCR, virus isolation	Airborne precautions	Wyeth calf lymph vaccinia vaccine (licensed) DOD cell-culture derived vaccinia vaccine (IND): scarification
Viral encehalitides	10-100 organisms	Serum VEE (BSL-3) EEE (BSL-2) WEE (BSL-2)	Viral isolation Serology: ELISA or hemogglutination inhibition	Standard precautions (mosquito control)	
Viral hemorrhagic fevers	1-10 organisms	Serum, blood Most viral hemorrhagic fevers (BSL-4) RVF, KHF, and YF (BSL-3)	Viral isolation Ag-ELISA RT-PCR Serology: Ab-ELISA	Contact precautions Consider additional precautions if massive haemorrhage	VEE DOD TC-83 live attenuated vaccine (IND):0.5mL SC31 dose; VEE DOD C-84 (formalin inactivated TC83)(IND): 0.5 mL SC for up to 3 doses;EEE inactivated (IND):0.5 mL SC at 0 & 28d;WEE inactivated (IND): 0.5mL SC at 0, 7, and 28 d

(Contd...)

(Contd...)

Botulinum	0.001 μg/kg (type A)	Nasal swab (possibly) (BSL-2)	Ag-ELISA, Mouse neutral	Standard precautions	AHF Candid #1 vaccine (x-protection for BHF)(IND) RVF inactivated vaccine (IND) DOD pentavalent Toxoid for serotypes A-E (IND): SC at 0, 2, & 12 wk, then yearly boosters
Staphylococcal enterotoxin B	30 ng/person (incapacitating); 1.7 μg/person (lethal)	1-6 h Nasal swab, serum, urine (BSL-2)	Ag-ELISA Serology: Ab-ELISA	Standard precautions	No vaccine available

*BSL indicates biosafety level; Rx, chemotherapy; Px, chemoprophylaxis; Ag, antigen; ELISA, enzyme-linked immunosorbent assay; IV, intravenously; q, every; IM, intramuscular; qd, each day; bid, twice a day; PO, by mouth; IFA, immunoflourescent assay; IND, Investigational New Drug; SC, subcutaneous; EM, electron microscopy; PCR, polymerase chain reaction; VIG, vaccinia immune globulin; DOD, Department of Defense; VEE, Venezuelan equine encephalitis; EEE, eastern equine encephalitis; WEE, western equine encephalitis; NA, not available; RVF, Rift Valley fever; KHF, Korean haemorrhagic fever; YF, yellow fever; RT-PCR, reverse transcriptase polymerase chain reaction; Ab, antibody; CCHF, Congo-Crimean haemorrhagic fever; AHF, Argentine haemorrhagic fever; BHF, Bolivian hemorrhagic fever; CDC, Centers for Disease Control and Prevention.

An overview of several BW threat agents, the disease syndromes resulting from exposure to them, and medical countermeasures available to clinicians are described briefly in this chapter.

ANTHRAX

Anthrax is the preferred biological warfare agent because it is, highly lethal, silent, invisible killer hundred million lethal doses per gram of anthrax material (100,000 times deadlier than the deadliest chemical warfare agent).

Anthrax is an acute infectious disease caused by the spore forming bacterium *Bacillus anthraces*. It most commonly occurs in wild and domestic lower vertebrates such as cattle, sheep, goats, camels, antelopes, and other herbivores, etc., but it can also occur in humans when they are exposed to infected animals or tissue from infected animals.

Anthrax is most common in agricultural regions where it occurs in animals. There include South and Central America, Southern and Eastern Europe, Asia, Africa, the Caribbean, and the Middle East.

When anthrax affects humans, it is usually due to an occupational exposure to infected animals or their products. Workers who are exposed to deal animals and animal products from other countries where anthrax is more common may become infected with *B. anthraces*. A lethal dose of anthrax is considered to be 10,000 spores; 80 per cent of a population that inhaled such a dose would die. Less than one millionth of a gram is invariably fatal within five days to a week after exposure.

Anthrax infection can occur in three forms: cutaneous (skin), inhalation, and gastrointestinal. *B. anthraces* spores can live in the soil for many years, and humans can become infected with anthrax by handling products from infected animals or by inhaling anthrax spores from contaminated animal products.

Anthrax can also spread by eating undercooked meat from infected animals.

i) *Cutaneous:* About 95 per cent of anthrax infectious occur when the bacterium enters a cut or abrasion on the skin, such as when handling contaminated wool, hides, leather, or hair products (especially goat hair) of infected animals. Skin infections begin as a raised itchy bump that resembles an insect bite but within one-two days develops into a vesicle and then a painless ulcer, usually one to three cm in diameter, with a characteristic black necrotic (dying) area in the centre, lymph glands in the adjacent area may swell. About 20 per cent of untreated cases of cutaneous anthrax will result in death. Deaths are rare with appropriate antimicrobial therapy.

ii) *Inhalations:* Initial symptoms may resemble a common cold. After several days, the symptoms may progress to severe breathing problems and shock; inhalation of anthrax is usually fatal.

iii) *Intestinal:* The intestinal disease form of anthrax may follow the consumption of contaminated meat and is characterised by an acute inflammation of the intestinal tract. Initial signs of nausea, loss of appetite, vomiting, fever, are followed by abdominal pain, vomiting of blood, and severe diarrhoea. Intestinal anthrax results in death in 25 per cent to 60 per cent of cases.

Direct person-to-person spread of anthrax is extremely unlikely to occur. Communicability is not a concern in managing or visiting with patients with inhalational anthrax.

The symptoms of anthrax begins after an incubation period varying from one to six days, presumably dependent upon the dose of inhaled organisms. Onset is gradual and nonspecific, with fever, malaise, and fatigue, sometimes in association with a non-productive cough and mild chest discomfort. In some cases, there may be a short period of improvement.

The initial symptoms are followed in two-three days by the abrupt development of severe respiratory distress with dyspnoea, diaphoresis, strider, and cyanosis. Physical findings may include evidence of pleural effasions, oedema of the chest wall, and meningitis. Chest x-ray reveals a dramatically widened mediastinum, often with pleural effusions, but typically without infiltrates.

Shock and death usually follow within 24-36 hours of respiratory distress onset. An epidemic of inhalation anthrax in its early stage with non-specific symptoms could be confused with a wide variety of viral, bacterial, and fungal infections.

Progression over two-three days with the sudden development of severe respiratory distress followed by shock and death in 24-36 hours in essentially all untreated cases eliminates diagnoses other than inhalation anthrax.

The presence of a widened mediastinum on chest X-ray, in particular, should alert one to the diagnosis. Other suggestive findings include chest-wall oedema, haemorrhagic pleural effusions, and haemorrhagic meningitis. Other diagnoses to consider include aerosol exposure to SEB; but in this case onset would be more rapid after exposure, and no prodrome would be evident prior to onset of severe respiratory symptoms. Mediastinal widening on chest X-ray will also be absent. Patients with plague or tularemia pneumonia will have pulmonary infiltrates and clinical signs of pneumonia.

Historically, penicillin has been regarded as the treatment of choice; with two million units given intravenously every two hours. Tetracycline and erythromycin have been recommended in penicillin sensitive patients. The vast majority of anthrax strains are sensitive *in vitro* to penicillin. However, penicillin resistant strains exist naturally, and one has been recovered from a fatal human case. Moreover, it is not difficult to induce resistance to penicillin, tetracycline, erythromycin, and many other antibiotics through laboratory manipulation of organisms.

Vaccines are available against some forms of anthrax, but their efficacy against abnormally high concentrations of the bacteria is uncertain. In countries where anthrax is common and vaccination levels of animal herds are low, humans should avoid contact with livestock and animal products and avoid eating meat that has not been properly slaughtered and cooked. Also, an anthrax vaccine has been licensed for use in humans. The vaccine is reported to be 93 per cent effective in protecting against anthrax.

The immunisation consists of three subcutaneous injections given two weeks apart followed by three additional subcutaneous infections given at six, 12 and 18 months. Annual booster injections of the vaccine of the vaccine are recommended thereafter.

Mild local reactions occur in 30 per cent of recipients and consist of slight tenderness and redness at the injection site. Severe local reactions are infrequent and consist of extensive swelling of the forearm in addition to the local reaction. Systemic reactions occur in fewer than 0.2 per cent of recipients.

Anthrax is diagnosed by isolating *B. anthraces* from the blood, skin lesions, or respiratory secretions or by measuring specific antibodies in the blood of persons with suspected cases. A licensed, alum-precipitated preparation of purified *B. anthraces* protective antigen (PA) has been shown to be effective in preventing or significantly reducing the incidence of inhalation anthrax. After completion of the first three doses of the recommended six-dose primary series (0, 2, 4 weeks, then 6, 12, 18 months), protection against both cutaneous and inhalation anthrax is afforded. As with all vaccines, the degree of protection depends upon the magnitude of the challenge dose; vaccine-induced protection is undoubtedly overwhelmed by extremely high spore challenge.

If there is information indicating that a biological weapon attack is imminent, prophylaxis with ciprofloxacin (500 mg po bid), or doxycycline (100 mg po bid) is recommended. If unvaccinated, a single 0.5 ml dose of vaccine should also be given subcutaneously.

PLAGUE

In a famous episode in World War II, the Japanese Army unleashed fleas infected with the *Yersinia pestic bacterium* on Chinese forces in Manchuria. It was reported that they worked on a plan for attacking enemy troops with the organism by releasing plague-infected fleas. This bacterium could be delivered theoretically as an aerosol. The attack backfired, inflicting heavy tolls on both sides.

Plauge is caused by *Yersinia pestis*, a rod-shaped, non-motile, non-sporulating, gram-negative, bipolar staining, facultative anaerobic bacterium. It is normally a zoonotic disease of rodents. Fleas which live on the rodents can sometimes pass the bacteria to human beings, who then suffer from the bubonic form of plague. The pneumonic form of the disease would be seen as the primary form after purposeful aerosol dissemination of the organisms. The bubonic form would be seen after purposeful dissemination through the release of infected fleas. All human populations are susceptible.

Recovery from the disease may be followed by temporary immunity. The organisms will probably remain viable in water and moist meals and grains for several weeks. At near freezing temperatures, it will remain alive from months to years but is killed by 15 minutes exposure to 72°C. It also remains viable for some time in dry sputum, flea feces, and buried bodies but is killed within several hours of exposure to sunlight.

Pneumonic plague incubates two-three days. High fever, chills, headache, hemoptysis, and toxemia, progressing rapidly to dyspnea, stridor, and cyanosis. Death from respiratory failure, circulatory collapse, and a bleeding diathesis. Bubonic plague incubates two-10 days. Malaise, high fever, and tender lymph nodes (buboes); may progress spontaneously to the septicemic form, with spread to the CNS, lungs, etc.

In man, plague normally appears in three forms: bubonic, primary septicemic, and pneumonic. The buboes in the bubonic form are normally seen in the inguinal lymph nodes as the legs are the most commonly flea-bitten part of the human body. Septicemia is common, as greater than 80 per cent of blood cultures are positive for the organism is bubonic plague, although primary septicemia may occur without lymphadenopathy. The pneumonic form is an infection of the lungs due either to inhalation of the organisms (primary pneumonic plague), or spread to the lungs from septicemia (secondary pneumonic plague). In man, the mortality of untreated bubonic plague is approximately 50 per cent, whereas in pneumonic plague the mortality rate is 100 per cent.

After an incubation period varying from two to three days for primary pneumonic plague, onset is acute and often fulminant. The presentation is one of malaise, high fever, chills, headache, myalgia, cough with production of a bloody sputum, and toxemia. The chest X-ray reveals a patchy or consolidates bronchopneumonia. The pneumonia progresses rapidly, resulting in dyspnea, stridor, and cyanosis. The terminal event is one of respiratory failure, circulatory collapse, and a bleeding diathesis.

In bubonic plague the incubation period ranges from two to 10 days with the onset also being acute and often fulminant. The presentation is one of malaise, high fever, and one or more tender lymph nodes. The liver and spleen are often tender and palpable. One quarter of patients will have various types of skin lesions. Occasionally a pustule, vesicle, eschar or papule containing leukocytes and bacteria will be apparent in the bubo distribution and presumably represents the site of the inoculating flea bite.

Bubonic plague may progress spontaneously to the septicemic form with organisms spreading to the central nervous system, lungs, and elsewhere. Black necrotic and purpuric lesions caused by endotoxemia are also often present. Laboratory findings include a leukocytosis, with a total WBC count up to 20,000 cells with increased bands, and greater than 80 per cent polymorphonuclear cells. One also often finds increased fibrin split products in the blood indicative of a low-grade DIC, and the ALT, AST, and bilirubin are also elevated.

Presumptive diagnosis of plauge can be made microscopically by identification of the gram-negative coccobacillus with safety-pin bipolar staining in Gram or Wayson's stained smears from a lymph node needle aspirate, sputum, or cerebrospinal fluid sample. When available, immunofluorescent staining is very useful. A definitive diagnosis can be readily made by culturing the organism from blood, sputum, and bubo aspirates. The organism grows slowly at normal incubation temperatures, and may be misidentified by automated systems because of delayed biochemical reactions. It may be cultured on blood agar, MacConkey agar or infusion broth. Most naturally occurring strains of *Y. pestis* produce an F1-antigen *in vivo*, which can be detected in serum samples by immunoassay. A fourfold rise in antibody titer in patient serum is also diagnostic.

Use standard precautions for health-care workers exposed to bubonic plague and droplet precautions for health-care workers exposed to pneumonic plague until the patient has been on antibiotic therapy for at least 48 hours and there has been a favourable clinical response to treatment. Streptomycin, tetracycline, chloramphenicol, and gentamicicn are highly effective, especially if begun early.

Plague pneumonia is almost always fatal if treatment is not initiated within 24 hours of the onset of symptoms. Streptomycin remains the drug of choice and is given 30 mg/kg/ day in two divided doses for 10 days. Gentamicin is acceptable if streptomycin is unavailable. While the patient is typically a febrile after three days, the extra week of therapy prevents relapses. Intravenous doxycycline 200 mg initially, followed by 100 mg every 12 hours of 10-14 days is also effective. Results obtained from laboratory animal, but not human, experience, indicate that quinolone antibiotics, such as ofloxacin and ciprofloxacin, may also be effective. The addition of chloramphenicol is required for the treatment of plague meningitis.

Usual supportive therapy required includes IV crystalloids and hemodynamic monitoring. Although low-grade DIC may occur, clinically significant haemorrhage is uncommon as is the need to treat with heparin. Finally, buboes rarely require incision and drainage or any form of local care, but instead recede with systemic antibiotic therapy. In fact, incision and drainage may pose a risk to others in contact with the patient.

A licensed, killed whole cell vaccine is available for use in those considered to be at risk of exposure. The primary series consists of three doses. The initial dose of 1.0 ml 1M is followed by 0.2 ml 1M at one and six months. Three booster doses of 0.2 ml 1M are given at six months intervals following the third dose of the primary series and then every one-two years thereafter. The current vaccine offers protection against bubonic plague, but is probably not effective against aerosolised *Y. pestis*.

Presently, 8-10 per cent of inoculations result in local reactions which include erythema, in duration, tenderness and oedema at the site of injection. These typically resolve within 48 hours. Approximately seven-10 per cent of inoculations will result in systemic symptoms including malaise, lymphadenopathy, fever and very rarely anaphylaxis, tachycardia, urticaria, or hypotension.

Due to oral administration and relative lack of toxicity, the choice of antibiotic for prophylaxis or for use in face-to-face contacts of patients with pneumonic plague or after a confirmed or suspected plague BW attack is doxycycline 100 mg orally twice daily, for seven days or the duration of risk of exposure, whichever is longer. Ciprofloxacin has also shown to be effective in preventing disease in exposed mice, and may be more available in a wartime setting as it is also distributed in blister-packs for anthrax post-exposure prophylaxis.

Q FEVER

Q fever or 'Query fever' was first described in Australia. It is called so because the causative agent was initially unknown. *Coxiella burnetii*, the causative agent, was discovered in 1937. This organism is a rickettsial agent that is resistant to heat and desiccation and highly infectious by the aerosol route. A single inhaled organism may produce clinical illness. For all of these reasons, Q fever could be used as a biological warfare agent. This organism could be employed by an adversary as an incapacitating agent due to its highly infectious nature and likelihood of causing disease if delivered by the respiratory route.

Coxiella burnetii's natural reservoirs are sheep, cattle and goats, and grows to especially high concentrations in placental tissues. Exposure to infected; animals at parturition is an important risk factor for endemic disease. The organisms are also excreted in animal milk, urine, and faeces. Humans acquire the disease by inhalation of aerosols contaminated with the organisms. Farmers and abattoir workers are at greatest risk occupationally. A biological warfare attack with Q fever would cause a disease similar to that occurring naturally. Q fever is also a significant hazard in laboratory personnel who are working with the organism.

Fever, cough, and pleuritic chest pain may occur as early as ten days after exposure. Patients are not generally critically ill, and the illness lasts from two days to two weeks.

Q fever generally occur as a self-limiting febrile illness lasting two days to two weeks. The incubation period varies according to the numbers of organisms inhaled, with longer periods between exposure and illness with lower numbers of inhaled organisms. The disease generally presents as an acute nondifferentiated febrile illness, with headaches, fatigue, and myalgias as prominent symptoms. Pneumonia manifested by an abnormal chest X-ray occurs in half of all patients, but only half of these, or 25 per cent of patients will have a cough or rates. Pleuritic chest pain occurs in about one-fourth of patients with Q fever pneumonia. Chest radiograph abnormalities, when present, are patchy infiltrates that may resemble viral or mycoplasma pneumonia. Rounded opacities and adenopathy have also been described. Uncommon complications include chronic hepatitis, culture negative endocarditis, aseptic meningitis, encephalitis and osteomyelitis.

Q fever is not a clinically distinct illness and, may resemble a viral illness or other types of atypical pneumonia. The diagnosis is confirmed serologically. As Q fever usually present as an undifferentiated febrile illness, or a primary a typical pneumonia, it may be difficult to distinguish from viral illnesses and must be differentiated from pneumonia cause by *Mycoplasma pneumoniae*, *Legionella pneumophila*, *Chlamydia psittaci*, and *Chlamydia pneumoniae*. More rapidly progressive forms of Q fever pneumonia may look like bacterial pneumonias such as tularemia or plague. Significant numbers of soldiers presenting over a one-to-two week period with a non-specific febrile illness, with associated pneumonic symptoms in about half of cases, should trigger the possibility of an attack with aerosolised Q fever in the minds of the treating physicians. The diagnosis will often rest on the clinical and epidemiologic picture in the setting of a possible biowarfare attack.

Isolation of the organism is impractical, as the organism is difficult to culture and a significant hazard to laboratory workers. Serological tests for Q fever include identification of antibody to *C.burnetii* by indirect fluorescent antibody (IFA), enzyme-linked immunosorbent assay (ELISA), and complement-fixation. Specific IgM antibodies may be detectable as early as the second week after onset of illness. ELISA testing is available at USAMRIID. A single serum specimen can be used to reliably diagnose acute Q fever with this test as early as one and a half to two weeks into the illness. The most commonly available serologic test is the complement fixation test (CF) which is relatively insensitive and may not be useful if sera have intrinsic anti-complement activity.

Standard precautions are recommended for healthcare workers. Most cases of acute Q fever will eventually resolve without antibiotic treatment. Tetracycline 500 mg every six hours or doxycycline 100 mg every 12 hours for five-seven days will shorten the duration of illness, and fever usually disappears within one to two days after treatment is begun. Successful treatment of Q fever endocarditis is much more difficult. Tetracycline or doxycycline given in combination with trimethoprim-sulfamethoxazole (TMP-SMX) or rifampin for 12 months or longer has been successful in some cases.

A formalin-inactivated whole cell vaccine is available for immunisation of a risk personnel on an investigational basis, although a Q fever vaccine is licensed in Australia. Vaccination with a single dose of this killed suspension of *C. burnetii* provides complete protection against naturally occurring Q fever, and greater than 95 per cent protection against aerosol exposure. Protection lasts for at least five years. The vaccine is generally safe in non-sensitised individuals.

Tetracycline or doxycyline given prophylactically after exposure can delay the onset of disease, or even prevent symptoms if administered late in the incubation period. When prophylaxis is started one day after exposure and continued for five days, clinical disease has been shown to occur about three weeks after stopping therapy.

TULAREMIA

Tularemia was recognised in Japan in the early 1800s. In the early 1900s American workers investigating suspected plague epidemics in San Francisco isolated the organism and named it *Bacterium tularense* after Tulare County where the work was performed. Dr. Edward Francis, USPHS, established the cause of deer-fly fever as *Bacterium tularense* and subsequently devoted his life to researching the organism and organism and disease, hence, the organism was later renamed *Francisella tularensis.*

Francisella tularensis was weaponised by the United States in the 1950s and 1960s during the US offensive biowarfare programme, and other countries and suspected to have weaponised this agent. This organism could potentially be stabilised for weaponisation by an adversary and theoretically produced in either a wet or dried form.

Francisella tularensis is a small, aerobic non-motile, gram-negative cocco-bacillus. Tularemia is a zoonotic disease which humans typically acquire after contact of their skin or mucous membranes with tissues or body fluids or infected animals, or from bites of infected deerflies, mosquitoes, or ticks. Less commonly, inhalation of contaminated dusts or ingestion of contaminated foods or water may produce clinical disease. Respiratory exposure by aerosol would cause typhoidal or pneumonic tularemia.

F. tularensis can remain viable for weeks in water, soil, carcasses, and hides, and for years in frozen rabbit meat. It is resistant for months to temperatures of freezing and below.

After an incubation period varying from one-21 days, presumably dependent upon the dose of organisms, onset is usually acute.

Tularemia may appear in several forms in man depending upon the route of inoculation: ulceroglandular, glandular, typhoidal, oculoglandular, pharyngeal, and pneumonic tularemia. In humans, as few as 10 to 50 organisms will cause disease if inhaled or injected intradermally, whereas approximately 108 organisms are required with oral challenge.

Ulceroglandular tularemia (75-85 per cent of cases) is most often acquired through inoculation of the skin or mucous membranes with blood or tissue fluids of infected animals. It is characterised by fever, chills, headache, and malaise, an ulcerated skin lesion and painful regional lymphadenopathy. The skin lesion is usually located on the fingers or hand.

Glandular tularemia (5-10 per cent of cases) results in fever and tender lymphadenopathy but no skin ulcer.

Typhoidal tularemia accounts for five-15 per cent of naturally occurring cases and occurs mainly after inhalation of infectious aerosols, but can occur after intradermal or gastro-intestinal challenge. It manifests as fever, prostration, and weight loss but without lymphadenopathy. Pneumonia may be associated with any form but is most common in typhoidal tularemia. Diagnosis of primary typhoidal tularemia is difficult, as signs and symptoms are non-specific and there frequently is no suggestive exposure history. Respiratory symptoms, substernal discomfort, and a non-productive cough may also be present. Radiologic evidence of pneumonia or mediastinal lymphadenopathy is most common with typhodial disease but may or may not be present in all other forms of tularemia.

Oculoglandular tularemia (1-2 per cent of cases) occurs after inoculation of the conjunctivae with infectious material. Patients have unilateral, painful, purulent conjunctivitis with preauricular or cervical lymphadenopathy. Chemosis, periorbital oedema, and small nodular lesions or ulcerations of the palpebral conjunctiva are noted in some patients.

Oropharyngeal tularemia refers to primary ulceroglandular disease confined to the throat. It produces an acute exudative or membranous pharyngotonsillitis with cervical lymphadeno-pathy.

Pneumonic tularemia is an illness characterised primarily by pneumonia. Pneumonia is common in tularemia. It is seen in 30-80 per cent of the typhoidal cases and in 10-15 per cent of the ulceroglandular cases. The case fatality rate without treatment is approximately five per cent for the ulceroglandular form and 35 per cent for the typhoidal form. All ages are susceptible, and recovery is followed by permanent immunity.

Identification of organisms by staining ulcer fluids or sputum is generally not helpful. Routine culture is difficult, due to unusual growth requirements and/or overgrowth or commensal bacteria. Isolation represents a clear hazard to laboratory personnel and should only be attempted in BL-3 laboratory. The diagnosis can be established retrospectively serologically. A fourfold rise in the tularemia tube agglutination or microagglutination titer is diagnostic of infection. A single convalescent titer of 1:160 or greater is diagnostic of past or current infection.

Standard precautions are recommended for healthcare workers. Streptomycin is the treatment of choice. Gentamicin is also effective. Tetracycline and chloramphenicol treatment are effective as well, but are associated with significant relapse rates. Although laboratory, related infections with this organism are very common, person-to-person spread is unusual and respiratory isolation is not required.

Attenuated tularemia vaccine is available as an investigational new drug (IND). It is given by scarification. This vaccine has been administered to more than 5,000 persons without significant adverse reactions. It is of proven effectiveness in preventing laboratory-acquired tularemia as well as in experimentally exposed human volunteers. As with all vaccines, the degree of protection depends upon the magnitude of the challenge dose; vaccine-induced protection could be overwhelmed by extremely high doses.

SMALLPOX

Eradicated from the wild in 1980, *variola major* is known to exist in only two restricted laboratories in Russia, and the United States. The United States stopped vaccinating its military population in 1989 and civilians in the early 1980s. These populations are now susceptible to *variola major*, although recruits immunised in 1989 many retain some degree of immunity. Variola may have been used by the British Army against native Americans by giving them contaminated blankets from the beds of smallpox victims during the eighteenth century. Japan considered the use of smallpox as a biological weapon in World War II and it has been considered as a possible threat agent against US forces for many years.

For the past century, two distinct types of smallpox were recognised. Variola minor was distinguished by milder systemic toxicity and more diminutive pox lesions, and caused one per cent mortality in unvaccinated victims. However, the prototypical disease variola major caused mortality of three per cent and 30 per cent in the vaccinated and unvaccinated, respectively. Other clinical forms associated with variola major, flat-type and haemorrhagic-type smallpox, were notable for severe mortality. A naturally occurring relative of variola, monkeypox, occurs in Africa, and is clinically indistinguishable from smallpox with the exception of notable enlargement of cervical and inguinal lymph nodes.

Variola virus is an orthopox virus and occurs in at least two strains, variola major and the milder disease, variola minor. Despite the global eradication of smallpox and continued availability of a vaccine, the potential weaponisation of variola continues to pose a military threat. This threat can be attributed to the aerosol infectivity of the virus, the relative ease of large-scale production, and an increasingly orthopox virus-naive populace. Although the fully-developed cutaneous eruption of smallpox is unique, earlier stages of the rash could be mistaken for varicella. Spread of infection constitutes a nosocomial hazard from the time of onset of a smallpox patient's exanthem until scabs have separated. Quarantine with respiratory isolation should be applied to secondary contacts for 17 days post-exposure.

The incubation period of smallpox averaged 12 days, and contacts were quarantined fora minimum of 16-17 days following exposure. Clinical manifestations began acutely with malaise, fever, rigours, vomiting, headache, and backache; 15 per cent of patients developed delirium. Approximately 10 per cent of light skinned patients exhibited an erythematous rash during this phase. Two to three days later, an exanthem appeared concomitantly with a discrete rash about the face, hands and forearms. Following eruptions on the lower extremities, the rash spread centrally to the trunk over the next week. Lesions quickly progress from macules to papules, and eventually to pustular vesicles. Lesions were more abundant on the extremities and face, and this centrifugal distribution is an important diagnostic feature.

In distinct contract to varicella, lesions on various segments of the body remained generally synchronous in their stage of development. From eight to 14 days after onset, the pustules formed scabs which leave depressed depigmented scars upon healing. Although variola concentrations in the throat, conjunctiva, and urine diminished with time, virus could readily be recovered from scabs throughout convalescence. Therefore, patients should be isolated and considered infectious until all scabs separate.

The usual method of diagnosis is demonstration of characteristic virions on electron microscopy of vesicular scrapings. Under light microscopy, aggregations of variola virus particles, called Guarnieri bodies, are found. Another rapid but relatively insensitive test for Guarnieri bodies in vesicular scrapings is Gispen's modified silver stain, in which cytoplasmic inclusions appear black. None of the above laboratory tests are capable of discriminating variola from vaccinia, monkeypox or cowpox. This differentiation classically required isolation of the virus and characterisation of its growth on chorioallantoic membrane. The development of polymerase chain reaction diagnostic techniques promises a more accurate and less cumbersome method of discriminating between variola and other orthopox viruses.

Medical personnel must be prepared to recognise a vesicular exanthem in possible biowarfare theatres as potentially variola, and to initiate appropriate counter-measures. Any confirmed case of smallpox should be considered an international emergency with immediate report made to public health authorities. Droplet and airborne precautions for a minimum of 16-17 days following exposure for all persons in direct contact with the index case, especially the unvaccinated. Patients should be considered infectious until all scabs separate. Immediate vaccination or revaccination should also be undertaken for all personnel exposed to either weaponised variola virus or a clinical case of smallpox. The potential for airborne spread to other than close contacts is controversial. In general, close person-to-person proximity is required for transmission to reliably occur. Nevertheless, variola's potential in low relative humidity for airborne dissemination was alarming in two hospital outbreaks.

Smallpox patients were infectious from the time of onset of their eruptive exanthem, most commonly from days three to six after onset of fever. Infectivity was markedly enhanced if the patient manifested a coughs. Indirect transmission via contaminated bedding or other formites was infrequent. Some close contacts harboured virus in their throats without developing disease, and hence might have served as a means of secondary transmission. Vaccination with a verified clinical 'take' (vesicle with scar formation) within the past three years is considered to render a person immune to smallpox. However, given the difficulties and uncertainties under wartime conditions of verifying the adequacy of troops prior vaccination, routine revaccination of all potentially exposed personnel would seem prudent if there existed a significant prospect of smallpox exposure.

Smallpox vaccine is most often administered by intradermal inoculation with a bifurcated needle, a process that became known as scarification because of the permanent scar that resulted. Vaccination after exposure to weaponised smallpox or a case of smallpox is effective in preventing disease if given within seven days after exposure. A vesicle typically appears at the vaccination site five-seven days post-inoculation, with surrounding erythema and in duration. The lesion forms a scab and gradually heals over the next one-two weeks. Side effects include low-grade fever and auxiliary lymphadenopathy. The attendant erythema and in duration of the vaccination vesicle is frequently misdiagnosed as bacterial superinfection. More severe first-time vaccine reactions include secondary inoculation of the virus to other sites such as the face, eyelid, or other persons and generalised vaccinia, which is a systematic spread of the virus to produce mocucutaneous lesions away from the primary vaccination site.

Vaccination is contraindicated in the following conditions: immunosuppression, HIV infection, history or evidence of eczema, or current household, sexual, or other close physical contact with persons possessing one of these conditions. In addition, vaccination should not be performed during pregnancy.

Vaccinia immune globulin is of value in post-exposure prophylaxis of smallpox when given within the first week following exposure, and concurrently with vaccination. Vaccination alone is recommended for those without contraindications to the vaccine, unless greater than one week has elapsed after exposure.

EBOLA HAEMORRHAGIC FEVER

Ebola haemorrhagic fever (HF) is a severe, often-fatal disease in humans and non-human primates that has appeared sporadically since its initial recognition in 1976. The *Ebola virus* causative of the disease is one of two members of a family of RNA viruses called the *Filoviridae*. Three of the four species of *Ebola virus* identified so far have caused disease in humans: Ebola-Zaire, Ebola-Sudan, and Ebola-Ivory Coast. The fourth, Ebola-Reston, has caused disease in non-human primates, but not in humans. The virus is zoonotic and is normally maintained in an animal host that is native to the African continent.

Confirmed cases of Ebola HF have been reported in the Democratic Republic of the Congo, Gabon, Sudan, the Ivory Coast, and Uganda. An individual with serologic evidence of infection but showing no apparent illness has been reported in Liberia, and a laboratory worker in England became ill as a result of an accidental needle-stick. No case of the disease in humans has ever been reported in the United States. *Ebola-Reston virus* caused severe illness and death in monkeys imported to research facilities in the United States and Italy from the Philippines; during these outbreaks, several research workers became infected with the virus, but did not become ill.

Ebola HF typically appears in sporadic outbreaks, usually spread within a health-care setting. It is likely that sporadic, isolated cases occur as well, but go unrecognised. Since the natural reservoir of the virus is unknown, the manner in which the virus first appears in a human at the start of an outbreak has not been determined.

The first patient becomes infected through contact with an infected animal. After the first case patient in an outbreak setting is infected, humans can transmit the virus in several ways. People can be exposed to *Ebola virus* from direct contact with the blood and/or secretions of an infected person. This is why the virus has often been spread through the families and friends of infected persons: in the course of feeding, holding, or otherwise caring for them, family members and friends would come into close contact with such secretions. People can also be exposed to *Ebola virus* through contact with objects, such as needles, that have been contaminated with infected secretions.

Nosocomial transmission has been associated frequently with Ebola HF outbreaks. It includes both types of transmission described above, but it is used to describe the spread of disease in a health-care setting such as a clinic or hospital. In African health-care facilities, patients are often cared for without the use of a mask, gown, or gloves, and exposure to the virus has occurred when health care workers treated individuals with Ebola HF without wearing these types of protective clothing. In addition, when needles or syringes are used, they may not be of the disposable type, or may not have been sterilised, but only rinsed before re-insertion into multi-use vials of medicine. If needles or syringes become contaminated with virus and are then reused, numbers of people can become infected. While all *Ebola virus* species have displayed the ability to be spread through airborne particles (aerosols) under research conditions, this type of spread has not been documented among humans in a real-world setting, such as a hospital or household.

The signs and symptoms of Ebola HF are not the same for all patients. Researchers do not understand why some people are able to recover from Ebola HF and others are not. However, it is known that patients who die usually have not developed a significant immune response to the virus at the time of death.

Diagnosing Ebola HF in an individual who has been infected only a few days is difficult because early symptoms, such as red and itchy eyes and a skin rash, are non-specific to the virus and are seen in other patients with diseases that occur much more frequently. If a person has the constellation of symptoms described in the table above, and infection with *Ebola* virus is suspected, several laboratory tests should be done promptly. These include a blood film examination for malaria and a blood culture. If the suspected patient has bloody diarrhoea, a stool culture should also be performed.

Antigen-capture enzyme-linked immunosorbent assay (ELISA) testing, IgG ELISA, polymerase chain reaction (PCR), and virus isolation can be used to diagnose a case of Ebola HF within a few days of the onset of symptoms. Persons tested later in the course of the disease or after recovery can be tested for IgM and IgG antibodies; the disease can also be diagnosed retrospectively in deceased patients by using immuno-histochemistry testing, virus isolation, or PCR.

There is no standard treatment for Ebola HF. Currently, patients receive supportive therapy. This consists of balancing the patient's fluids and electrolytes, maintaining their oxygen status and blood pressure, and treating them for any complicating infections. During the Kikwit outbreak, eight patients were given blood of individuals who had been infected with *Ebola* virus but recovered. Seven of the eight patients survived. However, because the study size was small, and participants characteristics predisposed them towards recovery, the efficacy of the treatment remains unknown.

The prevention of Ebola HF in Africa presents many challenges. Since the identity and location of the natural reservoir of *Ebola* virus are unknown, there are few established primary prevention measures. If cases of the disease do appear, current social and economic conditions favour the spread of an epidemic within health-care facilities. Therefore, health-care provider's must be able to recognise a case of Ebola HF should one appear. They must also have the capability to perform diagnostic tests and be ready to employ practical viral hemorrhagic fever isolation precautions, or barrier nursing techniques. These techniques include the wearing of protective clothing, such as masks, gloves, gowns, and goggles; the use of infection-control measures, including complete equipment sterilisation; and the isolation of Ebola HF patients from contact with unprotected persons. The aim of all of these techniques is to avoid any person's contact with the blood or secretions of any patient. If a patient with Ebola HF dies, it is equally important that direct contact with the body of the deceased patient be prevented.

Scientists and researchers are faced with the challenges of developing additional diagnostic tools to assist in early, diagnosis of the disease and ecological investigations of *Ebola* virus and the disease it causes. In addition, one of the research goals is to monitor suspected areas to determine the incidence of the disease. More extensive knowledge of the virus' reservoir and how the virus is spread must be acquired to prevent future outbreaks effectively.

CHOLERA

Cholera has been used as a biological weapon since early periods of fourteenth century. It does not easily spread from person-to-person. Therefore, to be an effective biological weapon, major drinking water supplies would need to be heavily contaminated. Recent naturally occurring cholera epidemics in South America have shown the devastating consequences of this disease. Cholera spread quickly in Peru and neighbouring countries, despite all attempts to curb the epidemic at an early stage. Over 250,000 symptomatic cases have been reported in Peru alone, and the epidemic has spread to other countries.

Cholera is an acute infectious disease, characterised by sudden onset with nausea, vomiting, profuse watery diarrhoea with 'rice water' appearance, the rapid loss of body fluids, toxemia, and frequent collapse. Mortality can range as high as 50 per cent in untreated cases.

Vibrio cholerae the causative is a short, curved, motile, gram-negative, non-sporulating rod. There are two serogroups, O-1 and O-139, that have been associated with cholera in humans. The O-1 serotype exists as 2 biotypes, classical and El Tor. The organisms are facultative anaerobes, growing best at a pH of 7.0, but able to tolerate an alkaline environment. They do not invade the intestinal mucosa, but rather adhere to it.

Cholera is the prototype toxigenic diarrhoea, which is secretory in nature. All strains elaborate the same enterotoxin, a protein molecule with a molecular weight of 84,000 daltons, The entire clinical syndrome is caused by the action of they toxin on the intestinal epithelial cell. Fluid loss in cholera originates in the small intestine with the colon being relatively insensitive to the toxin. The large volume of fluid produced; in the upper intestine overwhelms the capacity of the lower intestine to absorb. Transmission is made through direct or indirect fecal contamination of water or foods, and by heavily a soiled hands or utensils.

All populations are susceptible, while natural resistance to infection is variable. Recovery from an attack is followed by a temporary immunity which may furnish some protection for years. The organism is easily, killed by drying. It is not viable in pure water, but will survive up to 24 hours in sewage, and as long as six weeks in certain types of relatively impure water containing organic matter. It can withstand freezing for three to four days. It is readily killed by dry heat at 117°C, by steam and boiling, by short exposure to ordinary disinfectants, and by chlorination of water.

After an incubation period varying from four hours to five hours to five days, presumably dependent upon the dose of ingested organisms, onset is usually rather sudden, although the clinical manifestations range from an asymptomatic carrier state to severe illness. Initially the disease presents with intestinal cramping and painless diarrhoea. Vomiting, malaise and headache often accompany the diarrhoea, especially early in the illness. If fever is present, it is usually low grade. Diarrhoea may be mild or profuse and watery, with fluid losses exceeding five to 10 litres or more per day. Electrolyte loss can explain almost all clinical signs and symptoms. Without treatment, death may result from severe dehydration, hypovolemia and shock. On microscopic examination of stool samples there are few or no red cells or white cells and almost no protein. The absence of inflammatory cells and erythrocytes reflects the non-invasive character or *V. cholerae* infection of the intestinal lumen. The organism can be identified in liquid stool or enrichment broths by dark-field or phase contrast microscopy, and by identifying darting motile vibrio. The organism must be transported using Cary-Blair medium and then streaked for isolation onto TCBS (Thiosulfate Citrate Bile Salt Sucrose) medium.

Treatment of cholera depends primarily on replacement of fluid and electrolyte losses. This is best accomplished using oral rehydration therapy with the World Health Organisation solution (3.5 g NaCl, 2.5 g $NaHCO_3$ 1.5 g KCl and 20 g of glucose per litre). Intravenous fluid replacement is occasionally needed in patients with persistent vomiting or high rates of stool loss (>10ml/kg/hr). Antibiotics will shorten the duration of diarrhoea and thereby reduce fluid losses. Tetracycline (500 mg every 6 hours for 3 days) or doxycycline (300 mg once or 100 mg every 12 hours for 3 days) is generally adequate. However, due to widespread tetracycline resistance, ciprofloxacin (500 mg every 12 hours for 3 days) or erythromycin (500 mg every 6 hours for 3 days) should be considered. For paediatric treatment, tetracycline (50 mg/ kg/d divided into 4 doses × 3 days) can be used, as dental staining has only occurred after six courses of treatment lasting six or more days. Alternates are erythromycin (40 mg/ kg/d divided into 4 doses × 3 days), trimethoprim 8 mg and sulfamethoxazole 40 mg/kg/d divided into 2 doses × 3 days, and furazolidone (5 mg/kg/d divided into 4 doses × 3 days or 7 mg/kg × one dose).

A licensed, killed vaccine is available for use in those considered to be at risk of exposure, however, it provides only about 50 per cent protection that lasts for no more than six months. The vaccination schedule is an initial dose followed by a second dose four weeks later, with booster doses every six months. An inactivated oral vaccine (WC/ rBS), which is licensed in Europe, is safe and provides rapid short-term protection. Licensure in the US is anticipated. WC/rBS requires two doses and has approximately 85 per cent efficacy lasting two-three years for both El Tor and classical biotypes. Live attenuated oral vaccines show much promise, and one, CVD 103-HgR (classical biotype), will probably be available by 1999. There are no O-139 serogroup vaccines close to licensure, and none of the above-mentioned vaccines provide cross-protection against O-139. Primary infection with *V. cholerae* O-1 serogroup also provides no immunity against O-139.

Since the major biological threat from this organism appears to be sabotage of food and water supplies, it would seem justified to state that optimal prophylaxis in these circumstances would not be of a medical nature but would be proper safeguarding of these supplies to prevent the sabotage. The best way to prevent cholera in an endemic environment is to avoid contaminated water, ice, fruits, vegetables and also raw or undercooked seafood. Personal contact rarely causes infection because of the high inoculum required for infection; however, enteric precautions and careful hand-washing should be employed.

BRUCELLOSIS

Brucellosis is caused by *B. melitensis* among British soldiers on Malta during the Crimean War as Mediterranean gastric remittent fever. Work by the Mediterranean Fever Commission identified goats as the source of human brucella infection on Malta, and restriction of the ingestion of unpasteurised goats milk and cheese soon decreased the number of cases of brucellosis among military personnel. In 1997, most cases were associated with ingestion of unpasteurised dairy products and abattoir and veterinary work.

In US most cases are reported from Florida, California, Virginia, and Texas. It is a rare disease in US with an incidence of 0.5 per 100,000 population. In 1954, *Brucella suis* became the first agent weaponised by the US in the days of its offensive bioweapon programme at the newly constructed Pine Bluff Arsenal.

Brucella species are highly infectious via the aerosol route. Inhalation of only 10 to 100 bacteria is sufficient to cause disease in man. The relatively long and variable incubation period (5-60 days) and the fact that many infections are asymptomatic under natural conditions has made it a less desirable agent for weaponisation, although large aerosol doses may shorten the incubation period and increase the clinical attack rate. Brucellosis infection has a low mortality rate with most deaths caused by endocarditis or meningitis.

Brucellosis may present fever, headache, myalgia, arthralgia, back pain, sweats, chills, and generalised weakness and malaise are common complaints. Cough and pleuritic chest pain may occur in up to 20 per cent of cases, but these are usually not associated with acute pneumonitis. Pulmonary symptoms may not correlate with radiographic findings. The chest X-ray may be normal, or show lung abscesses, single or military nodules, bronchopneumonia, enlarged hailer lymph nodes, and pleural effusions. Gastrointestinal symptoms occur in up to 70 per cent of adult cases, and less frequently in children. These include anorexia, nausea, vomiting, diarrhoea and constipation. Ileitis, colitis and granulomatous or a mononuclear infiltrative hepatitis may occur. Lumbar pain and tenderness can occur in up to 60 per cent of cases and is due to various osteoarticular infections of the axial skeletal system. Paravertebral abscesses may occur and can be imaged by CT scan or MRI. CT scans often show vertebral sclerosis. Vertebral and disc space destruction may occur in chronic cases. One or less frequently, both sacroiliac joints may be infected causing low back and buttock pain that is intensified by stressing the sacroiliac joint on physical exam. Hepatomegaly and splenomegaly can occur in up to 45-63 per cent of cases.

Peripheral joint involvement may vary from pain on range of motion testing to joint immobility and effusion. Peripheral joint effusions usually show a mononuclear cell predominance and organisms can be isolated in up to 50 per cent of cases. The hip joints are the most commonly involved peripheral joints, but ankle, knee, and sternoclavicular joint infection may occur. Plain radiographs of involved sacroiliac joints usually show blurring of articular margins and widening of the joint space. Technetium or Gallium-67 bone scans are 90 per cent sensitive for detecting sacroileitis and will also detect other sites of bone and joint involvement.

In less than five per cent of cases meningitis occurs and may be an acute presenting illness of a chronic syndrome occurring late in the course of a persistent infection. The cerebrospinal fluid contains an increased number of lymphocytes and a low to normal glucose. Culture of the CSF has sensitivity of 50 per cent, and specific brucella antibodies can be detected in the fluid in a higher percentage of cases.

Encephalitis, peripheral neuropathy, radiculoneuropathy and, meningovascular syndromes have also been observed in rare cases. Behavioural disturbances in children and psychoses may occur in the meningoencephalitic form of the disease. Epididymo-orchitis may occur in men as the most frequent genitourinary form of brucellosis. Rashes occur in less than five per cent of cases and include macules, papules, ulcers, purpura, petechiae, etc.

In cases of brucellosis, the leukocyte count is usually normal but may be low. Anemia and thrombocytopenia may occur. Blood and bone marrow culture during the acute febrile phase of the illness will yield a positivity rate of 15-70 per cent and 92 per cent respectively. A biphasic culture method for blood (Castaneda bottle) may increase the number of isolates. The serum agglutination test (SAT) will detect both IgM and IgG antibodies. A titer of 1:160 or greater is indicative of active disease. The IgM titer can be measured by adding a reduced agent such as 2-mercaptoethanol to the serum. This will destroy the agglutinability of IgM allowing the IgM titer to be measured by subtracting the now lower titer from the total serum agglutinin titer.

A dot-ELISA using an autoclaved extract of *B. abortus* has been found to be a sensitive and specific screening test for detection of *Brucella* antibodies under field conditions. ELISA tests for antibody detection require standardisation using a specific antigen before they will be widely available. Antigen detection on DNA extracted from blood mononuclear cells has been accomplished using PCR analysis of a target sequence of the 31-kilodalton *B. abortus* protein BCSP31. This test has been proven to be rapid and specific and may replace blood culture in the future, since the latter may require incubation for up to six weeks.

Contact isolation is required for draining lesions. Person-to-person transmission is possible via contact with such lesion. Biosafety level 3 practices should be used for suspected brucella cultures in the laboratory because of the danger of inhalation infection. Antibiotic therapy is recommended as the sole therapy unless there are surgical indications for the treatment of localised diseases. The treatment recommended by the World Health Organisation for acute brucellosis in adults is doxycycline 200 mg/day p.o. plus rifampin 600-900 mg/day for a minimum of six weeks. The previously established regimen of intramuscular streptomycin along with an oral tetracycline may give fewer relapses but is no longer the primary recommendation. Ofloxacin 400 mg/day and rifampin 600 mg/day p.o. is also an effective combination. Combination therapy with rifampin, a tetracycline, and an aminoglycoside is indicated for infections with complications such as meningoencephalitis or endocarditis.

Animal vaccines are widely available. Consumption of unpasteurised milk and cheese should be avoided. No approved human brucella vaccine is available. An experimental human brucellosis vaccine has been tested on 271 subjects with a 25 per cent rate of unpleasant acute side effects.

VENEZUELAN EQUINE ENCEPHALITIS

Venezuelan Equine Encephalitis (VEE) was weaponised by the United States in the 1950s and 1960s before the US offensive biowarfare programme was terminated, and other countries have been or are suspected to have weaponised this agent. This virus could theoretically be produced in either a wet or dried from and potentially stabilised for weaponisation. This agent could then theoretically be delivered against friendly forces in a manner similar to the other agents already discussed. In natural human epidemics, disease in *Equidae* always precedes that in humans.

A biological warfare attack with virus disseminated as an aerosol would almost certainly cause human disease as a primary event. If *Equidae* were present, disease in these animals would occur simultaneously with human disease. However, during natural epidemics, illness or death in wild or free ranging *Equidae* may not be recognised before the onset of human disease, thus a natural epidemic could be confused with a BW event, and data on onset of disease should be considered with caution.

A more reliable method for determining the likelihood of a BW event would be the presence of VEE outside of its natural geographic range. Secondary spread by person-to-person contract has not been conclusively shown to occur; however, observations during a recent outbreak in Columbia suggest that it may occur often enough to sustain epidemics in the absence of *Equidae*.

VEE virus is an arthropod-borne alphavirus that is endemic in northern South America, Trinidad, Central America, Mexico, and Florida. Eight serologically distinct viruses belonging to the VEE complex have been associated with human-disease; the two most important of these pathogens are designated subtype 1, variants A/B, and C. These agents also cause severe disease in horses, mules, burros and donkeys. Natural infections are acquired by the bites of a wide variety of mosquitoes. *Equidae* serve as amplifying hosts and source of mosquito infection. In natural human epidemics, severe and often fatal encephalitis in *Equidae* always precedes disease in humans.

VEE is characterised by inflammation of the meninges of the brain and of the brain itself, thus accounting for the predominance of CNS symptoms in the small percentage of infections that develop encephalitis. The disease is usually acute, prostrating and of short duration. The case fatality rate is less than one per cent, although is somewhat higher in the very young or aged. Nearly 100 per cent of those infected suffer an overt illness. Recovery from an infection results in excellent short-term and long-term immunity.

The incubation period of the virus varies from one to five days. It is manifested by generalised malaise, spiking fever, rigours, severe headache, photophobia and myalgias in the legs and lumbosacral area. Nausea, vomiting, cough, sore throat, and diarrhoea may follow. This acute phase lasts 24-72 hours. A prolonged period of asthenia and lethargy may follow, with full health and activity regained after one-two weeks. Approximately four per cent of children during natural epidemics develop signs of central nervous system infection, with meningismus, convulsions, coma, and paralysis. Adults rarely develop neurologic complications. In children manifesting severe encephalitis, the fatality rate may reach 20 per cent. Permanent neurologic sequelae are reported in survivors.

The incidence of CNS disease and associated morbidity and mortality would be high after BW attack, as the VEE virus would infect the olfactory nerve and spread directly to the CNS. A VEE infection during pregnancy may cause encephalitis in the foetus, placental damage, abortion, or severe congenital neuro-anatomical anomalies. The white blood cell count shows a striking leukopenia and lymphopenia. In cases with encephalitis, the cerebrospinal fluid may be under increased pressure and contain up to 1,000 white cells/mm^3 and a mildly elevated protein concentration. Viremia during the acute phase of the illness is generally high enough to allow detection by antigen capture enzyme immunoassay. Virus isolation may be made from serum, and in some cases throat swab specimens, by inoculation of cell cultures or suckling mice. A variety of serological tests are applicable including the lgm ELISA, indirect FA, hemagglutination inhibition, complement-fixation; and neutralisation.

Person-to-person transmission may theoretically occur by means of respiratory droplet infection. There is no specific therapy. Patient with uncomplicated VEE infection may be treated with analgesics to relieve headache and myalgia. Patients who develop encephalitis may require anticonvulsants and intensive supportive care to maintain fluid and electrolyte balance, ensure adequate ventilation, and avoid complicating secondary bacteria infections. Patients should be treated in a screened room or in quarters treated with a residual insecticide for at least five days after onset, or until a febrile, as human cases may be infectious for mosquitoes for at least 72 hours. The virus can be destroyed by heat and disinfectants.

An investigational vaccine, designated TC-83, is a live, attenuated cell-culture-propagated vaccine which has been used in several thousand persons to prevent laboratory infections. The vaccine is given as a single 0.5 ml subcutaneous dose. Febrile reactions occur in up to 18 per cent of persons vaccinated, and may be moderate to severe in five per cent, with fever, myalgias, headache, and prostration. Approximately 18 per cent of vaccinated fail to develop detectable neutralising antibodies, but it is unknown whether they are susceptible to clinical infection if challenged. Contraindications for use include an intercurrent viral infection or pregnancy.

Another vaccine is the C-84 vaccine, prepared by formalin inactivation of the TC-83 strain. The vaccine is not used for primary immunisation, but is currently used to boost non-responders to three inoculations or until an antibody response is measured), and probably affords complete protection against aerosol infection from homologous strains in these individuals. As with all vaccines, the degree of protection depends upon the magnitude of the challenge dose; vaccine-induced protection could be overwhelmed by extremely high doses.

In experimental animals, alpha-interferon and the interferon-inducer poly-ICLC have proven highly effective for post exposure prophylaxis of VEE.

VIRAL HEMORRHAGIC FEVER

The viral hemorrhagic fevers are a diverse groups of human illness that are due to RNA virus from several different viral families: the Filoviridae, which consists of *Ebola* and *Marburg* viruses; the Arenaviridae, including Lassa fever, Argentine and Bolivian hemorrhagic fever viruses; the Bunyaviridae, including various members from the Hantavirus genus, Congo-Crimean hemorrhagic fever virus from the Nairovirus genus, and Rift Valley fever from the Phlebovirus genus; and Flaviviridae, such as yellow fever virus, dengue hemorrhagic fever virus, and others. The viruses may spread in a variety of ways, and for some there is a possibility that humans could be infected through a respiratory portal of entry.

These viruses are potential for aerosol dissemination or weaponisation, or likelihood for confusion with similar agents which might be weaponised. The clinical syndrome which these viruses may cause in humans is generally referred to as viral hemorrhagic fever or VHF. Not all infected patients develop VHF; there is both divergence and uncertainty about which host factors and virus strain differences might be responsible for clinically manifesting hemorrhagic disease.

For instance, an immunopathogenic mechanism has been identified for dengue hemorrhagic fever, which is seen only in patients previously infected with a heterologous, dengue serotype. Common presenting complaints are fever, myalgia, and prostration; clinical examination may reveal only conjunctiva injection, mild hypotension, flushing, and petechtal haemorrhages.

Full-blown VHF typically evolves to shock and generalised mucous membrane haemorrhage and often is accompanied by evidence of neurologic, hematopoietic, or pulmonary involvement. Apart from epidemiologic and intelligence information, some distinctive clinical features may suggest a specific etiologic agent: high AST elevation correlates with severity of illness from Lassa fever, and jaundice is a poor prognostic sign in yellow fever. Hepatic involvement is common among the VHFs, but a clinical picture dominated by jaundice and other evidence of hepatic failure is only seen in some cases of Rift Valley fever, Congo-Crimean HF, Marburg HF, Ebola HF, and yellow fever, Neurologic symptoms and thrombocytopenia are common in Argentine and Bolivian hemorrhagic fever. Kyanasur Forest disease and Omsk hemorrhagic fever and notable for a concomitant pulmonary involvement, and a biphasic illness with subsequent CNS manifestations. With regard to the Bonyaviruses, copious haemorrhage and nosocomial transmission are typical for Congo-Crimean HF, and retinitis is commonly seen in Rift Valley fever.

Renal insufficiency is proportional to cardiovascular compromise, except in haemorrhagic fever with renal syndrome

(HFRS) due to hantaviruses, where renal azotemia is an integral part of the disease process. Mortality may be substantial, ranging from five to 20 per cent or higher in recognised cases. *Ebola* outbreaks in Africa have been notable for the extreme prostration and toxicity of the victims, as well as frighteningly high case fatality rates ranging from 50 to 90 per cent. This particularly virulent virus could conceivably be chosen by an adversary as a biological warfare agent due to its probable aerosol infectivity and high mortality. A detailed travel history and a high index of suspicion are essential in making the diagnosis of VHF patients with arenaviral or hantaviral infections often recall having seen rodents during the presumed incubation period, but since the viruses are spread to man by aerosolised excreta or environmental contamination, actual contact with the reservoir is not necessary. Large mosquito populations are common during Rift Valley fever or flaviviral transmission, but a history of mosquito bite is sufficiently common to be of little assistance, whereas tick bites or nosocomial exposure are of some significance in suspecting Congo-Crimean hemorrhagic fever.

Large numbers of military personnel presenting with VHF manifestations in the same geographic area over a short time period should lead treating medical care providers to suspect either a natural outbreak if in an endemic setting, or possible a biowarfare attack, particularly if this type of disease does not occur naturally in the local area where troops are deployed. VHF should be suspected in any patient presenting with a severe febrile illness and evidence of vascular involvement who has travelled to an area where the virus is known to occur, or where intelligence information suggests a biological warfare threat.

For much of the world, the major differential diagnosis is malaria. It must be borne in mind that parasitemia in patients partially immune to malaria does not prove that symptoms are due to malaria. Typhoid fever, rickettsial, and leptospiral diseases are major confounding infections, with nontyphoidal salmonellosis, shigellosis, relapsing fever, fulminant hepatitis, and meningococcernia being some of the other important diagnoses to exclude. Any condition leading to disseminated intravascular coagulation could present in a confusing fashion, as well as diseases such as acute leukemia, lupus erythematosus, idiopathic or thrombotic thrombocytopenic purpura, and hemolytic uremic syndrome. Due to recent recognition of their worldwide occurrence, additional consideration should be given to infection with hantavirus. Classic HFRS (Korean hemorrhagic fever or epidemic hemorrhagic fever) has a severe course which progresses sequentially from fever through haemorrhage, shock, renal failure, and polyuria. This clinical form of HFRS is widely distributed in China, the Korean peninsula, and the Far Eastern USSR. Severe disease also is found in some Balkan states, including Bosnia/Serbia and Greece. However, the Scandinavian and most European virus strains carried by bank votes usually produce a milder disease with prominent fever, myalgia, abdominal pain, and oliguria, but without shock or severe hemorrhagic manifestations.

Diagnosis in an individual case rests on specific virologic diagnosis. Most patients have readily detectable viremia at presentation. Rapid enzyme immunoassays can detect viral antigens in acute sera from patients with Lassa, Argentine HF Rift Valley fever, Congo-Crimean HF, yellow fever and specific IgM antibodies in early convalescence. Lassa- and Hantaan-specific IgM often are detectable during the acute illness. Diagnosis by virus cultivation and identification will require three to 10 days or longer. With the exception of dengue, specialised microbiologic containment is required for safe handling of these viruses. Appropriate precautions should be observed in collection, handling, shipping, and processing of diagnostic samples.

Contact precautions required for healthcare workers. General principles of supportive care apply to hemodynamic, hematologic, pulmonary, and neurologic manifestations ofVHF, regardless of the specific etiologic agent concerned. Patients generally are either moribund or recovering by the second week of illness, but only intensive care will save the most severely ill patients. Health-care providers employing vigorous fluid resuscitation of patients with hemodynamic compromise must be mindful of the propensity of some VHF cases for pulmonary capillary leak. Pressor agents are frequently required. Invasive hemodynamic monitoring should be used where normal indications warrant, but extra caution should be exercised with regard to sharp objects and their potential for nosocomial transmission of a viral agent. Intramuscular injections, aspirin and other anticoagulant drugs should be avoided. Restlessness, confusion, myalgia, and hyperesthesia should be managed by conservative measures and judicious use of sedative, pain-relieving, and amnestic medications. Secondary infections may occur as with any patient undergoing intensive care and invasive procedures.

Management of clinical bleeding should follow the same principles as for any patient with a systemic coagulopathy, assisted by coagulation studies. DIC has been implicated specifically in Rift Valley fever and Marburg/Ebola infections, but in most VHF the etiology of the coagulopathy is multifactorial. Dengue HF is a notable case where antibody-mediated enhancement of dengue virus infection of monocytes and cytotoxic T-cell responses to these presented viral antigens precipitates vascular injury and permeability, complement activation, and a systemic coagulopathy. The investigational antiviral drug ribavirin is available via compassionate use protocols for therapy of Lassa fever, hemorrhagic fever with renal syndrome (HFRS), Congo-Crimean hemorrhagic fever, and Rift Valley fever. Separate Phase III efficacy trials have indicated that parenteral ribavirin reduces morbidity in both HFRS and Lassa fever, in addition to lowering mortality in the latter disease.

In the human field trial with HFRS, treatment was effective if begun within the first four days of fever, and was continued for seven days total. For Lassa fever patients, a compassionate use protocol utilising intravenous ribavirin as a treatment is sponsored by the CDC. Dosages used were slightly different, and continued for 10 days total; treatment is most effective if begun within seven days of onset. The only significant side effect of ribavirin is a modest anemia related to reversible block in erythropoiesis and mild hemolysis. Although ribavirin has demonstrated teratogenicity in animal studies, its use in a pregnant woman with grave illness from one of these VHFs must be weighed against potential benefit. Safety in infants and children has not been established. A similar dose of ribavirin begun within four days of disease may be effective in HFRS patients. Ribavirin has poor *in vitro* and *in vivo* activity against either the filoviruses (*Marburg* and *Ebola*) or the flaviviruses (dengue, yellow fever, omsk HF and kyanasur forest disease).

The only licensed virus-specific vaccine available for any of the haemorrhagic fever viruses is yellow fever vaccine, which is mandatory for travellers to endemic areas of Africa and South America. Argentine haemorrhagic fever (AHF) vaccine is a live, attenuated, investigational vaccine developed at USAMRIID, which has proved efficacious both in an animal model and in a field trial in South America, and seems to protect against Bolivian haemorrhagic fever (BHF) as well. Both inactivated and live-attenuated Rift Valley fever vaccines are currently under investigation.

Personal contacts or medical personnel extensively exposed to blood or secretions from VHF patients should be monitored for fever and other disease manifestations during a time equal to the established incubation period. Persons with percutaneous or mucocutaneous exposure to blood, body fluids, secretions, or excretions from a patient with suspected VHF should immediately wash the affected skin surfaces with soap and water. Mucous membranes should be irrigated with copious amounts of water or saline.

Strict adherence to contact precautions has halted secondary transmission in the vast majority of circumstances. With the exception of dengue (virus present, but no secondary infection hazard) and hantaviruses (infectious virus not present in blood or excreta at the time of diagnosis), VHF patients generally have significant quantities of virus in blood and often other secretions. Special caution must be exercised in handling sharps, needles, and other potential sources of parenteral exposure. Caution should be exercised in evaluating and treating the patient with a suspected VHF. Over, reaction on the part of health-care providers is inappropriate and detrimental to both patient and staff, but it is prudent to provide as rigorous isolation measures as feasible.

Marburg, Ebola, Lassa, and Congo-Crimean HF viruses may be particularly prone to aerosol nosocomial spread. Well-documented secondary infections among contacts and medical personnel who were not parenterally exposed have occurred. Sometimes this occurred when the acute haemorrhagic disease mimicked a surgical emergency such as a bleeding gastric ulcer, with subsequent exposure and secondary spread among emergency and operating room personnel.

CONGO-CRIMEAN HAEMORRHAGIC FEVER

The Congo-Crimean haemorrhagic fever (CCHF) is a viral disease caused by CCHF virus. The virus, first isolated in the Congo, is transmitted by ticks, principally of the genus Hyalomma, with intermediate vertebrate hosts varying with the tick species. The disease, next found in the Crimea, occurs also in the Middle East, the Balkans, the former USSP, and eastern China. In 1969 it was recognised that the pathogen causing Crimean haemorrhagic fever was the same as that responsible for an illness identified in 1956 in the Congo, and linkage of the 2 place-names resulted in the current name for the disease and the virus. Little is known about variations in the virus properties over the huge geographic area involved. Humans become infected through tick bites, crushing an infected tick, or at the slaughter of viremic livestock. Even in epidemics, cases do not show narrow clustering and person-to-person spread is rare. CCHF would probably be delivered by aerosol if used as a BW agent. The length of the incubation period for illness appears to depend on the mode of acquisition of the virus.

Following infection via tick bite, the incubation period is usually one to three days, with a maximum of nine days. The incubation period following contact with infected blood or tissues is usually five to six days, with a documented maximum of 13 days. Typical cases present with sudden onset of fever and chills three-12 days after tick exposure. There is severe headache, lumbar pain, nausea and vomiting, delirium, and prostration. Fatal cases are associated with extensive haemorrhage, coma, and shock. Mortality among cases recognised as hemorrhagic fever is 15-30 per cent with death occurring in the second week of illness. In those patients who recover, improvement generally begins on the ninth or tenth day after onset of illness.

Diagnosis of suspected CCHF is performed in specially-equipped, high biosafety level laboratories. Other viral haemorrhagic fevers, meningococcemia, rickettsial diseases, and similar conditions may resemble full-blown CCHF. Most fatal cases and half the others will have detectable antigen by rapid enzyme-linked immunosorbant assay (ELISA) testing of acute serum samples. IgM ELISA antibodies occur early in recovery. Supportive therapy with replacement of clotting factors is indicated. Crimean-Congo haemorrhagic fever virus is sensitive to ribavirin *in vitro* and clinicians have been favourably impressed in uncontrolled trials. Immune globulin has also been recommended but is available only in Bulgaria.

When patients with CCHF are admitted to the hospital adequate infection control measures be observed to prevent its disastrous spread. Patients with suspected or confirmed CCHF should be isolated and cared for using barrier nursing techniques. Due to several well-defined outbreaks within hospitals, protective measures for medical personnel are an issue. The weight of evidence points to large droplets or fomites as the mediators of transmission and so strict barrier nursing is indicated and probably sufficient for the care of naturally acquired disease. The virus is aerosol-infectious and additional precautions might be considered in a biological warfare setting. Although there is little field experience and no definitive data on efficacy, the sensitivity of the virus to ribavirin and the severity of disease suggests that prophylaxis of high-risk exposures is indicated. In the case of a suspected biological attack, ribavirin could be considered for prophylaxis, but there is insufficient information to make a firm recommendation for dosing.

MELIOIDOSIS

Melioidosis is an infectious disease caused by a bacteria called *Pseudomonas pseudomallei*. It is most frequently reported in South-east Asia and Northern Australia. The bacteria that causes the disease is found in the soil, rice paddies, and stagnant waters of the area. People get the disease by inhaling dust contaminated by the bacteria and when the contaminated soil comes in contact with abraded (scaped) area of the skin. The diseace most commonly involves the lungs where the infection can form a cavity of pus (abscess). It can spread from the skin through the blood to affect the heart, brain, liver, kidneys, joints, and eyes. Patients can have associated headaches, fever, chills, cough, chest pain, and/or loss of appetite.

Melioidosis is diagnosed with a microscopic evaluation of a sputum sample in the laboratory. A blood test is useful to detect early acute cases of melioidosis, but it cannot exclude the illness if it is negative. Treatment of melioidosis involves antibiotics and depends on the location of the disease. For patients with more mild illness, antibiotics such as chloramphenicol, doxycycline, sulfisoxazole, or trimethoprim-sulfamethoxazole are considered. The conventional treatment regimen for patients who are more severely ill is a combination of chloramphenicol, doxycycline, and cotrimoxazole. Even more severely ill patients may require intravenous antibiotics, including chloram-phenicol, and others. If sputum cultures remain positive for six months, surgical removal of the lung abscess with lobectomy is considered. Antibiotic treatments may be necessary from three to 12 months.

BOTULINUM TOXINS

Botulinum toxins haves caused numerous cases of botulism when ingested in improperly prepared or canned foods. Many deaths have occurred secondary to such incidents. It is feasible to deliver botulinum toxins as a biological weapon, and other countries have weaponised or are suspected to have weaponised one or more of this group of toxins. Iraq admitted to a United Nations inspection team in August of 1991 that it had done research on the offensive use of botulinum toxins prior to the Persian Gulf War, which occurred in January and February of that year. Further information given in 1995 revealed that Iraq had not only researched the use of this toxin as a weapon, but had filled and deployed over 100 munitions with botulinum toxin.

Botulinum toxins are proteins of approximately 150,000 kD molecular weight which can be produced from the anaerobic bacterium *Clostridium botulinum*. There are seven distinct but related neurotoxins, A through G, produced by different strains of the *Clostridial bacillus*. All seven types act by similar mechanisms. The toxins produce similar effects when inhaled or ingested, although the time course may vary depending on the route of exposure and the dose received. Although an aerosol attack is by far the most likely scenario for the use of botulinum toxins, theoretically the agent could be used to sabotage food supplies; enemy special forces or terrorists m might use this method in certain scenarios to produce foodborne botulism in those so targeted.

Botulinum toxin is the most toxic compound per weight of agent, requiring only 0.001 microgram per kilogramme of body weight to kill 50 per cent of the animals studied. As a group, bacterial toxins such as botulinum tend to be the most lethal of all toxins. The toxins act by binding to the presynaptic nerve terminal at the neuromuscular junction and at cholinergic autonomic sites. These toxins then act to prevent the release of acetylcholine presynaptically, and thus block neurotransmission. This interruption of neurotransmission causes both bulbar palsies and the skeletal muscle weakness seen in clinical botulism. Unlike the situation with nerve agent intoxication, where there is too much acetylcholine due to inhibition of acetylcholinesterase, the problem in botulism is lack of the neurotransmitter in the synapse.

The signs and symptoms may in fact not appear for several days when a low dose of the toxin is inhaled versus a shorter time period following ingestion of toxin or inhalation of higher doses. Bulbar palsies are prominent early, with eye symptoms such as blurred vision due to mydriasis, diplopia, ptosis, and photophobia, in addition to other bulbar signs such as dysarthria, dysphonia, and dysphagia. Skeletal muscle paralysis follows, with a symmetrical, descending, and progressive weakness which may culminate abruptly in respiratory failure.

Progression from onset of symptoms to respiratory failure has occurred in as little as 24 hours in cases of foodborne botulism. Physical examination usually reveals an alert and oriented patient without fever. Postural hypotension may be present. Mucous membranes may be dry and crusted and the patient may complain of dry mouth or even sore throat. There may be difficulty with speaking and with swallowing. Gag reflex may be absent. Pupils may be dilated and even fixed. Ptosis and extraocular muscle palsies may also be observed. Variable degrees of skeletal muscle weakness may be observed depending on the degree of progression in an individual patient. Deep tendon reflexes may be present or absent.

The occurrence of an epidemic of cases of a descending and progressive bulbar and skeletal paralysis in afebrile patients points to the diagnosis of botulinum intoxication. Foodborne outbreaks tend to occur in small clusters and have never occurred in soldiers on military rations such as MREs (Meals,

Ready to Eat). Higher numbers of cases in a theatre of operations should raise at least the consideration of a biological warfare attack with aerosolised botulinum toxin. Foodborne outbreaks are theoretically possible in troops on normal 'A' rations.

Individual cases might be confused clinically with other neuromuscular disorders such as Guillain-Barre syndrome, myasthenia gravis, or tick paralysis. The edrophonium or Tensilon test may be transiently positive in botulism, so it may not distinguish botulinum intoxication from myasthenia. The cerebrospinal fluid in botulism is normal and the paralysis is generally symmetrical, which distinguishes it from enteroviral myelitis Mental status changes generally seen in viral encephalitis should not occur with botulinum intoxication.

It may become necessary to distinguish nerve agent and/or atropine poisoning from botulinum intoxication. Nerve agent poisoning produces copious respiratory secretions and miotic pupils, whereas there is if anything a decrease in secretions in botulinum intoxication. Atropine overdose is distinguished from botulism by its central nervous system excitation even though the mucous membranes are dry and mydriasis is present. The clinical differences between botulinum intoxication and nerve agent poisoning are depicted in preceding pages.

Laboratory testing is generally not helpful in the diagnosis of botulism. Survivors do not usually develop an antibody response due to the very small amount of toxin necessary to produce clinical symptoms. Detection of toxin in serum or gastric contents is possible, and mouse neutralisation, remains the most sensitive test. Other assays include gel hydralisation or ELISA. Serum specimens should be drawn from suspected cases and held for testing at such a facility.

Respiratory failure secondary to paralysis of respiratory muscles is the most serious complication and, generally, the cause of death. Reported cases of botulism prior to 1950 had a mortality of 60 per cent. With tracheostomy or endotracheal intubation arid ventilatory assistance, fatalities should be less than five per cent. Intensive and prolonged nursing care may be required for recovery which may take several weeks or even months.

In isolated cases of foodborne botulism, circulating toxin is present, perhaps due to continued absorption through the gut wall. Botulinum antitoxin has been used in those circumstances, and is thought to be helpful. Animal experiments show that after aerosol exposure, botulinum antitoxin can be very effective if given before the onset of clinical signs. Administration of antitoxin is reasonable if disease has not progressed to a stable state.

A trivalent equine antitoxin has been available from the Centres for Disease Control and Prevention for cases of foodborne botulism. This product has all the disadvantages of a horse serum product, including the risks of anaphylaxis and serum sickness. A 'despeciated' equine heptavalent antitoxin against types A, B, C, D, E, F, and G has been prepared by cleaving the Fc fragments from horse IgG molecules, leaving $F(ab)_2$ fragments. This product is under advanced development, and is currently available under IND status.

A pentavalent toxoid of Clostridium botulinum toxin types A, B, C, D, and E is available under an IND status. This product has been administered to several thousand volunteers and occupationally at-risk workers, and induces serum antitoxin levels that correspond to protective levels in experimental animal systems. The currently recommended primary series of zero, two, and 12 weeks, then a one year booster induces protective antibody levels in greater than 90 per cent of vaccinees after one year. Adequate antibody levels are transiently induced after three injections, but decline prior to the one year booster. Contraindications to the vaccine include sensitivities to alum, formaldehyde, and thimerosal, or hypersensitivity to a previous dose.

Reactogenicity is mild, with two to four per cent of vaccines reporting erythema, oedema, or induration at the local site of injection which peaks at 24 to 48 hours, then dissipates. The frequency of such local reactions increases with each subsequent inoculation; after the second and third doses, seven to 10 per cent will have local reactions, with higher incidence after boosters. Severe local reactions are rare, consisting of more extensive oedema or induration. Systemic reactions are reported in up to three per cent, consisting of fever, malaise, headache, and myalgia. Incapacitating reactions are uncommon. The vaccine should be stored at refrigerator temperatures.

RICIN

Ricin is a potential biological warfare toxin and is widely availabile. Ricin is a potent protein toxin derived from the beans of the castor plant (*Ricinus communis*). Castor beans are ubiquitous worldwide, and the toxin is fairly easily produced. Worldwide, one million tons of castor beans are processed annually in the production of castor oil; the waste mash from this process is five per cent ricin by weight. The toxin is also quite stable and extremely toxic by several routes of exposure, including the: respiratory route.

When inhaled as a small particle aerosol, this toxin may produce pathologic changes within eight hours and severe respiratory symptoms followed by acute hypoxic respiratory failure in 36-72 hours. When ingested, ricin causes severe gastrointestinal symptoms followed by vascular collapse and death. This toxin may also cause disseminated intravascular coagulation, microcirculatory failure and multiple organ failure if given intravenously in laboratory animals. Ricin is said to have been used in the assassination of Bulgarian exile Georgi Markov in London in 1978. Markov was attacked with a specially engineered weapon disguised as an umbrella which implanted a ricin-containing pellet into his body.

The toxin is actually made up of two hemagglutinins and two toxins. The toxins, RCL III and RCL IV, are dimers of about

66,000 daltons molecular weight. The toxins are made up oaf two polypeptide chains, an A chain and a B chain, which are joined by a disulfide bond. Ricin can be produced relatively easily and inexpensively in large quantities in a fairly low technology setting. It is of marginal toxicity in terms of its LED_{50} in comparison to toxins such as botulinum and SEB (incapacitating dose), so an enemy would have to produce it in larger quantities to cover a significant area on the battlefield. This might limit large-scale use of ricin by an adversary.

Ricin can be prepared in liquid or crystalline form, or it can be lyophilised to make it a dry powder. It could be disseminated by an enemy as an aerosol, or it could be used as a sabotage assassination, or terrorist weapon. It is very toxic to cells. It acts by inhibiting protein synthesis. The B chain binds to cell surface receptors and the toxin-receptor complex is taken into the cell; the A chain has endonuclease activity and extremely low concentrations will inhibit protein synthesis. In rodents, the histopathology of aerosol exposure is characterised by necrotising airway lesions causing tracheitis, bronchitis, bronchiolitis, and interstitial pneumonia with perivascular and alveolar edema. There is a latent period of eight hours post-inhalation exposure before histologic lesions are observed in animal models. In rodents, ricin is more toxic by the aerosol route than by other routes of exposure. There is little toxicity data in humans. The exact cause of morbidity and mortality would be dependent upon the route of exposure. Aerosol exposure in man would be expected to cause acute lung injury, pulmonary oedema secondary to increased capillary permeability, and eventual acute hypoxic respiratory failure.

After aerosol exposure, signs and symptoms would depend on the dose inhaled. Accidental sublethal aerosol exposures which occurred in humans in the 1940s were characterised by onset of the following symptoms in four to eight hours: fever, chest tightness, cough, dyspnea, nausea, and arthralgias. The onset of profuse sweating some hours later was commonly the sign of termination of most of the symptoms.

Although lethal human aerosol exposures have not been described, the severe pathophysiologic changes seen in the animal respiratory tract, including necrosis and serve alveolar flooding, are probably sufficient to cause death if enough toxin is inhaled. Time to death in experimental animals is dose dependent, occurring 36-72 hours post inhalation exposure. Humans would be expected to develop severe lung inflammation with progressive cough, dyspnea, cyanosis and pulmonary edema. By other routes of exposure, ricin is not a direct lung irritant; however, intravascular injection can cause minimal pulmonary perivascular oedema due to vascular endothelial injury. Ingestion causes gastrointestinal haemorrhage with hepatic, splenic, and renal necrosis. Intramuscular administration causes severe local necrosis of muscle and regional lymph nodes with moderate visceral organ involvement.

An aerosolised ricin attack would be primarily diagnosed by the clinical and epidemiological setting. Acute lung injury affecting a large number of cases in a war zone should raise suspicion of an attack with a pulmonary irritant such as ricin, although other pulmonary pathogens could present with similar signs and symptoms.

Ricin intoxication would be expected to progress despite treatment with antibiotics, as opposed to an infectious process. There would be no mediastinitis as seen with inhalation anthrax. SEB would be different in that most patients would not progress to a life-threatening syndrome but would tent to plateau clinically. Phosgene-induced acute lung injury would progress much faster than that caused by ricin. Additional supportive clinical or diagnostic features after aerosol exposure to ricin may include the following: bilateral infiltrates on chest radiographs, arterial hypoxemia, neutrophilic leukocytosis, and a bronchial aspirate rich in protein compared to plasma which is, characteristic of high permeability pulmonary oedema. Specific ELISA testing on serum or immunohistochemical techniques for direct tissue analysis may be used where available to confirm the diagnosis.

Clinical management of ricin-intoxicated patients again depends on the route of exposure. Patients with pulmonary intoxication are managed by appropriate treatment for pulmonary oedema and respiratory support as indicated. Gastrointestinal intoxication is best managed by vigorous gastric decontamination with superactivated charcoal, followed by use of cathartics such as magnesium citrate. Volume replacement of GI fluid losses is important. In percutaneous exposures, treatment would be primarily supportive.

Although a vaccine is not currently available, candidate vaccines are under development which are immunogenic and confer protection against lethal aerosol exposures in animals. Prophylaxis with such a vaccine is the most promising defence against a ricin attack.

SAXITOXIN

Saxitoxin is a neurotoxins predominantly produced by marine dinoflagellates. They have also been identified in association with such diverse organisms as blue-green algae, crabs, and the blue-ringed octopus. Human intoxications are principally due to ingestion of bivalve molluscs which have accumulated dinoflagellates during filter feeding. The resulting intoxication, known as paralytic shellfish poisoning (PSP), is known throughout the world as a severe, life-threatening illness requiring immediate medical intervention.

In a BW scenario, the most likely route of delivery is by inhalation or toxic projectile. In addition, saxitoxin could be used in a confined area to contaminate water supplies. After oral exposure, absorption of toxins from the gastrointestinal tract is rapid. Onset of symptoms typically begins 10-60 minutes after exposure, but may be delayed several hours depending upon the dose and individual idiosyncrasy. Initial symptoms are numbness or tingling of the lips, tongue and fingertips, followed by numbness of the neck and extremities and general muscular incoordination. Nausea and vomiting may be present, but typically occur in a minority of cases. Respiratory distress and flaccid muscular paralysis are the terminal stages and can occur two-12 hours after intoxication. Death results from respiratory paralysis. Clearance of the toxin is rapid and survivors for 12-24 hours will usually recover.

Differential diagnosis may require toxin detection. Diagnosis is confirmed by detection of toxin in the food, water, stomach contents or environmental samples. Management is supportive and standard management of poison ingestion should be employed if intoxication is by the oral route. Toxins are rapidly cleared and excreted in the urine, so diuresis may increase elimination. Incubation and mechanical respiratory support may be required in severe intoxication Timely resuscitation would be imperative, albeit very difficult, after inhalation exposure on the battlefield. No vaccine against saxitoxin exposure has been developed for human use.

CLOSTRIDIUM PERFRINGENS TOXINS

Clostridium perfringens is an anaerobic bacterium associated with three distinct disease syndromes; gas gangrene or clostridial myonecrosis; enteritis necroticans (pig-bel); and clostridium food poisoning. Each of these syndromes has very specific requirements for delivering inocula of *C. perfringens* to specific sites to induce disease, and it is difficult to imagine a general scenario in which the spores or vegetative organisms could be used as a biological warfare agent. There are, however, at least 12 protein toxins elaborated, and one or more of these could be produced, concentrated, and used as a weapon. Waterborne disease is conceivable, but unlikely. The alpha toxin would be lethal by aerosol. This is a well characterised, highly toxic phospholipase C. Other toxins from the organism might be co-weaponised and enhance effectiveness.

Symptoms of the disease may be subtle before fulminant toxemia develops, and the diagnosis is often made at postmortem examination. The bacteria produce toxins that create the high mortality from *Clostridial myonecrosis*, and which produce the characteristic intense pain out of proportion to the wound. Within hours signs of systemic toxicity appear, including confusion, tachycardia, and sweating. Most *Clostridia* species produce large amounts of CO_2 and hydrogen that cause intense swelling hence the term gas gangrene, resulting in gas in the soft tissues and the emission of foul smelling gas from the wound.

Necrosis, dark red serous fluid, and numerous gas-filled vesicles are the major clinical features. The infection may progress up to 10 cm per hour, and early diagnosis and therapy are essential to prevent rapid progression to toxemia and death. Pulmonary findings might lead to confusion with staphylococcal enterotoxin B (SEB) initially. Liver damage, hemolytic anemia, and thrombocytopenia are not associated with SEB and the pulmonary findings should be reversible in SEB.

Early antibiotic treatment is effective, if undertaken before significant amounts of toxins have accumulated in the body. If not treated the bacteria enter the bloodstream causing systemic illness. The organism itself is sensitive to penicillin, and consequently, this is the current drug of choice. Recent data indicate that clindamycin or rifampin may suppress toxin production and provide superior results in animal models. Prompt surgical debridement and broad spectrum, intravenous antibiotics are the mainstay therapy. Hyperbaric oxygen has not been proven effective in prolonging survival. There is no available prophylaxis against most *C. perfringens* toxins. Toxoids are being used to prevent enteritis necroticans in humans, and veterinary toxoids are in wide use.

STAPHYLOCOCCAL ENTEROTOXIN B

Staphylococcal Enterotoxin B (SEB) has caused countless endemic cases of food poisoning. Often these cases have been clustered. Due to common source exposure in a setting such as a church picnic or other community event in which contaminated food is consumed. Although this toxin would not be likely to produce significant mortality on the battlefield, it could render up to 80 per cent or more of exposed personnel clinically ill and unable to perform their mission for one-two weeks. Therefore, even though SEB is not generally thought of as a lethal agent, it may severely incapacitate soldiers, making it an extremely important toxin to consider.

Staphylococcus aureus produces a number of exotoxins, one of which is Staphylococcal enterotoxin B, or SEB. Such toxins are referred to as exotoxins since they are excreted from the organism; however, they normally exert their effects on the intestines and thereby are called enterotoxins. SEB is one of the pyrogenic toxins that commonly causes food poisoning in humans after the toxin is produced in improperly handled foodstuffs and subsequently ingested. SEB has a very broad spectrum of biological activity. This toxin causes a markedly different clinical syndrome when inhaled than it characteristically produces when ingested. Significant morbidity is produced in individuals who are exposed to SEB by either portal of entry to the body.

Staphylococcal enterotoxins are extracellular products produced by coagulase-positive staphylococci. They are produced in culture media and also in foods when there is overgrowth of the staph organisms. At least five antigenically distinct enterotoxins have been identified, SEB being one of them. These toxins are heat stable. SEB causes symptoms when inhaled at very low doses in humans: a dose of several logs lower than the lethal dose by the inhaled route would be sufficient to incapacitate 50 per cent of those soldiers so exposed. This toxin could also be used (theoretically) in a special forces of terrorist mode to sabotage food or small volume water supplies.

Staphylococcal enterotoxins produce a variety of toxic effects. Inhalation of SEB can induce extensive pathophysiological changes to include widespread systemic damage and even septic shock. Many of the effects of staphylococcal enterotoxins are mediated by interactions with the host's own immune system. The mechanisms of toxicity are complex, but are related to toxin binding directly to the major histocompatibility complex that subsequently stimulates the proliferation of large numbers of T cell lymphocytes. Since there exotoxins are extremely potent activators of T cells, they are commonly referred to as bacterial superantigens. These superantigens stimulate the production and secretion of various cytokines, such as turnor necrosis factor, interferon, interleukin-1 and interleukin-2, from immune system cells: Released cytokines are thought to mediate many of the toxic effects of SEB.

Relevant battlefield exposures to SEB are projected to cause primarily clinical illness and incapacitation. However, higher exposure levels can presumably lead to septic shock and death. Intoxication with SEB begins three to 12 hours after inhalation of the toxin. Victims may experience the sudden onset of fever, headache, chills, myalgias, and a non-productive cough. More severe cases may develop dyspnea and restrosternal chest pain. Nausea, vomiting, and diarrhoea will also occur in many patients due to inadvertently swallowed toxin, and fluid losses can be marked. The fever may last up to five days and range from 103 to 106 degrees F, with variable degrees of chills and prostration. The cough may persist up to four weeks, and patients may not be able to return to duty for two weeks.

Physical examination in patients with SEB intoxication is often unremarkable. Conjunctival injection may be present and postural hypotension may develop due to fluid losses: Chest examination if unremarkable except in the unusual case where pulmonary oedema develops. The chest X-ray is also generally normal, but in severe cases increased interstitial markings, atelectasis, and possibly overt pulmonary oedema or an ARDS picture may develop.

As is the case with botulinum toxins, intoxication due to SEB inhalation is a clinical and epidemiologic diagnosis. Since the symptoms of SEB intoxication may be similar to several respiratory pathogens such as influenza, adenovirus, and mycoplasma, the diagnosis may initially be unclear. All of these might present with fever, non-productive cough, myalgia, and headache. SEB attack would cause cases to present in large numbers over a very short period of time, probably within a single 24-hour period. Naturally occurring pneumonias or influenza would involve patients presenting over a more prolonged interval of time. Naturally occurring staphylococcal food poisoning cases would not present with pulmonary symptoms. SEB intoxication tends to progress rapidly to a fairly stable clinical state, whereas pulmonary anthrax, tularemia pneumonia, or pneumonic plague would all progress if left untreated. Tularemia and plague, as well as Q fever, would be associated with infiltrates on chest radiographs. Nerve agent intoxication would cause fasciculations and copious secretions, and mustard would cause skin lesions in addition to pulmonary findings; SEB inhalation would not be characterised by these findings. The dyspnoea associated with botulinum intoxication is associated with obvious signs of muscular paralysis, bulbar palsies, lack of fever, and a dry pulmonary tree due to cholinergic blockade; respiratory difficulties occur late rather than early as with SEB inhalation.

Laboratory findings are not very helpful in the diagnosis of SEB intoxication. A non-specific neutrophilic leukocytosis and an elevated erythrocyte sedimentation rate may be seen, but these abnormalities are present in may illnesses. Toxin is very difficult to detect in the serum by the time symptoms occur however, a serum specimen should be drawn as early as possible after exposure. Data from rabbit studies clearly show that SEB in the serum is transient; however, it accumulates in the urine and can be detected for several hours post exposure. Therefore, urine samples should be obtained and tested for SEB. Since most patients will develop a significant antibody response to the toxin, acute and convalescent serum should be drawn which may be helpful retrospectively in the diagnosis.

Currently, therapy is limited to supportive care. Close attention to oxygenation and hydration are important, and in severe cases with pulmonary edema, ventilation with positive and expiratory pressure and diuretics might be necessary. Acetaminophen for fever, and cough suppressants may make the patient more comfortable. The value of steroids is unknown. Most patients would be expected to do quite well after the initial acute phase of their illness, but most would generally be unfit for duty for one to two weeks.

Although there is currently no human vaccine for immunisation against SEB intoxication, several vaccine candidates are in development. Preliminary animal studies have been encouraging and a vaccine candidate is nearing transition to advanced development and safety and immunogenicity testing in man.

EPIDEMIOLOGY OF BW ATTACKS

A sound epidemiologic investigation of a disease outbreak, whether natural or artificial, will assist medical personnel in identifying the pathogen, as well as instituting the appropriate medical interventions. The CDC realised this as early as 1951, when the Epidemic Intelligence Service was created to train epidemiologists in case a BW attack should take place against the United States during the cold war. Documenting who is affected, possible routes of exposure, signs and symptoms of disease, and the rapid identification of the causative agents will greatly increase the ability to plan an appropriate medical and public health response. Good epidemiologic information will allow the appropriate follow-up of those potentially exposed, as well as help determine public information guidelines and responses to the media.

Many diseases caused by weaponised biological agents present with nonspecific signs and symptoms that could be misinterpreted as natural occurrences. The disease pattern that develops is an important factor in differentiating between a natural and a terrorist or warfare attack. In most naturally occurring epidemics, there is a gradual rise in disease incidence, as people are progressively exposed to an increasing number of patients, vectors, or fomites that spread the pathogen. In contrast, those exposed to a BW attack would all come in contact with the agent at approximately the same time. Even taking into account varying incubation periods based on exposure dose and physiological differences, a compressed epidemic curve with a peakin a matter of days, or even hours, would occur. Most point source exposures will present in this fashion, including foodborne outbreaks, which may be natural or possibly intentionally induced. Therefore, further information should be obtained to help establish whether an outbreak is caused by an attack with a BW agent.

The general steps for epidemiologic assessment of any disease can be applied to a BW or terrorist attack. First, public health authorities and health care personnel should formulate a case definition to determine the number of actual cases and from that the approximate attack rate. The potential exists for hysteria to be confused with actual disease; therefore, objective criteria should be used to document the number of people affected. Once a case definition has been determined, description of the epidemic can be done with respect to the timing, place, and other characteristics of those who are ill. The investigation obviously needs to be done expeditiously, but even rudimentary information can be of assistance in determining the source and potential consequences of an outbreak. The unintended release of anthrax spores from a military compound in the former Soviet Union in 1979 demonstrated some of the epidemiologic indicators of an unnatural epidemic. The location of casualties followed a distinctive downwind pattern from the release site, animals in the same area were affected, and an unusual presentation of the disease, respiratory instead of cutaneous occurred. Other possible clues to a BW or terrorist attack include high disease rates among exposed individuals, more respiratory cases of disease if the agent is disseminated via aerosol, occurrence of a disease that is unusual in a given geographic area, a naturally vector-borne disease occurring in an area that lacks the appropriate vectors for normal transmission, more than one epidemic occurring at the same time, higher morbidity and mortality than normally expected for a disease, lower attack rates in personnel protected from exposure, and suspicious activity or discovery of a potential delivery system such as a spray device.

If an attack with biological agents is suspected, the proper authorities, whether military or civilian, should be notified immediately. To minimise the effects of a biological terrorist attack, health care professionals and public health authorities must be aware of the threat of biological warfare and terrorism and have an increased index of suspicion that such an attack can occur. They must have some understanding of the classes of agents that have been and can be weaponised and their effects after inhalation. Surveillance of background disease activity should be ongoing, and any unusual changes in disease occurrence or etiology should be promptly followed up with a directed examination of the facts regarding the increased rates.

Biological warfare agents would likely cause significant impacts on the medical care system too. Overwhelming number of patients, and demands for intensive care would overwhelm medical resources. Special medications or vaccines not generally available in standard pharmaceutical stocks would be required. Medical care providers and laboratory personnel might need added protection, and autopsy and interment of remains could present hazards not commonly dealt with. The medical response to the threat or use of biological weapons may be different depending on whether medical measures are employed prior to exposure, or whether exposure has already occurred and/orsymptoms are present. If provided before exposure, active immunisation or prophylaxis with antibiotics may prevent illness in those exposed.

Active immunisation may be effective against several potential biological warfare agents, and is probably the best modality for future protection of US military forces against a wide variety of biological threats. After exposure, active or passive immunisation as well as pretreatment with therapeutic antibiotics or antiviral drugs may ameliorate disease symptoms. After onset of illness, only diagnosis of the disease end general or specific treatment are left to medical care providers. The good news is that excellent vaccines and antitoxins exist for several of the most likely biological warfare agents, and more are under development.

REFERENCES

Acklund, J. R., Worswick, D. A., Marmion, B. P., Vaccine prophylaxis of Q fever, *Med., J. Aust,* 1994.

Arita, I., "Virological evidence for the success of the smallpox eradication programme", *Nature*, 1979.

Bauer, D.J., St. Vincent L., Kempe C.H., Downie, A.W., "Prophylactic treatment of smallpox contacts with N-methylisatin-thiosemicarbazone" (compound 33T57, Marboran), *Lancet*, 1963.

______________, Prophylaxis of smallpox with methisazone, *Am. J. Epidemiol*, 1969.

Bell, J.F., Lackman, D.B., Meis A., Hadlow W.J., Recurrent Reaction at Site of Q Fever Vaccination in a Sensitized *Person*, *Mil.Med.* 1964.

Benenson, A.S., *Q Fever Vaccine*, In Smadel, J.E., ed., *Symposium on Q Fever by the Committee on Rickettsial Diseases*, Washington, DC: Armed Forces Epidemiology Board; 1959.

______________, *Control of Communicable Diseases in Man*, 15th ed., Washington, DC: American Public Health Association; 1990.

Brachman, P.S., "Inhalation anthrax", *Ann NY Acad. Sci.*, 1980.

______________, Friedlander, A.M., *Anthrax*, In Plotkin SA, Mortimer EA Jr, eds., Vaccines, Philadelphia, Pa: WB Saunders Co; 1994.

Brouqui, P.B., Dupont, H.T., Drancourt, M., et al., Chronic Q Fever, *Arch. Intern. Med.*, 1993.

Butler, T., *Plague and Other Yersinia Infections*, New York, NY: Plenum Press; 1983.

Cavanaugh, D.C., Cadigan, F.C., Williams, J.E., Marshall, J.D., *General Medicine and Infectious Diseases*, In: Ognibene A.J., Barrett, O.N., eds., *Internal Medicine in Vietnam.* Washington,

DC: Office of the Surgeon General and Centre of Military History; 1982.

_______________, Elisberg, B.L., Llewellyn, C.H., et al., "Plague immunisation", *J.Infect. Dis.*, 1974.

Centers for Disease Control, "Management of patients with suspected viral hemorrhagic fever", *MMWR Morb. Mortal. Wkly. Rep.*, 1988;37 (suppl): 1-16.

Chan, R., Hardiman, R.P., "Endocarditis caused by Brucella melitensis", *Med. J.Aust.*, 1993.

Cochrane, R.C., *Biological warfare research in the United States*, In: *History of the Chemical Warfare Service in World War II*, Vol II. Frederick, Md: Historical Section, Plans, Training and Intelligence Division, Office of Chief, Chemical Corps, US Dept of the Army; 1947.

Crosby, E., Llosa, L., Miro, Q.M., Carrillo C., Gotuzzo E., "Hematologic changes in Brucellosis", *J.Infect. Dis.*, 1984.

Derrick, E.H., "The Course of Infection with Coxiella burnetii", *Med J.Aust.*, 1973.

Downie, A.W., Meiklejohn, M., St .Vincent, L., Rao, A.R., Sundara Babu, B.V., Kempe, C.H., "The recovery of smallpox from patients and their environment in a smallpox hospital", *Bull. World Health Organ*, 1965.

_______________, St. Vincent L., Meiklejohn G., et al., "Studies on the virus content of mouth washings in the acute phase of smallpox", *Bull. World Health Organ*, 1961.

Dupuis, G., Petite J., Olivier, P., Vouilloz, M., "An important outbreak of human Q fever in a Swiss alpine valley", *Int J.Epidemiol*, 1987.

Enria, D., Maiztegui, J.I., "Antiviral treatment of Argentine Hemorrhagic Fever", *Antiviral Res.*, 1994.

_______________, Fernandez, N.J., Briggiler, A.M., et al., "Importance of neutralising antibodies in treatment of Argentine haemorrhagic fever with immune plasma", *Lancet*, 1984.

Evans, A.C., "Comments on the early history of human brucellosis", In Larson CH, Soule MH, eds., *Brucellosis*, Baltimore, Md: Waverly Press; 1950.

Evans, M.E., Friedlander, A.M., *Tularemia*, In Zajtchuk R, ed., *Textbook of Military Medicine: Medical Aspects of Chemical and Biological Warfare*, Washington, DC: US Dept of the Army, The Surgeon General, and the Borden Institute; 1997.

Fenner, F., Henderson, D.A., Arita, I., Jezek, Z., Ladnyi, I.D., *Smallpox and Its Eradication*, Geneva, Switzerland: World Health Organisation; 1988.

Ferrante, M. A, and Dolan M.J., "Q fever meningo Encephalitis in a soldier returning from the Persian Gulf War", *Clin. Infect. Dis.*, 1993.

Franck, P.T., Johnson, K.M., "An outbreak of Venezuelan encephalitis in man in the Panama Canal Zone",*Am. J.Trop. Med. Hyg.*, 1970.

Franz, D.R., Pitt, L.M., Clayton, M.A., Hanes, M.A., Rose, K.J., "Efficacy of prophylactic and therapeutic administration of antitoxin for inhalation botulism", In Das Gupta B, ed., *Botulinum and Tetanus Neurotoxins and Biomedical Aspects*. New York, NY: Plenum Press, 1993.

______________, Parrott, C.D., Takafuji, E.T., "The US biological warfare and biological defence programs", In Zajtchuk R., ed., *Textbook of Military Medicine: Medical Aspects of Chemical and Biological Warfare*, Washington, DC: US Dept. of the Army, Surgeon General, and the Borden Institute, 1997.

Fraser, J.D., "High-affinity binding of staphylococcal enterotoxins A and B to HLA-DR", *Nature*, 1989.

Friedlander, A.M., "Anthrax", In Zajtchuk R., ed., *Textbook of Military Medicine: Medical Aspects of Chemical and Biological Warfare*. Washington, DC: US Dept. of the Army, Surgeon General, and the Borden Institute, 1997.

______________, Welkos SL, Pitt MLM, et al., "Postexposure prophylaxis against experimental inhalation anthrax", *J. Infect. Dis.*, 1993.

Goldfield, M., Welsh, J.N., Taylor, B.F., "The 1959 outbreak of eastern encephalitis in New Jersey", *Am.. J. Epidemiol,*1968.

Gotuzzo, E., Carrillo, C., Guerra, J., Llosa, L., "An evaluation of diagnostic methods for brucellosis", *J.Infect. Dis.*, 1986.

Grimont, F., Verger, J.M., Cornelis, P., et al., "Molecular typing of Brucella with cloned DNA probes", *Res Microbiol.*, 1992.

Harper, G.J., "Airborne microorganisms", *J. Hyg.* 1961.

Hayes, R.O., *Eastern and western encephalitis*, In Beran, G.W,, ed., *Handbook Series in Zoonoses: Viral Zoonoses*, I. Boca Raton, Fla: CRC Press, 1981.

Health Aspects of Chemical and Biological Weapons: Report of a WHO Group of Consultants, Geneva, Switzerland: World Health Organisation, 1970.

Hinman, A.R., McGowan, J.E., Henderson, B.E., "Venezuelan equine encephalomyelitis", *Am. J.Epidemiol*, 1971.

Horgan, E.S., Ali Haseeb, M., "Cross immunity experiments in monkey between variola, alastrim, and vaccinia", *J.Hyg.*, 1939.

Huggins, J.W., "Prospects for treatment of viral hemorrhagic fevers with ribavirin, a broad-spectrum antiviral drug", *Rev Infect. Dis.*, 1989; 11:S750- S761.

Huxsoll, D.L., Patrick, W.C., Parrott, C.D., Veterinary services in biological disasters, *J.Am.Vet Med Assoc.*, 1987.

Ibrahim, A.I.A., Shetty, S.D., Saad, M, Bilal, N.E., "Genitourinary complications of brucellosis", *Br. Journal*, 1988.

Ibrahim, M.S., Esposito, J.J., Jarhling, P.B., Lofts. R.S., "The potential of 5 nuclease PCR for detecting a single-base polymorphism in orthopoxvirus", Mol. Cell Probes, 1997.

Jahrling, P.B., Frame, J.D., Rhoderick, J.B., MoNson, M.H., "Endemic Lassa fever in Liberia", *Trans R. Soc. Trop. Med. Hyg.*, 1985.

Jahrling, P.B., Geisbert, J., Swearengen, J.R., et al., "Passive immunisation of Ebola virus-infected cynomolgus monkeys with immunoglobulin from hyper-immunehorses", *Arch.Virol.* 1996; (suppl 11):135-140.

______________, "Filoviruses and arena viruses". In: Murray, P.R., Baron, E.J., Pfaller M.A., Tenover, F.C., Yolken, R.H., eds., *Manual of Clinical Microbiology*, 6th ed., Washington, DC: ASM Press; 1995.

Jezek, Z., Fenner, F., "Human monkeypox", *Virol. Monogr.*, 1988.

Johnson, K.M., Martin, D.H., "Venezuelan equine encephalitis", *Adv. Vet. Sci. Comp. Med.*, 1974.

______________, Wiebenga, N.H., Mackenzie, R.B., et al., "Virusisolations from human cases of hemorrhagic fever in Bolivia", *Proc Soc Exp Biol Med.*, 1965.

Lackman, D.B., Bell, E.J., Bell, J.F., Pickens, E.G., "Intradermal sensitivity testing in man with a purified vaccine for Q fever", *Am. J.Public Health*, 1962.

Lee, H.W., "Hemorrhagic fever with renal syndrome in Korea", *Rev. Infect. Dis.*, 1989.

Leon, C.A., Jaramillo, R., Martinez, S., et al., "Sequelae of Venezuelan equine encephalitis in humans: a four-year follow-up", *Int. J.Epidemiol.,* 1975.

Luzzi, G.A., Brindle, R., Sockett, P.N., Solera, J., Klenerman, P., Warrell, D.A., "Brucellosis", *Trans R. Soc. Trop. Med. Hyg.*, 1993.

MacCallum, F.O., McDonald, J.R., "Survival of variola virus in raw cotton", *Bull. World Health Organ*, 1957.

Maiztegui, J., Feuillade, M., Briggiler, A., "Progressive extension of the endemic area and changing incidence of Argentine hemorrhagic fever", *Med. Microbiol Immunol.,* 1986.

Marmion, B.P., Ormsbee, R.A., Kyrkor, M., "Vaccine prophylaxis of abattoir-associated Q fever", *Epidemiol Infect.,* 1990.

Marrie, T.J., Langille, D., Papukna, V., Yates, L., "Truckin' pneumonia: an outbreak of Q fever in a truck repair plant", *Epidemiol Infect.*, 1989.

Martin, D.H., Eddy, G.A., Sudia, W.D., Reeves, W.C., Newhouse, V.F., Johnson, K.M., "An epidemiologic study of Venezuelan equine encephalomyelitis in Costa Rica, 1970, *Am. J.Epidemiol*, 1972.

McCormick, J.B., King, I.J., Webb, P.A., et al., Lassa fever: effective therapy with ribavirin", *N.Eng.l J. Med.*, 1986.

______________ , Webb, P.A., Krebs, J.W., Johnson, K.M., Smith E., "A prospective study of epidemiology and ecology of Lassa fever", *J.Infect Dis.*, 1987.

McCrumb, F.R. Jr., "Aerosol infection of man with Pasteurella tularensis", *Bacteriol Rev.*, 1961.

McGovern, T.W., Friedlander, A.M., *Plague*, In Zajtchuk R, ed., *Textbook of Military Medicine: Medical Aspects of Chemical and Biological Warfare*, Washington, DC: US Dept. of the Army, Surgeon General, and the Borden Institute, 1997.

McKendrick, G.D.W.,Velayudhan, L., Kamalakshi, K., "Assessment of an isothiazole thiosemIcarbazone in the prophylaxis of contacts of variola major", *Lancet*, 1966.

McKinney, R.W., Berge, T.O., Sawyer, W.D., Tigertt, W.D., Crozier, D., "Use of an attenuated strain of Venezuelan equine encephalomyelitis virus for immunisation in man", *Am. J.Trop. Med. Hyg.*, 1963.

Meikeljohn, G., Kempe, C.H., Downie, A.W., Berge, T.O., St. Vincent, L., Rao, A.R., "Air sampling to recover variola virus in the environment of a smallpox hospital", *Bull. World Health Organ*, 1961.

Miller, R.P., Bates, J.H., "Pleuropulmonary tularemia", *Am. Rev. Respir. Dis.*, 1969.

Mitra, A.C., Sarkar, J.K., Mukherjee, M.K, "Virus content of smallpox scabs", *Bull. World Health Organ*, 1974.

Mollick, J. A., Cook, R.G., Rich, R.R., "Class II MHC molecules are specific receptors for staphylococcal enterotoxin A", *Science*, 1989.

Moyer, N.P., Holcomb, L.A., *Brucella*, In Murray, P.R., Baron, E.J., Pfaller, M.A., Tenover, F.C., Yolken, R.F., eds., *Manual of Clinical Microbiology*, 6th ed. Washington, DC: ASM Press; 1995.

Penn, R.L., *Francisella tularensis (tularemia)*, In Mandell, G.A., Bennett, J.E., Dolen, R., eds.,*Principles and Practice of Infectious Diseases*, New York, NY: Churchill Livingstone Inc; 1995.

Report of the Investigation Into the Cause of the 1978 Birmingham Smallpox Occurrence, London, England: Her Majesty's Stationery Office, 1980.

Richmond, J.Y., McKinney, R.W., *Biosafety in Microbiological and Biomedical Laboratories*, Washington, DC: US Dept of Health and Human Services; 1993, HHS publication CDC 93-8395.

Salas, R., De Manzione, N., Tesh, R. B., et al., "Venezuelan haemorrhagic fever",*Lancet*, 1991

Sarkar, J.K., Mitra, A.C., Mukherjee, M.K., De, S.K., Mazumdar, D.G., "Virus excretion in smallpox",*Bull. World Health Organ,* 1973.

Tigertt, W.D., Benenson, A.S., "Studies on Q fever in man", *Trans. Assoc. Am. Physcians*, 1956.

Uhaa, I.J., Fishbein, D.B., Olson, J.G., et al., "Evaluation of specificity of indirect enzyme-linked immunosorbent assay for diagnosis of human Q fever",*J. Clin, Microbiol,* 1994.

Ulrich, R.G., Sidell, S., Taylor, T.J., Wilhelmsen, C.L., Franz, D.R., *Staphylococcal enterotoxin B and related pyrogenic toxins*, In Zajtchuk, R, ed., *Textbook of Military Medicine: Medical Aspects of Chemical and Biological Warfare*, Washington, DC: USDept of the Army, The Surgeon General, and the Borden Institute, 1997.

Waag, D., Chulay, J., Marrie, T., England, M., Willaims, J., "Validation of an enzyme immunoassay for serodiagnosis of acute Q fever",*Eur J.Clin. Microbiol. Infect. Dis.,* 1995.

Wehrle, P.F., Posch, J., Richter, K.H., et al., "An airborne outbreak of smallpox in a German hospital and its significance with respect to other recent outbreaks in Europe", *Bull. World Health Organ*, 1970.

World Health Organisation/International Study Team, Ebola haemorrhagic fever in Zaire, 1976, *Bull. World Health Organ*, 1978.

4

Cutaneous Manifestations

The term 'Biological Warfare' (BW) can be defined as the employment of biological agents to produce casualties in man or animals or damage to plants. While a biological attack could result in a made-made epidemic of unprecedented scale, the classical principles of clinical medicine and epidemiology would apply. Prompt diagnosis and early interventions could reduce morbidity and mortality, and mitigate the effects of a biological attack. In the aftermath of a biological attack, dermatologists could play a critical role in recognising the differential diagnosis of an epidemic exanthem and alerting public health officials, leading to prompt medical and public health interventions.

Perpetrators can escape long before BW agents cause casualties, due to the incubation periods of the agents. Weapons are easy and cheap to produce and can be used to selectively target humans, animals, or plants. The costs of conventional weapons ($2,000), nuclear armaments ($800), and chemical agents ($600) would far outstrip the bargain-base-ment price of biological weapons ($1) to produce 50 per cent casualties per square kilometre. Agents can be easily procured from the environment, universities, biological supply houses, and clinical specimens. Common fermentation techniques used for producing antibiotics, toxoid vaccines, foods, and beverages can be used to grow large quantities of biological agents. Simple aerosol generating devices mounted on planes or trucks, as used for crop-dusting, can generate one to five micron particles ideal for causing infectious aerosols. Aerosol particles half to five microns in diameter settle in the alveoli; larger particles are cleared by respiratory mucosa, and smaller particles float in and out of the alveoli without settling. BW agents are typically invisible in aerosol clouds and may not be detected until humans become ill. Disadvantages to using BW agents as weapons include hazards to the user, their dependence on optimal weather conditions to result in effective dispersal, and their possible inactivation by solar irradiation and other climatic conditions.

Biological agents may kill or incapacitate victims. Incapacitating agents may be more effective in battle by both preventing a unit from carrying out its mission and overwhelming medical and evacuation assets. Agents with short incubation times would be most effective in a tactical setting, while those with longer incubation periods would appeal more to terrorists.

BW attacks against large populations would most likely be disseminated by aerosol. A respiratory portal of entry may cause different clinical features than naturally occurring disease. The attacks could be attempted by contaminating food and water supplies, although modern water purification and the dilution effects in large volumes of water would negate the effectiveness of a waterborne attack. While intact skin is an excellent barrier to most biological warfare agents, some agents, such as trichothecene mycotoxins, can penetrate the integument and cause systemic illness. Ingestion and cutaneous penetration are currently considered unimportant potential routes of exposure. Person-to-person transmission of several agents—notably plague and smallpox—could perpetuate an epidemic. Nosocomial transmission could result from blood and body fluid exposures—haemorrhagic fever viruses, smallpox, and plague.

According to estimates of WHO a city of 500,000 people would be devastated following an aerosol release of as little as 50 kg of BW agent.

Table 4.1
Estimated casualties for BW attack on a city of 500,000

Agent	*Downwind reach (km)*	*Dead*	*Incapacitated*
Rift Valley fever	1	400	35,000
Tick-borne encephalitis	1	9500	35,000
Typhus	5	19,000	85,000
Brucellosis	10	500	100,000
Q-fever	>20	150	125,000
Tularemia	>20	30,000	125,000
Anthrax	>20	95,000	125,000

Despite the 1972 Geneva Biological Weapons Convention, at least 17 countries are known or suspected of having offensive biological weapons programmes. Clearly, BW is a credible threat to our military, as it was during Desert Shield/Storm. Terrorist use of BW agents could kill many people to create an unparalleled medical, political, and social crisis.

All BW agent work is limited to defensive measures such as developing immunisations, detection methods, personal protective equipment, decontamination, rapid diagnostic tests, and treatments. The US boidefence programme is centred at Fort Detrick, MD at the United States Army Medical Research Institute of Infectious Diseases (USAMRIID). Its mission is to conduct research to develop strategies, products, information, procedures, and training for medical defence against biological warfare agents and naturally occurring agents of military importance that require maximal containment for laboratory safety.

The agents listed in table 4.2 have detailed clinical data sheets in the NATO handbook on biological warfare defence, are included in the Textbook of Military Medicine Volume entitled *Medical Aspects of Chemical and Biological Warfare*, and/or are taught at the US Army's Management of Chemical and Biological Casualties Course.

Table 4.2
Potential BW threat agents

Agent class	*Natural reservoir*	*Likely BW route*	*Incubation, d*	*Personnel effect*	*Skin findings*	*Prevention*	*Treatment*
Bacterial							
Anthrax (*Bacillus anthracis*)	Soil, cattle, sheep, horses	R	1-6	L	E	C, V	1
Brucellosis (*Brucellaspecies*)	Goats, swine	R, P	5-60	I	...	C	1
Cholera (*Vibrio cholerae*)	Polluted water or food	G	1-5	I, L	...	C, V, X	1
Melioidosis (*Burkholderia pseudomallei*)	Soil	R	Weeks to years	I, L E	BW	C	1
Plague (*Yersinia pestis*)	Fleas	R	2-6	L E,	BW	C	1
Q fever (*Coxiella burnetii*)	Sheep, cattle, goats	R	10-40	I	...	C, X	1
Tularemia (*Francisella tularensis*)	Deerflies, mosquitoes, ticks	R	2-10	L	E	C, X	1

Contd . . .

Contd...

Viral							
Argentine HF (*Junin virus*)	Rodents	R	7-14	I E,	BW	...	2
Bolivian HF (*Machupo virus*)	Rodents	R	7-14	I E,	BW	...	2
Congo-Crimean HF	Ticks	R	3-12	L E,	BW	...	2
Ebola HF	Unknown	R	3-16	L E,	BW	...	
Hantaviruses	Rodents	R	9-35	I, L E,	BW	X	2
Lassa HF	Rodents	R	5-16	I, L E,	BW	...	2
Marburg HF	Unknown	R	3-16	L E,	BW	...	...
Rift Valley fever	Mosquitoes	R	2-5	L	...	X	...
Smallpox (*Variola major&minor*)	Human (eradicated)	R	7-17	L E,	BW	V	...
Venezuelan equine encephalitis	Mosquitoes	R	2-6	I	...	X	...

Contd...

Contd . . .

Toxins							
Botulinum (*Clostridium botulinum*)	Soil	R	1-5	L	. . .	X	3
Trichothecene mycotoxins (various moulds)	Soil	R, G, D	Minutes to hours	L	BW	. . .	. . .
Ricin	*Ricinus communis* (castor plant) seeds	R,G,P	4-6h	L	...	...	...
Staphylococcusenterotoxin B	Contaminated food	R, G	1-6 h	I	. . .	. . .	. . .

* Diseases in boldface cause cutaneous findings if disease is contracted from aerosol exposure. Underlined diseases cause cutaneous manifestations in endemic disease but not in aerosol-generated disease.

BW indicates biological warfare; R, respiratory; I,incapacitating; L, lethal; E, endemic disease; C, chemoprophylaxis; V, licensed vaccine; 1, antibiotics; P, percutaneous; G, gastrointestinal; D, dermal; X, investigational vaccine; 3, antiserum; HF, haemorrhagic fever; 2, investigational antiviral agents; and ellipses, not applicable.

In 1997, the economic impact of a bioterrorist aerosol attack on a city of 100,000 was estimated at $477 million for brucellosis to more than $26 billion for anthrax. One hundred and forty nations have ratified the 1972 Biological Weapons Convention. Signatories agreed to never develop, produce, stockpile, acquire, or retain BW agents or the means to deliver them. Despite this convention, BW has continued to cast its dark shadow.

The Iraqi regime had weaponised anthrax, botulinum toxin, and aflatoxin by 1991. Controversies regarding possible continued Iraqi offensive BW research and development have continued as the regime has alternately resisted and permitted the operations of the United Nations weapons inspection teams to verify compliance with United Nations Security Council Resolution 687 that mandates the dismantling of the Iraqi offensive BW programme. By 1995, at least 17 countries had been identified as nations harbouring biological weapons according to sources cited by the Office of Technology Assessment and at US Senate committee hearings. They included Iran, Iraq, Libya, Syria, North Korea, Taiwan, Israel, Egypt, Vietnam, Laos, Cuba, Bulgaria, India, South Korea, South Africa, China, and Russia. Clearly, BW remains a credible threat to our military, as it was during the Persian Gulf War. In addition, nonstate-sponsored terrorist organi-sations pose BW threats.

In 1995, the Aum Shinrikyo cult, who released sarin nerve gas in a Japanese subway, was found to possess a rudimentary biological weapons programme that included cultures of the etiologic agents of anthrax, botulism, and Q fever. The vulnerability of civilian populations to biological attack was illustrated by the successful use of *Salmonella typhimurium* to poison salad bars and cause 351 cases of gastroenteritis in Oregon by the Rajneeshee cult in 1984. Terrorist use of BW agents could kill many people to create an unparalleled medical, political, and social crisis. We must prepare for a new age of terrorism. Civilian health care providers must know how to recognise a BW attack in the event of the use of BW agents on civilian populations.

Many potential bioweapon agents have cutaneous manifestations that the trained eye of a dermatologist can recognise. Through early recognition of a BW attack, dermatologists can aid public health authorities in diagnosing the cause so that preventive and containment measures can be instituted to mitigate morbidity and mortality. They could play a critical role in recognising an epidemic exanthem.

Perpetrators can escape long before BW agents incubate and cause casualties. Weapons are easy and relatively inexpensive to produce and can be used to selectively target humans, animals, or plants. Agents can be easily procured from the environment, universities, biological supply houses, and clinical specimens.

Common fermentation techniques used for producing antibiotics, vaccines, foods, and beverages can be adapted to grow large quantities of biological agents. Simple aerosol-generating devices mounted on planes or trucks, like those used for crop dusting, can be adapted to generate 1- to 5-μm particles ideal for lodging in alveoli. Such aerosols would be undetectable by our senses, and an attack might not be noted until people became ill. Panic could result as medical capabilities become quickly overwhelmed.

Aerosolisation of biological agents often results in different clinical features of disease than those observed following natural infection. Biological attacks could be attempted by contaminating water supplies, although modern water purification and the dilution effects of large water volumes would negate the effectiveness of such an attack. While intact skin provides a barrier to most BW agents, the trichothecene mycotoxins can penetrate the skin and cause systemic effects. Ingestion and cutaneous penetration are currently considered as unimportant potential routes of exposure. Agents could be dispersed by releasing them in their natural arthropod vectors. Person-to-person aerosol transmission of several agents old perpetuate an epidemic.

Agents with cutaneous manifestations as a part of a BW presentation is decribed in this chapter.

BACTERIAL AGENTS

Bacterial agents who can cause cutaneous manifestations are:

i) *Burkholderia pseudomallei* (causative of melioidosis)

ii) *Yersinia pestis* (causative of plague)

Burkholderia pseudomallei

Burkholderia pseudomallei is a gram-negative bacillus that is often isolated from soil and causes epizootics in sheep, goats, swine, horses, and seals. Humans most commonly contract disease via inoculation of cutaneous abrasions with contaminated soil. Ingestion and inhalation of bacilli may also cause clinical infection. The disease is most commonly presents as an acute pulmonary infection, but it may also present as an acute, localised skin infection, septicemia, or a chronic disease with disseminated internal abscesses.

Inhaled organisms would commonly cause a mild bronchitis, but it could lead to severe, necrotising pneumonia, septicemia, and death. Pulmonary infection could also lead to a chronic disease with clinical and radiographic features indistinguishable from tuberculosis. Metastatic infection can involve numerous internal organs, and the disease can remain latent for years. The overall mortality rate remains near 40 per cent, despite antibiotic therapy. Before the antibiotic era, 95 per cent of patients died.

Severe urticaria may accompany pulmonary melioidosis. Flushing, cyanosis, and a pustular eruption may develop during septicemia. Patients often present with pustules and cutaneous abscesses associated with lymphangitis, cellulitis, or regional lymphadenitis. Draining sinuses from lymph nodes or bone may develop.

Burkholderia pseudomallei would most likely be delivered as an aerosol. The lack of a vaccine and its high mortality despite treatment could make it a plausible BW agent. Acute pneumonia could be confused with plague given the similar appearance of stained organisms, while a diffuse, pustular eruption could be mistaken for varicella or smallpox.

Yersinia pestis

Yersinia pestis, the causative agent of plague has been studied as a possible BW agent. Humans contract disease from flea bites, and less commonly from mammalian hosts or other humans via respiratory droplet transmission. After an incubation period of two to six days, bubonic plague acutely causes fever and prostration associated with painful lymphadenitis in the nodal basin draining the site of the flea bite. Buboes may point and drain spontaneously. Less than 10 per cent of patients complain of a prior flea bite. Untreated, bubonic plague progresses to septicemic plague within two to six days.

Patients exhibit shock, ecchymoses, and small artery thromboses resulting in digital gangrene. Both septicemic and pneumonic forms of plague can occur primarily, without antecedent bubonic disease, or, secondarily, due to dissemination of bubonic disease. Abdominal pain is the only presenting symptom more common in septicemic plague than in bubonic plague.

The case-fatality rate of untreated bubonic plague is approximately 60 per cent, but less than five per cent with antibiotic therapy. The case-fatality rate for untreated septicemic and pneumonic plague approaches 100 per cent. The currently licensed, inactivated, whole-cell vaccine prevents bubonic plague. However, it does not reliably protect against primary pneumonic plague, and thus it would not be helpful in a BW context. Candidate live-attenuated vaccines are no more immunogenic than the killed vaccine, and they may revert to virulent, wild-type bacteria.

Patients with terminal pneumonic and septicemic plague would develop livid cyanosis and large ecchymoses. The petechiae and ecchymoses can mimic meningococcemia. Dark areas of cyanosis, ecchymoses, or acral necrosis probably gave rise to the Medieval epithet, "the Black Death." Rose-coloured purpuric lesions gave rise to the nursery rhyme "Ring around the rosy." The "pocket full of posies" referred to the sweet-smelling flowers carried into the homes of the sick, in an effort to ward off the stench and transmission of disease. Rare cases of ecthyma gangrenosum like lesions and carbuncles due to *Y. pestis* have been reported. Pharyngitis associated with cervical lymphadenopathy has been reported in contacts of patients with bubonic plague.

In China, during World War II, the Japanese allegedly tested plague as a BW agent. Human fleas (*Pulex irritans*) were bred and infected with *Y pestis.* Infected fleas were released into several Chinese cities where small epidemics of bubonic plague ensued. Normally, animal hosts die in epizootics before humans are infected, but in these cases, humans died of plague before animals did. Plague would likely be released as an aerosol during a modern BW attack and could generate many cases of highly lethal and contagious pneumonia. Bubonic plague would not ensue after aerosol release, but it could occur after transmission by fleas. The possibility of rapid death combined with potential person-to-person transmission makes plague an ominous BW threat.

There are some other bacterial agents producing cutaneous manifestations naturally. They are:

i) *Bacillus anthracis*

ii) *Francisella tularensis.*

Bacillus anthracis

Bacillus anthracis bacterium can survive in extremes of heat, cold, drying, and chemical disinfection, and in nature, they retain viability for years. Anthrax is endemic in western Asia and western Africa. Disease is transmitted from infected animals or their products via skin abrasions in more than 90 per cent of cases. Approximately 95 per cent of cases present as cutaneous disease.

Gastrointestinal anthrax follows ingestion of poorly cooked meat obtained from infected livestock and results in mucosal ulcers that can perforate viscera to cause abdominal pain, diarrhoea, and sepsis. Inhalational anthrax, or wool-sorter's disease, is an extraordinarily rare form of anthrax; only 18 cases were reported in the United States between 1900 and 1980. Inhaled spores germinate in hilar nodes and cause a deadly haemorrhagic mediastinitis, not a primary pneumonia. Inhalational anthrax would follow a biological attack using anthrax spores. The illness begins with a vague prodrome featuring low-grade fever, malaise, myalgias, and non-productive cough with transient improvement in some patients after two to four days. This is followed by the acute phase, manifesting with abrupt onset of respiratory distress, shock, and death. Metastatic infection results in haemorrhagic meningitis in up to 50 per cent of cases. Radiographic findings may include hilar adenopathy, a widened mediastinal shadow, and pleural effusions.

Cutaneous anthrax begins as a small, painless, red macule that progresses to a papule that vesiculates, ruptures, ulcerates, and forms a classic one to five cm brown or black eschar surrounded by significant oedema. This coal black eschar gave rise to the term anthrax that is derived from the Greek anthrakos meaning "coal."

Lesions usually appear within two weeks after handling sick animals or eating their meat; however, incubation periods of more than eight weeks have been observed. Lesions are not purulent in the absence of superinfection, thus the term malignant pustule ascribed to this lesion is a misnomer.

Even with prompt antibiotic therapy, cutaneous lesions progress through the eschar phase. While 80 per cent to 90 per cent of lesions heal spontaneously, 10 per cent to 20 per cent of untreated patients develop malignant oedema, septicemia, shock, renal failure, and death.

Anthrax spores would most likely be disseminated as an aerosol. In April and May 1979, at least 66 people died during an epidemic of inhalational anthrax in Sverdlovsk, Russia, following the accidental release of aerosolised spores. It has been estimated that the release of less than one gram of spores caused the outbreak. All 42 victims undergoing autopsy demonstrated hemorrhagic mediastinitis. This accident demonstrated the silent and deadly nature of an aerosol BW attack.

Anthrax spores were weaponised by Japan, the United Kingdom. and the United States in the 1940s, 1950s, and 1960s before their offensive BW programmes were terminated. Iraq admitted to a United Nations inspection team in 1995 that it had weaponised anthrax. A Food and Drug Administration-licensed vaccine has proven safe and effective in preventing anthrax among textile workers, veterinarians, and laboratory workers at risk. The toxoid vaccine also protects non-human primates against aerosol challenge with anthrax spores.

Francisella tularensis

Francisella tularensis the causative agent of tularemia is a gram-negative, pleomorphic coccobacillus maintained in numerous mammalian reservoirs and spread by dozens of biting and blood-sucking arthropods. Skin or mucous membranes serve as the portal of entry for arthropod bites or abrasions.

As few as 10 organisms are necessary to cause cutaneous or pulmonary infection. Each of six possible clinical forms (ulceroglandular, glandular, oculoglandular, gastrointestinal, typhoidal, and pulmonary) begins with the sudden onset of a flulike syndrome. An ulcer is commonly seen at a bite site, and the ulcer may persist for several months.

Cutaneous multiplication of *F. tularensis* can allow organisms to spread to lymph nodes and then to the blood. Inhalation of organisms may result in typhoidal disease (septicemia) or a primary pneumonia. Pneumonic tularemia is the primary concern in a BW scenario. Patients complain of fever, cough, minimal or no sputum production, and pleuritic chest pain.

Physical findings are variable, and they may include rales, pleural friction rubs, and signs of consolidation or effusions. Radiographic findings are also variable, and they may include infiltrates, cavitation, hilar adenopathy, and pleural effusions. The clinical course may be rapidly progressive and fulminant. While four per cent of patients with the most common form, ulceroglandular tularemia, die if untreated, fully 35 per cent die from typhoidal disease, and 30 per cent to 60 per cent succumb to the pulmonary form.

A cancer-like ulcer with heaped-up borders forms at the site of bacterial inoculation in 60 per cent of patients. About 85 per cent of patients develop tender lymphadenopathy 112 that sometimes presents as fluctuant buboes. Pharyngeal ulcers may accompany aerosol-induced disease. A morbilliform eruption has been reported in a minority of patients with systemic disease.

Tularemia was weaponised by the United States in the 1950s and 1960s. Other countries may have weaponised tularemia for aerosol delivery. Both typhoidal and pulmonary tularemia can result from inhalation, and mucosal lesions could accompany inhalational disease. The rapid onset of action, non-specific nature of complaints in those affected, and the difficulty in identifying and culturing the organism make it a potential threat agent.

VIRAL AGENTS

Viral agents who can cause cutaneous manifestations are:

i) Poxviridae
ii) Haemorrhagic fever viruses

Poxviridae

The *Poxviridae* family includes variola, the etiologic agent of smallpox, and a number of animal poxviruses that occasionally cause human disease. Thirty years ago, smallpox was endemic in 31 countries, resulting in 15 million illnesses and two million deaths annually. A 10-year World Health Organisation (WHO) programme eradicated the disease as of October 1977. Unfortunately, smallpox still lingers as a potential BW threat. Variola can remain viable for one year in dust and cloth. Person-to-person spread requires close contact, typically via a respiratory route. Only 30 per cent of close contacts develop disease with infectivity peaking between days four and six of illness.

Monkeypox, caused by a closely related virus was first identified in 1958 as a pathogen in cynomolgus monkeys; in 1971 it was first linked to human disease. Unlike smallpox, monkeypox is maintained in an animal reservoir, an arboreal squirrel of tropical rain forests in western and central Africa.

Following a seven to 17-day incubation period, a flulike prodrome lasting two to four days ensues during which 10 per cent of light-skinned patients exhibit an erythematous exanthem. Most patients develop a buccal and pharyngeal enanthem that shed virus and enhance respiratory transmission.

Cutaneous lesions typically appear first on the face, then on the forearms and hands, and finally on the lower limbs and trunk within one week. Lesions favour ventral surfaces and begin as macules that progress to papules, vesicles, pustules (often umbilicated, like molluscum contagiosum lesions), and crusts. This synchronous progression of centrifugal lesions results in crusts within one to two weeks. The deep crusts then detach after two to four weeks leaving depressed, hypopigmented scars. Virus can be cultured from crusts throughout convalescence.

There are two different recognised strains of variola. The more virulent strain (variola major) caused death in 20 per cent to 5 per cent of the unvaccinated. The less virulent strain (variola minor), also known as *alastrim*, led to death in less than one per cent of unvaccinated patients. Four clinical forms of smallpox were described: ordinary, flat, haemorrhagic, and modified. Either strain of variola could bring about any one of these clinical pictures.

Ordinary smallpox presented in 80 per cent of patients and led to death in 30 per cent of unvaccinated and three per cent of vaccinated individuals. When ordinary smallpox was caused by variola minor, illness was milder and lesions were more diminutive.

The most virulent form, hemorrhagic smallpox, accounted for three per cent of infections and caused death in 99 per cent of unvaccinated and 94 per cent of vaccinated patients, usually before they developed typical pox lesions.

Flat smallpox occurred in four per cent of patients and caused severe systemic toxic effects during the slow evolution of macular, soft or velvety, focal skin lesions. Case-fatality rates were 66 per cent among the vaccinated and 95 per cent among the unvaccinated.

Modified smallpox accounted for the remaining 13 per cent of cases. It usually occurred among vaccinees and was composed of a mild prodrome, rapid development and crusting of lesions, and frequent absence of a pustular stage. The extent of the eruption was not necessarily any different than in the other types.

Variola sine eruption occurred in 30 per cent to 50 per cent of vaccinated contacts of patients with smallpox. While no cutaneous changes occurred, patients often developed conjunctivitis following a mild prodrome. The cause of such cases was confirmed by serologic studies.

In the case of monkeypox patients develop fever, respiratory symptoms, and synchronised lesions just like patients with smallpox. They seem more prone to develop inguinal and cervical lymphadenopathy and appear to have a lower mortality rate. Pneumonia secondary to monkeypox has a 50 per cent mortality rate.

A search for monkeypox in the Democratic Republic of the Congo in February 1997 found 92 cases among 4,000 inhabitants of 12 villages yielding an attack rate of two per cent. Of these, 18 per cent had smallpox vaccination scars. Vaccinia seems to provide some cross-protection against monkeypox.

Though has been eradicated, the Centres for Disease Control and Prevention in Atlanta, Ga, and the Russian State Research Centre of Virology and Biotechnology in Koltsovo still maintain viable variola. The extent of clandestine stockpiles remains a matter of debate and concern.

The World Health Organisation has recommended the destruction of remaining stocks by June 30, 1999. If variola were released by an enemy or by terrorists, morbidity and mortality could be devastating. Its person-to-person communicability, high mortality, and stability make variola a significant potential BW threat. In addition, animal poxviruses that are virulent to humans or recombinant poxviruses could be developed as BW weapons.

Haemorrhagic Fever Viruses

Viral haemorrhagic fever (VHF) is a syndrome which includes fever, malaise, myalgias, haemorrhage, and sometimes hypotension, shock, and death. The haemorrhagic fever viruses belong to four families of lipid-enveloped viruses with single-stranded RNA genomes. The taxonomy, ecology, and epidemiology of these viruses are summarised in Table 4.3.

Animal reservoirs have been identified for three of these families (*Arenaviridae*, *Bunyaviridae*, and *Flaviviridae*); however, the reservoirs for the *Filoviridae* are unknown. Transmission may occur via arthropod vectors or from inhalation of aerosolised rodent excreta. Person-to-person spread often occurs via direct contact with blood and bodily fluids. All haemorrhagic fever viruses except dengue can be transmitted via aerosol. Four VHFs carry a high risk of nosocomial transmission and are quarantinable: Lassa fever, Congo-Crimean hemorrhagic fever, Ebola fever, and Marburg disease.

Table 4.3

Taxonomy, ecology, and epidemiology of Haemorrhagic Fever Viruses

Disease	*Geography*	*Source of Human Infection*	*Incubation*
CCHF Europe	Africa, Asia	Tick	3-12 days
Dengue HF	Asia, Amer., Africa	Mosquito	3-15 days
HFRS	Worldwide	Rodent	9-35 days
Junin/Machupo	X	Rodent	7-14 days
KFD	Omsk India/Russia	Tick	3-8 days
Lassa	Africa	Rodent, Nosocomial	5-16 days
Marburg/Ebola	Africa	Unknown, Nosocomial	3-16 days
RVF	Africa	Mosquito	2-5 days
Yellow Fever	Trop. Africa, S.Am	Mosquito	3-15 days

VHFs present as acute febrile illnesses with non-specific constitutional symptoms including fever, headache, sore throat, malaise, myalgia, nausea, and vomiting. Initial signs include flushing, conjunctival injection, periorbital oedema, petechiae, and hypotension. Disease may progress to prostration, shock, haemorrhage, and organ system failure. Sequelae of infections include alopecia, Beau lines, and deafness (Lassa and Ebola fevers), retinitis (Rift Valley fever, Kyasanur Forest disease), uveitis (Rift Valley fever, Marburg disease), encephalitis (Argentine haemorrhagic fever, Bolivian haemorrhagic fever, Rift Valley fever, Kyasanur Forest disease, and Omsk haemorrhagic fever), pericarditis (Lassa fever), and renal insufficiency (haemorrhagic fever with renal syndrome).

VHFs produce a variety of cutaneous findings that are mostly due to vascular instability and bleeding abnormalities. All these diseases, except Rift Valley fever, may manifest flushing, petechiae, purpura, ecchymoses, and oedema. The Old World Arena virus responsible for Lassa fever causes an extensive capillary leak syndrome without clotting abnormalities. Thus oedema, without petechiae or haemorrhage, is most commonly seen. The South American Arena viruses (Junin, Machupo, Sabia, and Guanarito) more commonly cause petechiae, purpura, ecchymoses, palatal hyperemia, and haemorrhage from mucosal surfaces.

The Bunyavirus causing Congo-Crimean haemorrhagic fever results in the most severe haemorrhagic complications among all VHFs. The hanta-viruses of the Bunyaviridae cause hemorrhagic fever with renal syndrome. Around day three, patients develop a petechial eruption on the neck, anterior and posterior axillary folds, arms, and thorax. A morbilliform eruption may also appear. A sunburn flush is commonly seen about the head, neck, and upper torso accompanied by facial oedema. Dermatographism is often present, and severe haemorrhages on oral and conjunctival mucosae may be seen.

The highly feared Filoviruses Marburg and Ebola frequently exhibit characteristic exanthems noted best in light-skinned patients. Disease typically presents with an acute, flulike syndrome with soft-palate reddening spreading to the hard palate. The most reliable diagnostic sign is a non-pruritic, centripetal, pinhead-sized papular, erythematous eruption appearing between days five and seven.

Sometimes, scrotal or labial erythema and dermatitis accompany this. After 24 hours, this eruption develops into large, well-demarcated, coalescent macules and papules that are sometimes haemorrhagic. In severe cases, a dark, livid erythema with or without cyanosis develops on the face, trunk, and extremities. Patients have expressionless, ghostlike faces. With progressive disease, haemorrhage exudes from mucous membranes, venipuncture sites, and body orifices. After one to two more weeks, desquamation of the palms, soles, dorsal feet, and extremities follows. Death occurs owing to a combination of haemorrhage, capillary leak, shock, and end-organ failure. The mortality rate for Marburg disease is 23 per cent and for Ebola fever, 70 per cent.

The most common Flavivirus disease is the dengue fever and causes approximately 100 million annual cases of an erythematous exanthem with notable islands of sparing. Infection due to one of the four serotypes grants lifelong immunity to that serotype only and predisposes one to develop dengue haemorrhagic fever or dengue shock syndrome following infection with a heterologous strain. Only patients infected sequentially with different dengue serotypes will develop the life-threatening haemorrhagic fever or shock syndrome. This occurs in one million people annually resulting in approximately 100 000 deaths. Typically, yellow fever's only cutaneous manifestation is jaundice. The tick-borne Flavivirus diseases can cause any of the haemorrhagic manifestations listed earlier.

The VHF viruses cause high morbidity and, in some cases, high mortality. Some replicate well enough in cell culture to permit weaponisation. With the exception of dengue, all the haemorrhagic fever viruses are transmissible by aerosol, underscoring their possible role as BW agents. For example, Marburg virus can be stabilised in 10 per cent glycerin so that viral inactivation occurs at a rate of 1.5 per cent per minute instead of 11.5 per cent per minute. This rate of inactivation is similar to that for influenza virus that spreads naturally via aerosol. The susceptibility of Bunyaviruses to heat, drying, and UV light make them poor candidates as BW agents. Hantaviruses replicate poorly in cell culture. The Flaviviruses are unlikely to be used since dengue is not infectious by aerosol and troops are routinely immunised for yellow fever. A live-attenuated junin vaccine provides protection against infection with both junin and machupo viruses.

TOXIN THREAT

The only potential BW toxins with cutaneous activity and manifestations are trichothecene mycotoxins (yellow rain). These are a diverse group of small-molecular-weight compounds mainly produced by fungi of 5 genera: *Alternaria*, *Aspergillus*, *Claviceps*, *Fusarium*, and *Penicillium*.

Toxic levels may develop in mouldy grains. If eaten or inhaled, such grain may cause human or animal disease. Alimentary toxic aleukia, reported in Russia since the nineteenth century, is thought to result from ingesting mycotoxins while eating foods prepared from moldy grain. Symptoms and signs include vomiting, diarrhoea, skin inflammation, leukopenia, and haemorrhage.

Trichothecene mycotoxins are thought to have caused fatal pulmonary haemorrhage in Cleveland, Ohio, area infants. In all cases, the fungus *Stachybotrys atra* was found growing in water-saturated cellulose in the walls of poorly maintained homes. In one area of Cleveland, mycotoxins may have accounted for five per cent of cases of sudden infant death syndrome between 1993 and 1995. At low doses most trichothecene mycotoxins, including T-2 mycotoxin, cause cutaneous erythema, edema, vesicles, bullae, and necrosis in guinea pigs. Maximal vesiculation occurs at 48 hours in guinea pigs. Similar findings have occurred in humans accidentally exposed to T-2 mycotoxins. T-2 mycotoxin is estimated to be 400 times more potent than mustards in producing skin injury in laboratory animals. T-2 mycotoxins can be absorbed percutaneously, and they can cause death in animals with a median lethal dose of only 2 to 12 mg/kg compared with 37 mg/kg for lewisite and 4500 mg/kg for mustards.

In Afghanistan and South-east Asia during the late 1970s the United States accused the Soviet Union and its proxies of using mycotoxins as biological weapons. However, these accusations were never conclusively proven and they are regarded as controversial.

Aerosolised mycotoxins could be adapted for BW use. At microgram levels, trichothecene mycotoxins can induce tearing, eye pain, conjunctivitis, and blurred vision lasting eight to 14 days in humans exposed to aerosols containing T-2, HT-2, and/ or anguidine. Higher doses induce emesis and diarrhoea. Aerosols cause death in humans within minutes to hours by destroying alveoli. The toxins kill rapidly proliferating tissues by inhibiting protein and RNA synthesis. They gain access to all rapidly proliferating tissues following cutaneous absorption. Washing the skin with soap and water within four to six hours of exposure removed 80 per cent to 98 per cent of T-2 mycotoxin and prevented cutaneous necrosis.

COMPLICATIONS OF BW PREVENTION

Scientists have developed numerous strategies to prevent an dtreat the diseases that could develop after a BW attack. These include vaccines, antibiotic prophylaix, and protective measures such as the use of gas masks. Cutaneous complications were at least 10 times more common in primary vaccinees than revaccinees. The most severe cutaneous complication, vaccinia necrosum, occurred in 12.3 per million primary vaccinees. Vaccinees with cellular immunodeficiencies developed relentlessly progressive pox lesions and even metastatic lesions. Fatal cases showed no evidence of resolution, no adenopathy, and no erythema. Death occurred in 13/17 (76 per cent) of documented cases.

Vaccinia

Vaccinia, which would be used as a preventive measure if smallpox was released, causes a variety of cutaneous adverse effects in a small percentage of vaccinees. The Orthopox virus vaccinia, used as the first live vaccine, was essential for the global eradication of smallpox. Vaccinia has recently been studied as a vector for experimental recombinant vaccines. Vaccinia may have developed from an extinct animal poxvirus, such as horsepox, or it may represent a cowpox mutant that emerged during multiple human passages as vaccine was passed from arm-to- arm during the early vaccine era. Vaccinia has little virulence for immunocompentent humans and would not be an effective BW agent, but it could cause disease when used to prevent smallpox.

Vaccinia can cause serious complications in those with impaired cellular immunity, widespread dermatitis, and exfoliative dermatoses. Vaccine is administered percutaneously with a bifurcated needle. Primary vaccinees usually develop a two to four cm pustule surrounded by induration six to eight days after vaccination. This is accompanied by low-grade fever and axillary lymphadenopathy that indicate viral replication. This major reaction was required to confer protective immunity and occurred in 95 per cent of primary vaccinees. All other reactions were termed equivocal. The pustule would evolve into an ulcer with an overlying eschar that would eventually separate. This process became known as scarification because of the ensuing permanent scar. Vaccination by intramuscular injection induces a threefold to 10-fold reduction in the immune response.

Vaccinees, usually with impaired cell-mediated immunity, developed relentlessly progressive pox lesions and metastatic lesions. Fatal cases demonstrated no evidence of immune response. *Eczema vaccinatum* featured hundreds of pox lesions and occurred in patients with active atopic dermatitis who were either vaccinated or exposed to a recent vaccinee. Mortality was 10 per cent to 14 per cent.

Patients were treated with vaccinia immune globulin (0.6 mL/kg per day) until no new lesions appeared. Only 1.5 cases per million primary vaccinees were reported in the United States. This low rate is best explained by the fact that atopic dermatitis was identified as a contraindication to vaccination. Accidental vaccinia infection occurred among 242 per million primary vaccinees by autoinoculation to another body site or to another individual via intimate contact.

Ocular vaccinia was one of the most morbid complications since it resulted in conjunctivitis, keratitis, or corneal perforation. Generalised vaccinia presented as a vesicular eruption one to two weeks after primary vaccination. Afebrile and nontoxic-appearing patients developed many small vesicles on erythematous bases. This self-limited complication resolved in about one week in the 39 people per million primary vaccinees who contracted it. Other patients developed erythematous urticarial eruptions that resembled enterovirus or roseola exanthems. Other complications included the formation of melanoma or basal cell carcinomas in vaccination scars.

CONFRONTINF THE BW THREAT

The primary threat from BW agents today is from terrorists, civilians in densely populated regions would be likely targets. Therefore, civilian medical personnel need to be aware of how a BW attack would present to minimise its effects. We cannot presume that such an attack would never happen.

With current technology, an enemy could complete a BW attack before the local commander or medical officer would know anything had happened. Large and steadily increasing numbers of casualties would present in a shorter period than for a natural epidemic. There may be a large number of rapidly fatal cases with few recognisable signs and symptoms. Multiple diseases could present simultaneously. Vector-borne diseases will appear without natural outbreaks in animals.

BW agents would likely have a high attack rate among exposed individuals, and the disease would often be unusual for the geographic area. Since most agents would be delivered in aerosol clouds, many patients would have pulmonary disease caused by agents that don't usually cause pulmonary disease. Owing to the incubation periods of most BW agents, an enemy could complete a BW attack before health care providers and public health officials would be aware that an attack had occurred. Large and steadily increasing numbers of casualties could present within a shorter period than during a natural epidemic. There could be large numbers of rapidly fatal cases with few specific signs and symptoms depending on the agent(s) used. Multiple diseases could present simultaneously. Vector-borne diseases could appear without natural outbreaks in animals. The disease(s) would typically be unusual for a given geographic area and attack a high proportion of those exposed. Since most agents would be delivered in aerosol clouds, patients could develop pulmonary disease caused by agents that usually do not involve the respiratory tract.

BW attacks would generally allow time for an effective emergency response to save many lives. Due to the vulnerability of the civilian population to a biological attack, civilian medical personnel need to be aware of how such an attack would present so that they could ameliorate its effects. The US Army Chemical and Biological Defence Command, supported by the US Army Medical Research Institute of Infectious Diseases and the US Army Medical Research Institute of Chemical Defence, in accord with the Nunn-Luger-Domenici legislation of 1996, is conducting training for emergency responders and caregivers in more than 100 cities over five years so that these responders can recognise and respond to a BW assault.

Scientist have developed strategies to prevent and treat the diseases that could develop after a BW attack. These include vaccines, antibiotic prophylaxis, and protective measures such as the use of gas masks. The dermatologist should be aware of the ecchymotic and purpuric changes seen in septicemic plague and various haemorrhagic fevers. Prompt recognition of the dermatologic features of BW-associated diseases can lead to a more rapid mobilisation of public health and medical assets, leading to implementation of vaccines, chemoprophylaxis, and appropriate therapy.

REFERENCES

Arms Control and Disarmament Agency, *Signatories and Ratifications of the Biological and Toxin Weapons Convention*, Available at: http://www.stimson.org/ cwc/bwcsigs.htm. Accessed February 24, 1997.

Bamburg, J.R., Marasas WFO, Riggs, N.V., Smalley, E.B., Strong, F.M., "Toxic spiroepoxy compounds from fusaria and other hyphomycetes", *Biotechnol, Bioeng.*, 1968.

Baxby, D., "Poxviruses", In Belshe RB, ed., *Textbook of Human Virology*, Littleton, Mass: PSG Publishing, Co; 1984.

Cavanaugh, D.C., Cadigan, F.C., Williams, J.E., Marshall, J.D., *Plague*, In Ognibene A.J., Barrett, O.N., eds., *General Medicine and Infectious Diseases*, Washington, DC: Office of the Surgeon General and Centre of Military History; 1982.

Chaowagul, W., "Melioidosis: a treatment challenge", *Scand. J. Infect. Dis.Suppl.* 1996;101:14-16.

Eitzen, E.M., *Use of biological weapons*, In Sidell, F.R., Takafuji, E.T., Franz, D.R., eds., *Medical Aspects of Chemical and Biological Warfare*, Falls Church, Va: Office of the Surgeon General, US Dept of the Army; 1997.

Fenner, F., Henderson, D.A., Arita, I., Jezek, Z., Ladnyi, I.D., *Small pox and Its Eradication*, Geneva, Switzerland: World Health Organisation, 1988.

Franz, D.R., Jahrling, P.B., Friedlander, A.M., et al., *Clinical Recognition and Management of Patients Exposed to Biological Warfare Agents*, JAMA, 1997.

Jahrling, P.B., "Viral hemorrhagic fevers", In Sidell, F.R., Takafuji, E.T., Franz, D.R., eds., *Medical Aspects of Chemical and Biological Warfare*, Falls Church, Va: Office of the Surgeon General, US Dept of the Army; 1997.

McClain, D.J., Harrison, S., Yeager, C.L., et al., "Immunologic responses to vaccinia vaccines administered by different parenteral routes", *J.Infect. Dis.,* 1997.

Meyer, K.F., Cavanaugh, D.C., Bartelloni, P.J., Marshall, J.D. Jr., "Plague immunization: Past and present trends", *J. Infect. Dis.,* 1974;129(suppl):S13-S18.

Neff, J.M., "Vaccinia virus" (cowpox), In Mandell, G.L., Bennett, J.E., Dolin, R., eds.,*Principles and Practice of Infectious Diseases*, New York, NY: Churchill Living-stone Inc; 1995.

Perry, R.D., Fetherston, J.D., "Yersinia pestis:etiologic agent of plague", *Clin.Microbiol. Rev.*, 1997;10:35-66.

Pile, J.C., Malone, J.D., Eitzen, E.M., Jr, Friedlander, A.M., "Anthrax as a potential biological warfare agent", *Ann. Intern. Med.*, 1998;158:429-434.

Ricketts, T.F., *The Diagnosis of Smallpox*, London, England: Cassell; 1908.

5

Understanding the Massive Global Destruction

Biology has been a field of exponential discovery today. By the late 1990s, a massive pool of bioengineers, equipped with genetic blueprints to guide their efforts, had emerged. Determining the genetic sequence of a virus, such as Ebola, was no longer much of a feat. In 1998, scientists at the Frederick Cancer Research Centre in Maryland determined, at the genetic level, exactly how anthrax kills human cells. In response to such advances, Western militaries hardened their defences against biological warfare as they vaccinated troops, stockpiled antitoxins, stored appropriate antibiotics, purchased protective suits and masks, practised war-game drills involving biological weapons, and supported research on potential microbe-detecting devices. But no one had a master plan for dealing with the collateral impact of biological weapons on civilians and located around the combat zone or the deliberate impact of bioterrorist damage inflicted on an unsuspecting community.

The potential of biological weapons to cause death and suffering is similar to that of nuclear weapons. A bioweapons attack could, like nuclear attack, push a nation beyond the "point of non-recovery". Reaction to a bioweapons attack could conceivably generate sufficient fear and urgency to threaten fundamental democratic principles and even confidence in government. The sophistication of biological weaponry has improved by leaps and bounds. Until 1985, all of the world's biological weapons makers were stuck with the same lists of pathogens and toxins that could kill thousands of enemies and be delivered with missiles or large-scale aerosol systems. Each nation knew the list and stocked antidotes and vaccines.

The threat of bioterrorism has origanted from the 14th century itself. Since 1346, when the Mongols catapulted corpses contaminated with plague over the walls into Kaffa (Crimea) and forced the besieged Genoans to flee, there have been many documented cases of the use of biological agents against people. In the ninenteenth century, biological agents such as plague-infested fleas, cholera, anthrax, glanders, etc., have been used or field tested by aggressor nations in times of war and hostility.

The threat of biological terrorism is real and growing. An accident at a Soviet biological weapons facility in 1979 released a plume of anthrax that killed 66 people and livestock up to 100 kilometres downwind. An airborne release of 250 pounds of anthrax spores over Washington, DC, could cause more deaths than a one-megaton hydrogen bomb. The economic impact of an anthrax attack could range from $478 million to $26 billion for every 100,000 people affected. Recent events in Iraq, Japan, and Russia cast an ominous shadow. The magnitude of the problems and the gravity of the scenarios associated with release of these organisms have been vividly portrayed by two epidemics of smallpox in Europe during the 1970s and by an accidental release of aerosolised anthrax from a Russian bioweapons facility in 1979.

Terrorist organisations prey on deficiencies in national infrastructure and planning. The September 11, 2001 terrorist attacks on the World Trade Centre and the Pentagon made starkly clear how vulnerable people are to terrorism at home. But as devastating as those attacks were, the likelihood is growing that terrorists may soon decide to use biological agents as weapons to extract even higher death tolls. Evidence of this includes the startling fact that the number of criminal investigations in the United States related to the use of biological materials as weapons of mass destruction more than doubled between 1997 and 1998: In 1997, 22 of the 74 criminal investigations—or 30 per cent—involved biological materials. In 1998, 112 of the 181 criminal investigations—or 62 per cent—involved biological materials. As the facts about possible biological agents and the figures about their potential effects become known, the challenges for terrorists in mounting a biological attack against America may appear daunting, but they are not impossible to meet.

According to the US Centres for Disease Control and Prevention (CDC), biological agents pose a risk to the security of the people, because they are easily disseminated; cause high mortality, which would have a major impact on public health systems; cause panic and social disruptions; and require special action and funding to increase public preparedness. They can be spread by airborne release; by injection or direct contact; through food, pharmaceutical, and water contamination; or by animal vectors such as fleas and hair. They can be produced from widely available pathogens that are manufactured for legitimate biomedical research or obtained from soil or infected animals and humans. In fact, many of the infectious diseases that are associated with biological warfare are endemic to the same countries that are most often suspected of trying to develop biological weapons. And because biological agents may be cheap and easy to obtain, any nation with a basic industry or facility such as a brewery has a *de facto* capability to produce biological weapons.

The effectiveness of an attack can be affected by the particle size of the agent itself, the stability of the agent under desiccating conditions, exposure to ultraviolet light, wind speed and direction, and atmospheric stability. In most terrorist incidents that involved chemical or biological contamination, the method of dissemination is unknown. In cases where the method has been identified, the terrorists have relied on airborne dissemination (17 per cent); pharmaceutical contamination (16 per cent); food or drink contamination (15 per cent); injection or direct contact (13 per cent); and water contamination (11 per cent).

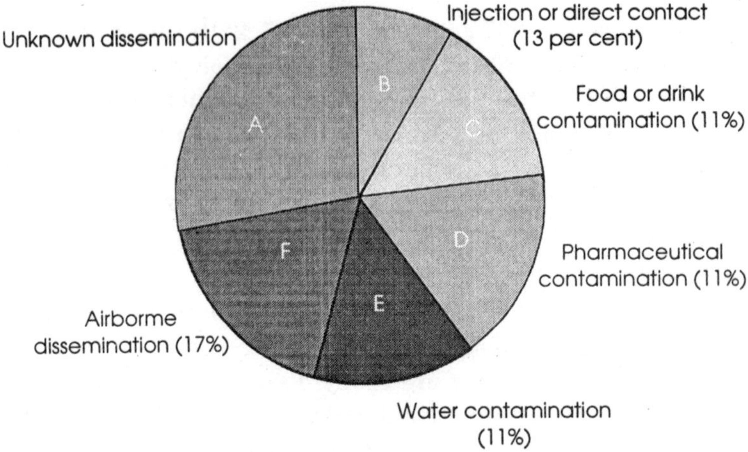

Figure 5.1: Terrorist incident involvong chemical or biological contamination

There are several other factors regarding delivery of biological weapons that counter-terrorism planners must consider. They are:

i) No reliable fixed means exist for detecting biological agents released into the atmosphere over large areas such as cities. Biological attacks are likely to be recognised only after affected people start to become sick. In some cases, this may not occur for weeks after an attack.

ii) There are various plausible scenarios for biological and chemical contamination of agricultural products. These include infecting livestock with hoof and mouth disease, pigs with African Swine fever, chicken with the Newcastle disease virus, or crops with Karnal Bunt, stem rust, or leaf rust.

iii) Imported materials could be used by terrorists to introduce pathogens into a country. These include straw, animal feed, and fertiliser. Imports infected before they leave the country of origin could facilitate multiple outbreaks over large geographic areas in recipient countries, mimicking a natural event.

iii) The greatest number of potential casualties involves the airborne release of biological and chemical agents. Releases within enclosed spaces require less of these agents but are likely to be quite lethal because the agent remains concentrated in the confined airspace. Such releases would require less than about one gram of biological agents.

iv) Open-air release of biological and chemical weapons can affect the broadest area with the highest number of casualties. Temperature inversions, in particular, could trap these agents close to the ground, substantially increasing the level of surface doses. Rain washes most of these agents out of the air. Some biological and chemical agents may remain harmful in groundwater for a period of time; however, most become harmless.

v) Biological agents may be aerosolised by explosion or by use of a spray nozzle. Explosive release tends to be inefficient, with the heat and shock of the explosion destroying much of the agent.

vi) Being indoors during an airborne attack can lessen the exposure depending on the building. The degree of exposure for people inside a closed building when a biological or chemical plume passes outside is reduced by a factor of two or more for typical American homes and by a factor of as much as 10 or more for hermetically sealed office buildings, depending on the quality of the air filters in the heating, ventilation, and air-conditioning system.

Today, offensive biological weapons programmes exist in a dozen countries, particularly in the Middle East and Asia. Countries currently listed as 'proliferation concerns' include China, Iraq, Iran, Libya, North Korea, India, Pakistan, Syria, Taiwan and Egypt.

China's offensive biological weapons programme had started in the 1950s. It possesses biotechnology infrastructure sufficiently advanced to allow it to develop and produce biological agents. Its munitions industry is sufficient to allow it to weaponise such agents, and it has a variety of means that could be used for delivery. China's offensive biological warfare capability is believed to be based on technology developed before its accession in 1984 to the Biological and Toxin Weapons Convention (BWC). Since then, China has claimed that it has never researched, produced, or possessed any biological weapons and would never do so.

Iraq is famous for its bioweapon programmes. Iraq may have produced up to 10 billion doses of anthrax, botulinum toxin, and aflatoxin; however, its scientists apparently have had difficulty developing efficient spray nozzles, forcing them to rely on explosive release by Scud missiles equipped with these toxins. Under supervision by the UN team of inspectors (UNSCOM), 38,537 filled and unfilled munitions, 690 tons of agents, 3,000 tons of chemical precursors to chemical weapons agents, and thousands of pieces of production equipment and analytical instruments were destroyed in Iraq before UNSCOM was expelled in December 1998.

Iran's biological weapons programme began during the Iran-Iraq war. Iran is believed to be pursuing offensive biological warfare capabilities, and its effort may have evolved beyond agent research and development to the ability to produce small quantities of agents. The country has a growing biotechnology industry, significant pharmaceutical experience, and the overall infrastructures to support a biological warfare programme. Tehran has expanded its efforts to seek considerable dual-use biotechnical materials and expertise from entities in Russia and elsewhere, ostensibly for civilian purposes. Outside assistance, which Iran needs, is difficult to prevent because of the dual-use nature of the materials and equipment it seeks and the many legitimate end uses for these items.

Libya' biological warfare programme has not advanced significantly beyond research and development, though it may be capable of producing small quantities of biological agents. It has been hindered by a poor scientific and technological base, equipment shortages, a lack of skilled personnel, and UN sanctions from 1992 to 1999. Without foreign assistance and technical expertise on dual-use materials, Libya's biological warfare programme is not likely to make significant progress.

Although North Korea has acceded to the BWC, it has pursued biological warfare capabilities since the 1960s. Pyongyang's resources include a rudimentary biotechnical infrastructure that could support the production of infectious biological warfare agents and toxins such as anthrax, cholera, and plague. North Korea is believed to possess a munitions-production infrastructure that would allow it to weaponise biological warfare agents.

Having many well-qualified scientists, numerous biological and pharmaceutical production facilities, and biocontainment facilities suitable for research and development of dangerous pathogens, India use some of these facilities to support research and development for biological warfare defence work.

Pakistan has ratified the BWC and participates actively in compliance protocol negotiations. Pakistan is believed to have the resources and capabilities to support limited biological warfare research and development. It may continue to seek foreign equipment and technology to expand its biotechnical infrastructure.

Efforts in the United States to deal with possible incidents involving bioweapons in the civilian sector have only recently begun and have made only limited progress. Only with substantial additional resources at the federal, state, and local levels can a credible and meaningful response be mounted. For longer-term solutions, the medical community must educate both the public and policy makers about bioterrorism and build a global consensus condemning its use.

The points of view prevalent among national policy circles and the academic community at various times have served to dismiss biological terrorism as nothing more than a theoretical possibility.

i) Biological weapons have so seldom been deployed that precedent would suggest they will not be used.

ii) Their use is so morally repugnant that no one would deign to use them.

iii) The science of producing enough organisms and dispersing them is so difficult that it is within the reach of only the most sophisticated laboratories.

iv) Like the concept of a nuclear winter, the potential destructiveness of bioweapons is essentially unthinkable and so to be dismissed. Each of these arguments is without validity.

The materials needed to construct bioweapons are relatively inexpensive and readily available. Moreover, widespread dissemination of the knowledge necessary to create such weapons renders bioweapons accessible to subnational groups and individuals to a degree that nuclear weapons are not. Nations and dissident groups exist that have both the motivation and access to skills to selectively cultivate some of the most dangerous pathogens and to deploy them as agents in acts of terrorism or war. After the Gulf War, Iraq was discovered to have a large biological weapons programme. In 1995, Iraq confirmed that it had produced, filled, and deployed bombs, rockets, and aircraft spray tanks containing *Bacillus anthraces* and botulinum toxin; its work force and technologic infrastructure are still wholly intact.

In 1995, the Japanese cult, Aum Shinrikyo, released the nerve gas Sarin in the Tokyo subway. The cult also had plans for biological terrorism; included in its arsenal were large quantities of nutrient media, botulinum toxin, anthrax cultures, and drone aircraft equipped with spray tanks. Members of this group had travelled to Zaire in 1992 to obtain samples of Ebola virus for weapons development.

The bombing of the World Trade Centre and the Oklahoma City Federal Building have dramatised the serious problems even small dissident groups can cause. Of more recent concern is the status of one of Russia's largest and most sophisticated former bioweapons facilities, called Vector, in Koltsovo, Novosibirsk. Through the early 1990s, this was a 4,000-person, 30-building facility with ample biosafety level four laboratory facilities, used for the isolation of both specimens and human cases. Situated on an open plain surrounded by electric fences and protected by an elite guard, the facility housed the smallpox virus as well as work on Ebola, Marburg, and the haemorrhagic fever viruses. A visit in the autumn of 1997 found a half-empty facility protected by a handful of guards who had not been paid for months. No one can say where the scientists have gone, nor is there confidence now that this is the only storage site for smallpox virus outside the Centres for Disease Control and Prevention.

Preventing or countering bioterrorism will be extremely difficult. Recipes for making biological weapons are now available on the internet, and even groups with modest finances and basic training in biology and engineering could develop, should they wish, an effective weapon at little cost.

Detection or interdiction of those intending to use biological weapons is next to impossible. The first evidence of such weapons will almost certainly be cases in hospital emergency rooms. Specialists in infectious diseases thus constitute the front line of defence. The rapidity with which they and emergency room personnel reach a proper diagnosis and the speed with which they apply preventive and therapeutic measures could spell the difference between thousands and perhaps tens of thousands of casualties. Indeed, the survival of physicians and health-care staff caring for the patients may be at stake.

However, today few have ever seen so much as a single case of smallpox, plague, or anthrax, or, for that matter, would recall the characteristics of such cases. Of a long list of potential pathogens, only a handful are reasonably easy to prepare and disperse and can inflict sufficiently severe disease to paralyse a city and perhaps a nation.

Health professional would be morally obliged to respond to the illness and suffering caused by a bioterrorism attack. The US (CDC) programme has made great strides since starting the Bioterrorism Preparedness and Response Programme in 1999. Its agenda is ambitious, complex, and depends heavily on cooperation and resources from states and local health departments as it must. Although progress has been impressive, especially in the upgrading of the capacity of state laboratories and the raising of awareness bioterrorism among public-health professional, much remains to be done.

In the USA, public-health authority rests largely with the states. It is not apparent that state health departments have the resources to implement the actions needed to respond to major and epidemics of infectious disease. Continued attention and funding from Congress could create some viral public-health capacities. A robust capacity to respond to a possible bioterrorist attack will also require that the lack of elasticity in the US health-care system be addressed. As in the case in the UK, the US health-care system's quest for efficiency has eliminated virtually all its capacity.

The biomedical research community—the universities, the pharmaceutical companies, and biotechnology firms—must come together and create meaningful ways to prevent the misuse of the knowledge now being created. Finally, it is apparent that avoiding the development and use of biological weapons will demand now approaches to arms control.

Today the US government stores only about 15.4 million doses of the smallpox vaccine—enough for less than seven per cent of the American population. The World Health Organisation (WHO) keeps another 500,000 doses in the Netherlands, and other national stockpiles total about 60 million more doses of varying quality and potency. If the smallpox virus were released today, the majority of the world's population would be defenceless, and given the virus's 30 per cent kill rate, nearby two billion people could die.

The picture worsened in 1999, when scientists discovered that the US samples of the smallpox vaccine had severely deteriorated. Originally made in the 1970s by the Wyeth Pharmaceutical Company, the samples were stored at the Centres for Disease Control and Prevention (CDC) in Atlanta in the form of freeze-tied crystals parcelled out in 100-dose quantities inside vacuum-sealed glass tubes. The tubes were further sealed with rubber stoppers secured by metal clamps. To their dismay, CDC investigators discovered condensation in many of the glass tubes indicating that the rubber stoppers had decayed and the vacuum pressure had been lost. Such vaccine supplies can no longer be considered safe for human use. Although the rest of the world's vaccine reserves have not undergone similar scrutiny, experts do not have much confidence in those either. Furthermore, the world's supplies of bifurcated needles—uniquely designed for scratch-administering the smallpox vaccine on human skin—have been depleted, and companies are no longer interested in manufacturing such specialised devices.

The world is, thus, completely vulnerable to a smallpox attack. The last time a mass emergency vaccination took place in the United States was 1947, when a traveller from Mexico spread smallpox to New York City. Vaccines were then readily available, and 6.35 million New Yorkers were immunised in less than four weeks. In 1961, a similar vaccination campaign was administered following a smallpox outbreak in a England: 5.5 million people were immunised in a month's time. A decade later, smallpox cases in Yugoslavia prompted the rapid vaccination of 20 million people in that country. Were a smallpox crisis to emerge today, none of these efforts could be repeated.

Even if large stockpiles of the smallpox vaccine could be collected immediately, they would be of limited value for two reasons: only several days after infection would individuals develop recognisable symptoms, by which time thousands—even millions—would have been exposed and only several days or weeks after vaccination would individuals develop sufficient antibodies to stave off infection.

For other diseases preventable by vaccine, such as anthrax, the time between inoculation and the development of powerful antibodies could be far longer—up to a year, even with boosters. Immunisation efforts would be useless against vaccine-resistant pathogens, such as created by Russian scientists working on anthrax weapons. Furthermore, a determined bioterrorist could simply try a succession of microbial weapons—or use a cocktail at the outset, defying even the best-organised vaccination programme.

The cost of a delayed response to an anthrax attack would be staggering. Cities—large and small—should start stock-piling relevant antibiotics, vaccines, and general medical supplies. But even if cities were well equipped for a bioterrorist attack, they would still have a difficult time recognising that such an attack had occurred.

Local authorities probably are not going to be able to recognise it has happened until the incubation period is over. If the pathogen were fairly common, like *Clostridium botulinum*, local hospital laboratories could probably identify the culprit first. But if the microbe were rare, like those that cause anthrax, Q-fever, Ebola, smallpox, or plague, and local facilities would probably be unable to diagnose the problem.

In a large urban centre, the true costs of a bioterrorist attack might be the consequences of panic, such as a stock market in New York or a commodities market crash in Chicago. In February 1999, the Johns Hopkins Centre for Civilian Defence Studies enacted an elaborate bioterrorist scenario in Crystal City, Virginia. The details were played out over a tense eight-hour period in a room packed with public health, military, and law enforcement personnel. Under the scenario, the Vice President of the United States makes a speech at a prestigious university located in a fictional town dubbed North-east. It is April 1. Eleven days later, a 20-year-old student who attended the Vice President's speech shows up in the university hospital's emergency room with flu-like symptoms; high fever, muscle aches, fatigue, headache. She is sent home with aspirin and the old maxim, get some rest and drink plenty of fluids. Two days later, the young woman returns to the hospital, now fighting for her life. And a janitor who cleaned up after the Vice President's speech turns up with the same symptoms. By six o'clock that night, April 11, the hospital's infectious disease expert gingerly voices an outrageous conclusion: both patients have smallpox.

Since smallpox was officially eradicated in 1977, and remaining samples of the virus exist only in Atlanta and Siberia under lock and key, there can be but one conclusion; someone has stolen laboratory samples of the virus and deliberately released them in a bioterrorist attack aimed at the Vice President of the United States. Under this scenario, more than 15,000 people die of smallpox worldwide within two months, and epidemics rage out of control in 14 nations. All global supplies of the smallpox vaccine are depleted, and it will take years to manufacture enough to save humanity. The global economy teeters on the brink of collapse as nations close their borders and flee into isolation, barring all Americans from entering their countries.

In the city of North-east, utter chaos reigns, and the National Guard enforces martial law over the city's two million residents. Similarly, government authority either breaks down or reverts to military-style control in cities all over the world as smallpox claims lives and pits terrified citizens against one another. Meanwhile, back in North-east, a top smallpox expert scribbles projections on the back of an envelope and gently slides it in front of the state governor; within 12 months 80 million people worldwide will be dead.

Although most people remain ignorant of the issues raised in that scenario, handfuls of internet-hooked extremists, right-wing militia members, psychologically imbalanced belligerents, and post-modern fascists are well versed in the fine points of bioterrorism. Recipes for producing botulinum and anthrax are posted on the web. Books describing biological-warfare assassination techniques are readily available. Some private militia groups train to use biological weapons.

It is a well-known fact that religious cults and militant political groups are likely to engage in biological terrorism. The first bioterrorist attack in America was carried out by members of an Oregon-based religious cult led by Bhagwan Shree Rajneesh. The cult members, hoping to disrupt an upcoming country election, contaminated local salad bars with salmonella, infecting hundreds of Oregonians. Perhaps, it is the tone of some militant's rhetoric that sparks the most concern.

US Congress has sought technological solutions as well, allocating money for Department of Defence (DoD) research on devices that might sniff out bugs and sanitise contaminated areas. First in line was the Navys TagMan, a sophisticated gene scanner that could, in less than half an hour, determine whether a liquid sample contained any of several known pathogens. But the system had significant limitations; weighing 300 pounds, it was hardly portable. And it could not detect pathogens of high 'biohazard levels'—precisely the cost worrisome microbes. Most significant, the device could not analyse air samples.

In 1998, Congress also gave the DoD's Defence Advanced Research Projects Agency (DARPA) two billion dollars to sponsor wild and crazy science projects—ideas so far out that standard civilian funding sources would not consider them. These projects included $ 61.6 million of bioweapons defence efforts, the foremost of which was the development of a fast, cheap, safe, and portable way to sample air for the presence of nasty pathogens. Most of the research focused on unique genetic attributes of bacteria and viruses. One project involved trying to grow human nerve cells on microscopic chips that would change colour or light up if they detected a neuretoxin, such as botulinum. Several laboratories, notably the Argonne, would be manned by the public health workers who would track down and treat the patients, dispense appropriate drugs, determine whether the outbreak was spreading from the Bourse source, and analyse the microorganism for any special attributes.

It is obvious that public health, law enforcement, and defence officials have very different priorities in the event of a bioterrorist attack. For public health workers, the paramount concerns are limiting the spread of infection, identifying the cause of the disease and, if possible, treating and vaccinating the public. Law enforcement agents, however, are in the business of stopping and solving crimes—and the scene of any bioterrorist incident is, first and foremost, a source of evidence. Managing a response to an outbreak, thus, poses a conflict of interest, since the police would, by mandate, focus on detaining witnesses and obtaining evidence, even if those efforts ran counter to public health needs.

What is even less clear is how a public health system can respond to bioterrorism without destroying the basis of its credibility. When a public health system needs to intrude on individuals' lives to protect the larger community it does so in limited ways and usually under the hard-and-fast promise of confidentiality. During an epidemic, for example, individuals may be asked to submit to blood tests and medical exams, and their medical charts may be scrutinised but all under the promise of confidentiality. In the long term, a public health system protects the community by monitoring disease trends, which requires tracking who has diseases. Again, this information is generally stored under confidential or anonymous terms.

On a global level, the WHO and a variety of other groups keep count of nations' diseases, monitoring for the emergence of new epidemics. After the 1995 Ebola outbreak in Zaire, for example, the WHO sought to create a more rigorous surveillance system and pushed countries to be more open about epidemics in their populations. All of these functions, in all tiers of public health systems, require the maintenance of a crucial social contract; the individual or country agrees to openly disclose information for the sake of the larger community's health. In return, public health authorities promise never to abuse this trust, maintaining discretion and protecting patient privacy.

But the fear of bioterrorism threatens to destroy the vital social contract, which is not shared by law enforcement and defence officials. The closer a public health system draws to the other two systems, the greater the danger that it will lose credibility in the eyes of the public. Indeed, suspicions already run high in many American minority communities, prompting widespread belief that such microbes as the AIDS virus were created by the US Public Health Service, the US Institutes of Health, or the CIA with the intention of obliterating key minority populations.

Some public health advocates are convinced that no marriage between their profession and law enforcement could ever work and have denounced all efforts to heighten concerns about bioterrorism. For many older public health leaders, the bioterrorism scare evokes nasty memories of Cold War cover-ups and censorship. By adopting the bioterrorism issue, they warn, public health officials are buying into a similar framework of paranoid thinking. Public health system's role in the fight against bioterrorism can be comfortable only if it is an equal partner of the law enforcement and defence communities.

The threat of a bioagricultural attack could have a devastating effect on the economy. For example, an anonymous caller to the US embassy in Santiago, Chile, in 1989 claimed that Chilean grapes destined for US and Japanese markets were contaminated with cyanide. The United States placed a quarantine on Chilean grapes and forced the growers to recall those that had been shipped, causing approximately $333 million in damage to the Chilean grape industry. A 1993 OTA report estimated that 250 pounds of anthrax spores, spread efficiently over the Washington, DC, metropolitan area, could cause up to three million deaths, more than from a one-megaton hydrogen bomb. A senior-level war game in June 2001, called "Dark Winter", looked at the national security, intergovernmental, and information challenges of a biological attack on the US homeland. One conclusion of the war game, hosted by the Centre for Strategic and International Studies, the Johns Hopkins Centre for Civilian Biodefense Studies, the ANSER

Institute for Homeland Security, and the Oklahoma National Memorial Institute for the Prevention of Terrorism: Within three months of a biological attack on Oklahoma City using smallpox, over three million Americans could be infected, and over a million would be killed.

According to a recent US General Accounting Office (GAO) report, coordination of federal terrorism research, preparedness, and the responsible programmes thus far has been fragmented. Several agencies are responsible for coordinating functions, and this both limits accountability and hinders unity of effort. Moreover, several agencies have not been included in bioterrorism-related policy and response planning meetings, and different agencies have developed lists of biological agents as well as disaster response assistance programmes for state and local governments. An inter-agency health-care group, led by the US Department of Health and Human Services (HHS), chose four biological agents for the CDC to begin developing vaccine stockpiles for civilian populations. These are inhalation anthrax, pneumonic plague, smallpox, and tularemia, which have the ability to affect large numbers of people and to tax the medical system should bioterrorism occur.

Government agencies have begun to look more closely at the threat of biological terrorism, and some have already instituted policies and programmes to prevent such attacks or limit the damage should one occur. However, numerous loopholes still exist. The Achilles' heel of government programmes to combat bioterrorism will be a lack of real coordination through a national strategy that outlines the roles of federal, state, and local agencies after an attack. Without such a strategy, the risk for chaos increases as does the likelihood that resources will be squandered by overlapping efforts and insufficient bureaucratic attention.

Today there is no country in this world which is prepared to deal with a terrorist attack that employs biological weapons. In countering civilian terrorism, the focus has been almost wholly on chemical and explosive weapons. A chemical release or a major explosion is far more manageable than the biological challenges posed by smallpox or anthrax. After an explosion or a chemical attack,. the worst effects are quickly over, the dimensions of the catastrophe can be defined, the toll of injuries and deaths can be ascertained, and efforts can be directed to stabilisation and recovery.

The medical community should educate the public and policy makers about the threat. We need to build on the 1972 Biological and Toxin Weapons Convention to strengthen measures prohibiting the development and production of biological weapons and to ensure compliance with existing agreements. In a broader sense, we need a strong moral consensus condemning biological weapons. In the longer term, we need to be as prepared to detect, diagnose, characterise epidemiologically, and respond appropriately to biological weapons use as to the threat of new and re-emerging infections. We need at international, state, and local levels a greater capacity for surveillance; a far better network of laboratories and better diagnostic instruments; and a more adequate cadre of trained epidemiologists, clinicians, and researchers.

REFERENCES

Flanagin, A., Lederberg, J., "The Threat of Biological Weapons: Prophylaxis and Mitigation: Call for Papers", *JAMA*, 1996;276:419-420.

Henderson, D.A., "Bioterrorism as a public health threat", *Emerging Infectious Diseases*, 1998; 4:488-492.

Kahn, H., *Thinking About the Unthinkable*, London, England: Weidenfeld & Nicolson; 1962.

Kupperman, R. H., Smith, D.M., "Coping with Biological Terrorism", In Roberts, B., ed. , *Biological Weapons: Weapons of the Future*? Washington, DC: Centre for Strategic and International Studies; 1993.

Simon, J.D., "Biological Terrorism: Preparing to Meet the Threat", *JAMA*, 1997; 278:428-430.

__________ , *The New Age of Terrorism*, Boston Globe, April 19, 1996:19.

6

Impact of Bioterrorist Attacks

As a result of the recent and developing terrorist events the world population is now experiencing the emergence of professional and amateur terrorists. We are compelled to evaluate and adjust our business and personal lifestyles in an effort to protect our lives and our commercial assets. Terrorism is the unlawful use of force and violence against persons or property to intimidate or coerce a government, the civilian population, or any segment thereof, in furtherance of political or social objectives. Bioterrorism is the use of biological organisms to inflict life-threatening illnesses on a large scale within a designated population. Biological weapons are considered to be weapons of mass destruction, along with chemical and radioactive weapons.

Today, approximately 17 countries may have active research and development programmes for biologic weapons. Moreover, groups and individuals with grievances against the government or society have been known to use or plan to use biologic weapons to further personal causes. Only modest microbiologic skills are needed to produce and effectively use biologic weapons. The greatest, but not insurmountable, hurdle in such an endeavour may be gaining access to a virulent strain of the desired agent. Production costs are low, and aerosol dispersal equipment from commercial sources can be adapted for biologic weapon dissemination.

Bioterrorists operating in a civilian environment have relative freedom of movement, which could allow them to use freshly grown microbial suspensions. The impact of a bioterrorist attack depends on the specific agent or toxin used, the method and efficiency of dispersal, the population exposed, the level of immunity in the population, the availability of effective postexposure and/or therapeutic regimens, and the potential for secondary transmission. Understanding and quantifying the impact of a bioterrorist attack are essential to developing an effective response. Therefore, it is essential to analyse the impact of biologic warfare agents.

According to a United States Department of Health and Human Services fact sheet, concern about deliberate use of disease agents presently focuses on anthrax, smallpox, pneumonic bubonic plague, tularemia and haemorrhagic fevers. All of these agents are colourless, odourless, silent and invisible, making them difficult and time consuming to detect. Unlike explosions or chemical releases, a bioterrorist attack would be undetectable prior to victims presenting themselves at hospitals with symptoms of these diseases. Symptoms might not occur among the victims for days or weeks, and those initially presenting themselves to physicians and medical care centres might be geographically dispersed.

A bioterrorist attack could be carried out by a lone terrorist who could be far from the scene of the attack at the time it is discovered. Bioterrorist attacks may be delivered through a mass aerosolised release of a biological agent or a limited release through means such as mail. Other methods of bioterrorist attacks could include releases of biological agents over food supplies by crop dusting planes or sabotage and infiltration of water sources and food processing facilities.

Every major state BW programme has included an anti-agricultural component, from the WWI German use of anthrax and glanders against animals to the Iraqi programme on wheat cover smut. For most agents, effective use would require large stockpiles and extensive delivery efforts; however, there is potential for delivery by secret agent to initiate point-source epidemics of highly contagious agents. The relevance of this to terrorist use is slight; however, BW proliferator states are likely to include anti-animal and anti-plant agents in their developing arsenal, and if they also support terrorist groups, there is a slim chance that such groups might be allowed access to anti-agricultural agents for the purpose of bioterrorism. Disruption of the agricultural sector can cause profound dislocation of societies. Direct losses of plants or animals could cause food shortages, rises in food prices, and unemployment. All of these could, if severe, have serious destabilising effects on social and political structures.

Many developed countries are quite vulnerable to disruption of the agricultural sector, although their social and political institutions are fairly robust and the resulting discontent is probably unlikely to cause institutional collapse. Nevertheless, the potential for immense economic damage is high in a well-planned attack, and the consequences for the food supply, export trade, and financial markets could be very serious. A widespread epidemic, or any outbreak that triggered the imposition or relaxation of trade restrictions, could result in significant changes of supply of the affected plant or animal materials on domestic and international markets. This in turn would open up or close markets for others.

Biological attack could also be used to manipulate futures, and for other manipulations of the financial markets. The use of legitimate, peaceful biocontrol is expanding steadily, and provides an unfortunate body of knowledge and range of ready-made delivery technologies for the interested agricultural bioterrorist or biowarfare programme. There are programmes to develop pathogens of drug crops as biocontrol agents. These have been conducted under UNDCP auspices, funded and performed by the US (fungal pathogens of coca), and funded by the US and UK and performed by Uzbekistan (fungal pathogens of poppy). Both of these programmes involve the development of biological agents and delivery devices, and both are presumably intended for use principally or entirely in other countries.

However, none of the potential target states has agreed to allow the use of these agents for biocontrol, and several have now stated explicitly that they will not allow it. As a result of this refusal, UNDCP has now withdrawn its sponsorship of the anti-coca project. Although there is no evidence that the agents are being developed for hostile use, the absence of target country approval makes it equally difficult to demonstrate that they are being developed for peaceful purposes. This ambiguity raises legitimate concerns about compliance with Article I of the BTWC.

Furthermore, once effective agents have been developed, the intense concern over the drug trade in drug-consuming states may lead to pressure to use them covertly, regardless of target country approval. Terrorists and individuals might also be interested in biocontrol agents. The deliberate and illegal 1997 importation of Rabbit Haemorrhagic Disease Virus (RHDV) into New Zealand constitutes a past instance. And biological attack on genetically engineered plants might be considered by the more extreme activist groups opposed to such technology, a use that could in their view be a form of biocontrol. Countries might consider agricultural attack for military, political, ideological, or economic reasons. Since there could be quite severe consequences of being recognised as responsible for a biological attack, such efforts would likely be covert. This would entail an effort to make the outbreak appear natural-most probably a point-source outbreak, or multiple outbreaks with an apparently natural common source. Countries that are actively pursuing a secret military BW capability are probably developing anti-agricultural agents for strategic use in the event of war. Agricultural corporations, including producers, processors, and shippers, could benefit immensely from the economic impacts, market share changes, and financial market effects of a successful biological attack. Many also employ expert plant pathologists or veterinarians and have large collections of pathogens. The combination of motivation, expertise, and materials within a single, closed organisation is worrisome. Of course, corporations, like countries, would run enormous legal risks if they perpetrated a biological attack, so if they were to choose to do this, it would be expertly designed to mimic a natural outbreak.

For both corporations and governments, decision to use bioweapons would be expected to require approval at the very highest level, thus reducing its likelihood. However, in both the possibility of mid- or lower-level zealots initiating unauthorised action has to be considered. Due to the huge financial stakes in the agricultural sector, and because the foundation of the drug industry involves crop cultivation, organised crime may take an interest in biocriminal activities with agricultural targets. Terrorist groups might be interested in agricultural bioweapons for a variety of reasons: international terrorist organisations for the harm they could do to enemy states or peoples, millennial groups for their potential contribution to societal collapse, anti-GMO groups for their potential value in deterring farmers from the use of genetically engineered crops or animals.

In many cases of ideologically-motivated terrorist attack there would be willing assumption of responsibility by the perpetrator; in other cases there could be an attempt to disguise the outbreak as natural.

Individual perpetrators (biocriminals) could include disgruntled employees or ex-employees in the agricultural sector, ideologically motivated individuals, speculators on the commodities market, or individuals with a profit motive. Direct financial loss due to mortality or morbidity of domestic animals or crop plants can vary from insignificant to catastrophic. In many cases the direct losses would be modest and would fall on a small number of farms.

One of the major determinants of the magnitude of the direct losses will be the rapidity with which the disease is noticed and diagnosed. In developed countries most of the foreign diseases of greatest concern would likely be identified fairly early, allowing the direct disease losses to be kept modest.

The control of an outbreak of an imported, highly contagious animal or plant disease is routinely controlled by destruction of all potentially exposed healthy host organisms. With animal diseases, this normally means the slaughter of all host animals in the immediate vicinity. With plants, thousands of acres of crop plants may have to be destroyed to contain an outbreak. Thus the losses attendant on outbreak control can exceed, often by several orders of magnitude, the direct losses due to the disease itself.

Destruction of exposed hosts is often the only option when the agent is bacterial or viral. However, for fungal agents destruction of exposed crops may be reduced by the use of fungicides. However, this is an expensive process itself, so it adds significantly to the cost of the outbreak, and it may cause environmental damage. A number of important threats to crop plants are from insect pests, rather than microbial pathogens. These outbreaks are usually controlled by use of pesticides rather than destruction of exposed plants, which, as with control of fungal disease, can cost large amounts.

Widespread broadcast of insecticide may also cause environmental or human health damage as well. The BTWC certainly could cover pests as well as pathogens, as Article I refers to microbial or other biological agents, and the consultative process of the BTWC has been used to address concerns about a pest infestation in Cuba. However, this coverage has never been made explicit, and it would be useful to do so since there are so many insect pests of great potential for agricultural biowarfare or bioterrorism. Under the World Trade Organisation, member states are allowed to impose import restrictions on agricultural products to prevent the importation of pests or disease agents. Thus importing countries free of a particular disease are usually quick to block imports from countries in which that disease breaks out. This happens frequently, as these diseases periodically resurface in areas that they have been absent from; trade restrictions typically last a month or two when control of the outbreak is rapid, or they may endure much longer if disease control is slow and difficult. Thus major agricultural exporters are parti-cularly vulnerable.

The introduction of a disease into a country previously free of it would undermine the legitimacy of that country's import restrictions under the WTO, forcing the lifting of the restrictions and opening up the market. This could bring significant additional losses to domestic producers. The substantial market effects of a widespread outbreak, or one that has major impacts on international trade, could have secondary effects, such as shareholder losses, revenue losses to processors and shippers, etc. In the extreme, if losses are very large and if future losses appear likely, significant levels of investor panic could lead to market destabilisation. With the exception of a few agents of zoonotic disease, most of the diseases that are likely to be considered for an attack on the agricultural sector are completely harmless to humans.

There is an innate human revulsion to the use of disease as a weapon; if so, this could constitute an important disincentive to bioterrorism and biowarfare. However, it is unlikely that this sentiment extends to biological attack on plants or animals. Furthermore, the response after a biological attack on plants or animals would be less substantial than if the attack involved human victims, and the penalties of being identified as the perpetrator would be lighter. If the goal is to disrupt trade by introducing a highly contagious disease into territory from which it is absent, then the attack does not have to be constructed to cause a large number of cases—a handful of cases may be sufficient. Because of the high background of naturally-occurring disease, a deliberately instigated outbreak could be mistaken for a natural one. If avoiding detection is important, an attack would be constructed to take advantage of this confusion. Especially if the goal is disruption of international trade, where few cases are necessary, it is feasible to construct an attack to appear to be a natural point-source outbreak. Multiple point source outbreaks can be initiated by contaminating imported feed or fertiliser, without even entering the country. Many countries import materials such as straw, animal feed, or fertiliser. This provides an opportunity for introducing serious pathogens, without having to even enter the target country. It also allows the possibility of initiating multiple outbreaks over a large geographic area, in a way that mimics a natural event.

Emerging sciences of genomics and proteomics are already beginning to transform biology and medicine. One outcome will be the possibility of constructing genotype-specific biological control or weapons agents. Although there has been much concern about the possibility of ethnic weapons targeting specific groups of humans, the likelihood is that this will prove impossible. In many developed countries, agriculture several properties that make it vulnerable to attack with genotype-specific weapons. It employs monocropping of large acreages with genetically identical cultivars, and high-density husbandry of genetically inbred animal strains. These agronomic practices reduce the genetic variability that makes populations resistant to genotype-specific weapons, and it creates conditions that facilitate disease spread. High-tech agent design is an option available only to sophisticated players, e.g., states and multinational corporations. At least for the near future, the construction of novel toxin weapons or genetically engineered microbes as genotype-specific weapons would require a substantial scientific infrastructure, ranging from molecular biology to genomics to agronomy.

The states most vulnerable to economic attack on the agricultural sector are those with several or most of the following attributes:

i) high-density, large area agriculture.
ii) heavy reliance on monoculture of a restricted range of genotypes.
iii) free of specific serious animal and plant pathogens or pests.
iv) major agricultural exporter, or heavily dependent on a few domestic agricultural products.

v) suffering serious domestic unrest, or the target of international terrorism, or an unfriendly neighbour of states likely to be developing BW programmes.

vi) weak plant and animal epidemiological infrastructure.

The threat of biological attack against at-risk states and their agricultural sector should be taken quite seriously, and preventative and punitive measures put in place. Enactment of legislation implementing the BTWC is required of all States parties; however, many have not yet done so. Such legislation can be a significant deterrent to biological attack on the agricultural sector. The legislation should, among other provisions, provide for substantial criminal penalties for the hostile use anywhere of biological agents against plants or animals as well as people, and it should provide for extradition for anyone charged with using such agents against the agricultural sector of another state. States that already have enacted such legislation should review its provisions to ensure that it adequately covers biological attack on plants and animals.

Biological attack on the agricultural sector will be options for perpetrators only to the extent that they maintain plausibility as natural events. Increased epidemiological capacity, especially in strain identification from molecular sequence data, makes it increasingly difficult to escape detection, and thus would act as a substantial deterrent. A BTWC Protocol that establishes effective measures to deter states from developing or possessing biological weapons would provide a powerful tool in making progress towards the goal of complete biological disarmament. This would reduce the likelihood of BW in regional conflicts, and the chance that state-supported terrorist organisations would ever get bioweapons.

Provision for internationally sponsored epidemiological investigation of possible agricultural attacks would deter covert use in the same manner as national epidemiological capacity. States that engage in high intensity agriculture of a limited range of varieties could reduce their vulnerability to both deliberate and natural disease outbreaks by increasing the use of intercropping, expanding the diversity of genotypes utilised, reducing the size of plots, and a variety of other agricultural changes designed to reduce susceptibility to disease outbreaks.

IMPACT OF BIOAGENTS: AN ANALYTICAL STUDY

Here we are going to discuss a study conducted by Centres for Disease Control and Prevention (CDC), Atlanta, on the comparative analysis of three major biologic warfare agents (*Bacillus anthraces*, *Brucella melitensis*, and *Francisella tularensis)* when released as aerosols in the suburbs of a major city and compare the benefits of systematic intervention with the costs of increased disease incidence from the economic point of view used in society.

The study compared the impact of a theoretical bioterrorist attack on a suburb of a major city, with 100,000 population exposed in the target area. The attack was made by generating an aerosol of an agent (*B. anthraces spores*, *B. melitensis*, or *F. tularensis*) along a line across the direction of the prevailing wind. The meteorologic conditions—thermal stability, relative humidity, wind direction and speed—were assumed to be optimal, and the aerosol cloud passed over the target area within two hours.

The study projected impact on the basis of 10 per cent and 100 per cent of the target population being exposed to the aerosol cloud. It was assumed that, when inhaled, the infectious dose 50 (ID50) was 20,000 spores for *B. anthraces* and 1,000 vegetative cells for *B. melitensis* and *F. tularensis*. The rate of physical decay for airborne particles five mm or less in diameter was estimated to be negligible during the two-hour transit time. The rate of biologic decay of the particulate agents was estimated to be negligible for the *B. anthraces* spores and two per cent per minute for the *B. melitensis* and *F. tularensis* vegetative cells. Viability and virulence did not dissociate.

Persons who were exposed to the *B. anthraces* cloud at any point during the two-hour transit time inhaled one ID50 dose, and persons who were exposed to either the *B. melitensis* or *F. tularensis* cloud inhaled one to 10 ID50 doses, depending on their proximity to the origination point of the aerosol cloud.

Epidemic curve for anthrax by days after exposure was assumed to be < 1 day, 0 per cent of cases; 1 day, 5 per cent; 2 days, 20 per cent; 3 days, 35 per cent; 4 days, 20 per cent; 5 days, 10 per cent; 6 days, 5 per cent; and 7 or more days, 5 per cent (3-5). Case-fatality rates were also assumed to vary by the day symptoms were first noted. The case-fatality rate was estimated as 85 per cent for patients with symptoms on day 1; 80 per cent for patients with symptoms on day 2; 70 per cent for those with symptoms on day 3; 50 per cent for those with symptoms on days 4, 5, and 6; and 70 per cent for those with symptoms on and after day 7. The increased death rate in persons with an incubation period of 7 or more days is calculated on an assumption of delayed diagnosis, with resultant delayed therapy.

When estimating days in hospital and outpatient visits due to infection, the study assumed that 95 per cent of anthrax patients were hospitalised, with a mean stay of 7 days. Patients not admitted to a hospital had an average of seven outpatient visits, and surviving hospitalised patients had two outpatient visits after discharge from the hospital. Persons who received only outpatient care were treated for 28 days with either oral ciprofloxacin or doxycycline. No significant long-term sequelae resulted from the primary infection, and no relapses occurred.

Epidemic curve for brucellosis by days after exposure was assumed to be 0 to 7 days, 4 per cent of cases; 8 to 14 days, 6 per cent; 15 to 28 days, 14 per cent; 29 to 56 days, 40 per cent; 57 to 112 days, 26 per cent, and 113 or more days, 10 per cent. The case-fatality rate was estimated to be 0.5 per cent. Fifty per cent of patients were hospitalised, with an average stay of 7 days. Non-hospitalised patients had an average of 14 outpatient visits, and hospitalised patients had seven outpatient visits after discharge from the hospital. Outpatients received a combination of oral doxycycline for 42 days and parenteral gentamicin for the first 7 days of therapy. Five per cent of patients had a relapse or long-term sequelae, and required 14 outpatient visits within 1 year.

Epidemic curve for tularemia by days after exposure was assumed to be: <1 day, 0 per cent of cases; 1 day, 1 per cent; 2 days, 15 per cent; 3 days, 45 per cent; 4 days, 25 per cent; 5 days, 10 per cent; 6 days, 3 per cent; and 7 or more days, 1 per cent. The estimated case-fatality rate was 7.5 per cent; and 95 per cent of patients were hospitalised, with an average stay of 10 days.

Non-hospitalised patients had an average of 12 outpatient visits, and hospitalised patients who survived the acute illness had two outpatient visits after discharge from the hospital. Outpatients received oral doxycycline for 14 days and parenteral gentamicin for 7 days. Five per cent of patients had a relapse or long-term sequelae and required an average of 12 outpatient visits.

The projected intervention programme for anthrax was either a 28-day course of oral ciprofloxacin or doxycycline (assumed to be 90 per cent effective), or a 28-day course of oral ciprofloxacin or doxycycline plus three doses of the human anthrax vaccine (assumed to be 95 per cent effective); for brucellosis, a 42-day course of oral doxycycline and rifampin (assumed to be 80 per cent effective), or a 42-day course of oral doxycycline, plus 7 days of parenteral gentamicin (assumed to be 95 per cent effective); for tularemia, the intervention programme was a 14-day course of oral doxycycline (assumed to be 80 per cent effective), or a 14-day course of oral doxycycline plus 7 days of parenteral gentamicin (assumed to be 95 per cent effective). Only 90 per cent of persons exposed in the target area were assumed to effectively participate in any intervention programme.

To check the economic factors involved in establishing an intervention programme, the costs to the potential savings from such an intervention, were compared. Following the recommendation of the Panel of Cost-Effectiveness in Health and Medicine (PCEHM), estimates of actual costs were used. It calculated the net savings (cost reductions) by using the following formula:

> Net savings = (number of deaths averted x present value of expected future earnings) + (number of days of hospitalisation averted × cost of hospitalisation) + (number of outpatient visits averted × cost of outpatient visits) – cost of intervention.

When calculated the costs of hospitalisation and outpatient visits, it was assumed that only persons with symptoms would use medical facilities. The remainder of the exposed and potentially exposed populace would receive post-exposure prophylaxis. Cost of a premature human death was nominally valued at the present value of expected future earnings and housekeeping services, weighted by the age and sex composition of the work force in the United States. The undiscounted average of future earnings is $1,688,595. As recommended by PCEHM, the stream of future earnings was discounted at 3 per cent and 5 per cent, to give values of $790,440 and $544,160, respectively. The present value of expected future earnings was estimated with 1990 dollars, adjusted for a 1 per cent annual growth in productivity. In 1993, the average charge for a single day of hospitalisation was $875.

To true cost was derived by multiplying the average charge by the cost-to-charge ratio of 0.635. On this basis, it was estimated that true hospitalisation costs at $556/day. Hospital costs included all professional services, drugs, X-rays, and laboratory tests. Lost productivity during hospital stay was valued at $65/day.

A patient, after discharge from the hospital, was assumed to have follow-up outpatient visits, the number of which varied by disease. Outpatient visit costs were valued by using the Medicare National Average Allowance, which was chosen to represent the equivalent of bulk purchase discounted 's.

Table 6.1
Costs of hospitalisation and outpatient visits following a BW attack

	Anthrax		*Tularemia*		*Brucellosis*	
	Base	*Upper*	*Base*	*Upper*	*Base*	*Upper*
Hospitalised patient						
Days in hospital	7	7	10	10	7	7
Cost per day ($)[a]	556	669	556	669	556	669
Lost productivity ($/day)	65	65	65	65	65	65
Follow-up OPVs (no.)	2	2	2	2	7	7
Cost 1st OPV ($)	28	44	28	44	28	44
Cost other OPVs, ea. ($)	13	24	13	24	13	24
OPV laboratory ($)[b,c]	87	174	87	174	131	261
OPV x-rays costs ($)[d]	66	66	0	0	0	0
Lost productivity ($/OPV)[e]	16	16	16	16	16	16
Total costs ($)	4,541	5,380	6,338	7,582	4,584	5,587
Avg. costs/day ($/day)	649	769	634	758	655	798
% increase:						
Base to upper estimate		18		20		22
Non-hospitalised patient						
Number of OPVs	7	7	12	12	14	14
Cost 1st OPV ($)	28	44	28	44	28	44
Cost other OPVs, ea. ($)	13	24	13	24	13	24
Lost productivity ($/OPV)[e]	16	16	16	16	16	16
Laboratory costs ($)[b,f]	131	174	261	522	261	522
X-ray costs ($)[d]	66	66	66	66	66	66
Drugs used g	D	C	D+G	D+G	D+R	D+R+G
Cost of drugs ($)	6	181	29	29	220	246
Total costs ($)	422	810	722	1,120	972	1,418
Avg. costs/day ($/day)	60	116	60	93	69	101
%increase:						
Base to upper estimate		93		55		46

All costs rounded to the nearest whole dollar.

[a] Hospital costs assumed to include all costs such as drugs, laboratory tests, and x-rays.

[b] Laboratory tests consists of general health panel and an antigen or antibody test .

[c] Follow-up OPVs for hospitalised patients included two laboratory test sets for anthrax and tularemia patients and three laboratory test sets for brucellosis patients.

[d] X-ray costs (CPT code 71021), included two sets taken at different OPVs.

[e] Productivity lost due to an OPV was assumed to be one-quarter of an unspecified day's value.

[f] For OPVs of non-hospitalised patients, one set of laboratory tests is assumed for every two visits.

[g] Drugs used: D = doxycycline; C = ciprofloxacin; R = rifampin.

The first visit has a Current Procedural Terminology (CPT) code of 99201, which is classified as a "level 1" visit, requiring a physician to spend an average of 10 minutes with a patient. Subsequent level 1 visits, with the physician spending an average of 5 minutes with each patient, have a CPT code of 99211.

During outpatient visits, a general health panel test incorporating clinical chemistry tests and complete blood counts and a single antigen or antibody detection test were assumed to be ordered. Although data on Medicare allowances for office visits and many other procedures were available, data on Medicare allowances for laboratory tests were not. Thus, to establish the costs of the tests, the lowest allowable charge for each test in half, were arbitrarily divided.

X-rays were valued according to the Medicare National Average Allowance. In terms of lost productivity, it was assumed that each outpatient visit cost the equivalent of 2 hours, or one-quarter, of the value of an unspecified day. For non-hospitalised outpatients, the cost of each visit, laboratory test, X-ray, and lost productivity was the same as an outpatient visit for discharged hospital patients and varied by disease. It was assumed that one set of laboratory tests would be ordered every other visit and that two sets of X-rays would be ordered during the therapeutic course.

> Costs of an intervention can be expressed as follows: Cost of intervention = (cost of drugs used) × ([number of people exposed × multiplication factor] – number killed – number hospitalised – number of persons who require outpatient visits).

Costs of intervention per person depend directly on the costs of the antimicrobial agents and vaccines used in a prophylaxis programme. The project obtained drug prices from the 1996 *Drug Topics Red Book* and used the lowest cost available for each drug.

Table 2
Costs of prophylaxis following a bioterrorist attack

Level of effectiveness	*Anthrax*	*Tularemia*	*Brucellosis*
Lower			
Effectiveness (%)	90	80	80
Drugs used[a]	D or C	D	D+R
Cost of drugs ($)[b]	6 or 181	3	220
No. of visits[c]	4	2	6
Total cost/ person ($)	51 or 226	28	285
Upper			
Effectiveness (%)	95	95	95
Drugs used[a]	D+V or		
C+V	D+G	D+G	
Cost of drugs ($)[b]	17 or 193	29	36
No. of visits[c]	4	7	12
Total cost/ person ($)	62 or 238	104	161
Minimum No. participants[d]	451,912	418,094	423,440
Maximum No. participants	1,492,750	1,488,037	1,488,037

[a] Drugs used: D = doxycycline; C = ciprofloxacin; V = anthrax vaccine; G = gentamicin; R = rifampin.

[b] See text for explanation of drug costs.

[c] Cost of visit to drug-dispensing site: 1st visit = $15/person; follow-up visits = $10/person/visit.

[d] Estimate assumed that the prophylaxis programme was initiated on postattack day 6 for anthrax and tularemia and postattack day 113 for brucellosis, that the prophylaxis programme had the lower effectiveness level, and that the multiplication factor for unnecessary prophylaxis given to unexposed persons was 5.

[e] Estimate assumed that prophylaxis was initiated on postattack day 0 (day of release), that prophylaxis had the upper effectiveness level, and that the multiplication factor for unnecessary prophylaxis given to unexposed persons was 15.

The cost of doxycycline ($0.22 per 200 mg total daily dose) was the Health Care Financing Administration cost, whereas the cost of gentamicin ($3.76 per 160 mg total daily dose), ciprofloxacin ($3.70 per 1,000 mg total daily dose), and rifampin ($5.01 per 900 mg total daily dose) were wholesale costs from pharmaceutical companies. The cost of anthrax vaccine was $3.70 per dose. The cost of administering one vaccine dose or gentamicin injection was estimated at $10 on the basis of the 1992 cost of administering a vaccine in a clinical setting. In estimating the cost of administering oral antimicrobial agents, it was assumed that it was weekly visits, during which the drug would be distributed and counselling would be given.

According to the study, more people would receive prophylaxis than were actually exposed because of general anxiety and uncertainty about the boundaries of the attack, the timing of the attack, and the time it would take non-residents to travel through the attack area. Three different multiplication factors were used to construct within the population. Finally, ongoing intelligence gathering would detect possible bioterrorist threats. The cost of these prerequisite activities can be calculated if they are seen as a form of insurance, the goal of which is to "purchase" the maximum net savings through preparedness to manage the consequences of an attack and reduce the probability of an attack. The "actuarially fair premium" for the "insurance" can be defined as follows:

$$\text{Actuarially fair premium} = \text{reduction of loss probability} \times \text{value of avoidable loss.}$$

The term "reduction of loss probability" indicates that, although increased surveillance and related activities can reduce the odds of an attack, they cannot guarantee absolute protection.

The term "avoidable loss" refers to the fact that, even if a post-exposure prophylaxis programme were implemented on the day of release, some deaths, hospitalisations, and outpatient visits would be unavoidable.

Various reductions of attack probability illustrated the impact of these estimates on the calculation of actuarially fair premiums. Such reductions included reducing the probability from 1 in 100 years (0.01) to 1 in 1,000 years (0.001), a reduction of 0.009, and reducing a probability from 1 in a 100 years (0.01) to 1 in 10,000 years (0.0001), and from 1 in 100 years (0.01) to 1 in 100,000 years (0.00001). The attack probability of 0.01 in the absence of enhanced preventive actions was selected for illustrative purposes and does not represent an official estimate. A range of minimum and maximum values of avoidable loss was derived from the net savings calculations. The values reflect differences in effectiveness of the various prophylaxis regimens, the reduced impact of delayed prophylaxis on illness and death, and the two discount rates used to calculate the present value of earnings lost because of death.

Besides the above scenario, other sensitivity analyses also were conducted. First, the impact of increasing the cost of hospitalisation and outpatient visits were assessed by using a set of upper estimates. The cost of a hospital day was increased to $669 by increasing the cost-to-charge ratio from 0.634 to 0.764 (the ratio for Maryland). The costs of outpatient visits (first and follow-up) were increased by assuming each visit was a "level 2" visit, doubling the average time a physician spends with each patient. The alternative cost-of-intervention scenarios took into account persons who were not at risk but participated in the prophylaxis programme. Thus, if 100,000 people were exposed, it was assumed that the maximum number seeking prophylaxis was 500,000, 1,000,000, or 1,500,000.

The analyses outlined above consider only the economics of an intervention after an attack and include several assumptions:

i) stockpiles of drugs, vaccines, and other medical supplies would be available and could be rapidly moved to points of need.

ii) civil, military, and other organisations would be in place and have the capability to rapidly identify the agent, dispense drugs, treat patients, and keep order costs of laboratory tests were increased to the full amount of the allowable charge.

The second sensitivity analysis considered a reduced impact, in which only 10 per cent of the original 100,000 target population were considered exposed. All other estimates were held constant.

The third sensitivity analysis considered the threshold cost of an intervention, given differences due to the effectiveness of various drug regimens, and discount rates used to calculate the present value of expected lifetime earnings lost to a death. The threshold cost occurs when net savings equal $0. Thus, the threshold value represents the maximum that could be spent per person on an intervention without having the intervention cost more than the loss from no intervention.

In this study, we have seen that all three biologic agents would cause high rates of illness and death. In the absence of an intervention programme for the 100,000 persons exposed, the *B. anthraces* cloud would result in 50,000 cases of inhalation anthrax, with 32,875 deaths; the *F. tularensis* cloud in 82,500 cases of pneumonic or typhoidal tularemia, with 6,188 deaths; and the *B. melitensis* cloud in 82,500 cases of brucellosis requiring extended therapy, with 413 deaths. The speed with which a post-attack intervention programme can be effectively implemented is critical to its success. For diseases with short incubation periods such as anthrax and tularemia, a prophylaxis programme must be instituted within 72 hours of exposure to prevent the maximum number of deaths, hospital days, and outpatient visits.

Some benefit, however, can be obtained even if prophylaxis is begun as late as day 6 after exposure. The relative clinical efficacy of the intervention regimen has a lesser but definite impact on observed illness and death rates. A disease with a long incubation period such as brucellosis has a similar pattern; an important difference is the time available to implement an intervention programme. Having more time available to implement an intervention programme can make a marked difference in its effectiveness.

Table 6.3
Costs[a] ($ millions) of a bioterrorist attack with no post-exposure prophylaxis programme

	Anthrax	*Tularemia*	*Brucellosis*
Direct costs			
Medical: Base estimates[b]			
Hospital	194.1	445.8	170.3
OPV[c]	2.0	10.5	48.9
Medical: Upper estimated			
Hospital	237.1	543.3	211.7
OPV[c]	4.4	18.5	78.3
Lost productivity			
Illnesses			
Hospital	21.6	50.9	18.8
OPV[c]	0.7	3.9	15.0
Death			
3 % discount[f]	25,985.7	4,891.2	326.5
5 % discount[f]	17,889.3	3,367.3	224.7
Total costs			
Base estimates			
3 % discount[f]	26,204.1	5,402.4	579.4
5 % discount[f]	18,107.7	3,878.4	477.7
Upper estimates			
3 % discount[f]	26,249.7	5,507.9	650.1
5 % discount[f]	18,153.1	3,983.9	548.4

[a] Assuming 100,000 exposed.
[b] Medical costs are the costs of hospitalisation (which include follow-up outpatient visits) and outpatient visits (Table 1).
[c] OPV = outpatient visits.
[d] Upper estimates calculated with data in Table 1.
[e] Lost productivity due to illness is the value of time spent in hospital and during OPVs.
[f] Discount rate applied to calculate the present value of expected future earnings and housekeeping services, weighted by age and sex composition of the United States workforce (16), lost due to premature death.

The differences between agents in medical costs as a percentage of total estimated costs are due to the large differences in death rates attributed to each agent. If the post-exposure prophylaxis programme is initiated early, it reduces the economic impact of all three diseases, especially anthrax. Regardless of drug costs, the largest cost reductions are obtained through a combination of the most effective prophylaxis regimen, the smallest multiplication factor to adjust for persons who unnecessarily receive prophylaxis, and a 3 per cent discount rate to calculate the present value of the expected value of lifetime earnings. In the case of anthrax, either doxycycline or ciprofloxacin could be used in the intervention programme, but the use of doxycycline generated the largest savings. The largest difference in net savings between the two drugs was approximately $261.6 million. This difference occurred when it was assumed that the programme began on day zero, each drug was used in combination with the anthrax vaccine, a 3 per cent discount rate was used, and a multiplication factor of 15 for unnecessary prophylaxis was used. This amount is equal to approximately 1.2 per cent of the maximum total net savings generated by using a regimen of doxycycline plus the anthrax vaccine.

In the case of tularemia, at a 5 per cent discount rate, net losses of $10.7 to $115.1 million occurred when a post-exposure programme was delayed until day 6 after exposure, and a prophylaxis regimen of doxycycline and gentamicin was used. For the same scenario, but with a 3 per cent discount, a net savings of $1,513.3 million was observed when a multiplication factor of five for unnecessary prophylaxis was used. However, multiplication factors of 10 and 15 generated net losses of $49.8 and $102.0 million, respectively. With the same drug combination, beginning the programme 1 day earlier resulted in net savings in all scenarios except when a multiplication factor of 15 and a discount rate of 5 per cent were used. Under the latter two assumptions, net savings result only for prophylaxis initiated by day 4 after exposure.

In the case of brucellosis, the use of a doxycycline-rifampin regimen, a multiplication factor of 15 for unnecessary prophylaxis, and a discount rate of either 3 per cent or 5 per cent generated net losses regardless of when intervention began. The doxycycline-gentamicin regimen generated net losses only when the study assumed that the start of a programme was delayed until 113 or more days after exposure.

The annual actuarially fair premium that can be justifiably spent on intelligence gathering and other attack prevention measures increases with the probability that a bioterrorist attack can be decreased by such measures. However, the potential net savings attributed to reduced probability are minor compared with the potential net savings from implementing a prophylaxis programme. Depending on the level of protection that can be achieved, the annual actuarially fair premium in an anthrax scenario would be $3.2 million to $223.5 million. The lower premium would be justifiable for measures that could reduce the risk for an attack from 0.01 to 0.001 and provide the ability to mount an intervention programme within 6 days of the attack. The higher premium would be justifiable for measures that could reduce the risk from 0.01 to 0.00001 and allow immediate intervention if an attack occurred.

Upper estimates of the cost of hospitalisation increased average costs per day by 18 per cent to 22 per cent, and upper estimates of the cost of outpatient visits increased average costs per day by 46 per cent to 93 per cent. However, the upper estimates only increased medical costs by 1 per cent to 6 per cent of the total medical costs associated with a bioterrorist attack. The largest increase was for brucellosis, for which upper estimates increased medical costs from 38 per cent to 44 per cent of total costs. When the number of persons infected during an attack was reduced tenfold, the patient-related costs were reduced proportionately. In most cases, however, the net savings in total costs are less than 10 per cent of the net savings when 100 per cent of the target population was presumed infected. The shortfall in savings is caused by an increase in the number of unexposed persons receiving prophylaxis.

In the case of anthrax, when intervention programmes are initiated within 3 days of exposure, savings are 4.1 per cent to 10 per cent of those in the original scenario. Delaying initiation of prophylaxis until days 4, 5, or 6 after exposure, however, results in net losses of $13.4 to $283.1 million. Losses occur regardless of prophylaxis regimen, discount rate, or multiplication factor used to adjust for unnecessary prophylaxis by unexposed persons.

In scenarios in which a multiplication factor of 15 was used to adjust for unnecessary prophylaxis, the threshold value of intervention was always above the prophylaxis cost for anthrax but not above the prophylaxis costs for tularemia and brucellosis. For tularemia, the threshold intervention costs exceeded disease costs up to day 5 in the scenario with 95 per cent effectiveness and a 5 per cent discount, and for brucellosis, at all levels in the scenarios with 80 per cent effectiveness and up to day 56 in the scenarios with 95 per cent effectiveness. This is consistent with the lower range of estimated net savings. Reducing the number of unexposed persons receiving prophylaxis increases the cost thresholds, making the programme cost beneficial. For example, changing the multipli-cation factors for unnecessary prophylaxis to 5 and 10 increases the cost thresholds to $659 and $319, respectively, for a brucellosis prophylaxis programme initiated 15 to 28 days after exposure, with a 5 per cent discount rate. If a discount rate of 3 per cent is used instead of 5 per cent, the cost thresholds increase to $799 and $387. All these cost thresholds are above the estimated prophylaxis cost of $285 per person for the doxycycline-rifampin regimen and $161 per person for the doxycycline-gentamicin regimen.

Economic impact of a bioterrorist attack can range from $477.7 million per 100,000 persons exposed in the brucellosis scenario to $26.2 billion per 100,000 persons exposed in the anthrax scenario. These are minimum estimates. Delay in starting a prophylaxis programme is the single most important factor for increased losses. This observation was supported by the actuarially fair premium for preparedness analysis.

Table 6.4
The maximum annual actuarially fair premium by reduction in probability of event and size of avoided loss: Anthrax

Days post-attack[a]	Preventable loss ($millions)	Actuarially fair annual premium ($ millions)		
		0.01 tp 0.001	0.01 to 0.00001	0.01 to 0.0001
Maximum loss estimate[b]				
0	22,370.5	201.3	221.5	223.5
1	20,129.4	181.2	199.3	201.1
2	15,881.5	142.9	157.2	158.7
3	8,448.0	76.0	83.6	84.4
4	4,200.1	37.8	41.6	42.0
5	2,076.1	18.7	20.6	20.7
6	1,013.8	9.1	10.0	10.1
Minimum loss estimate[c]				
0	14,372.4	128.9	141.8	143.1
1	12,820.1	115.4	126.9	128.1
2	10,049.1	90.4	99.5	100.4
3	5,200.1	46.8	51.5	51.9
4	2,429.7	21.9	24.1	24.3
5	1,004.2	9.4	10.3	10.4
6	351.2	3.2	3.5	3.5

[a] No. of days from attack to effective initiation of prophylaxis.

[b] Maximum loss preventable (potential net savings) occurs with the doxycycline-anthrax vaccine prophylaxis regimen, a multiplication factor of 5 for unnecessary prophylaxis, and a discount rate of 3 per cent (Table 6.2).

[c] Minimum loss preventable (potential net savings) occurs with the ciprofloxacin prophylaxis regimen, a multiplication factor of 15 for unnecessary prophylaxis, and a discount rate of 5 per cent (Table 6.2).

Reductions in preventable loss due to early intervention had significantly greater impact on the amount of an actuarially fair premium than reductions in probability of an attack through intelligence gathering and related activities. Although implemented at different times in a threat-attack continuum, both attack prevention measures and prophylaxis programmes are

Table 6.5
Cost thresholds[a] of interventions ($ / person) by day of intervention initiation, prophylaxis effectiveness, and discount rates.

	Threshold costs for intervention ($ / person, multiplication factor of 15[b])							
	Anthrax		*Tularemia*			*Brucellosis*		
Post-attack day[d]	*Disc. rate[c] 5%*	*3%*	*Post-attack day*	*Disc. rate 5%*	*3%*	*Post-attack day*	*Disc. rate 5%*	*3%*
	90% effectiveness[e]		*80% effectiveness[e]*			*80% effectiveness[e]*		
0	9,838	14,238	0	1,	2,633	0-7	233*	282*
1	8,851	12,809	1	1,873	2,609	8-14	224*	272*
2	7,022	10,162	2	1,599	2,227	15-28	211*	255*
3	3,775	5,463	3	756	1,053	29-56	179*	217*
4	1,893	2,739	4	258	366	57-112	86*	104*
5	944	1,366	5	79	110	113 +	24*	30*
6	468	677	6	20 *	28			
Prophylaxis cost[c]	$226				$28			$285
	95% effectiveness[e]		*95% effectiveness[e]*			*95 % effectiveness[e]*		
0	10,370	15,007	0	2,229	3,104	0-7	274	333
1	9,359	13,544	1	2,207	3,074	8-14	264	320
2	7,427	10,948	2	1,898	2,644	15-28	248	301
3	3,995	5,782	3	898	1,251	29-56	211	256
4	2,004	2,900	4	328	457	57-112	102 *	124 *
5	1,000	1,447	5	93 *	131	113 +	29 *	35 *
6	496	718	6	23 *	32	*		
Prophylaxis cost[e]		$238			$104			$161

* Threshold value is below estimated cost of prophylaxis.

[a] Cost threshold is the point where cost of intervention and net savings due to the intervention are equal.

[b] Multiplication factor to adjust for persons who participated in the prophylaxis programme but were unexposed.

[c] Applied to present value of expected future earnings and housekeeping services (weighted average for age and sex).

[d] Post-attack day on which prophylaxis was effectively implemented.

[e] See table 2 for prophylaxis regimens assumed to give the stated levels of effectiveness and cost/person prophylaxis.

forms of preventive medicine. Attack prevention measures seek to prevent infection, while prophylaxis programmes prevent disease after infection has occurred.

Using an actuarially fair premium analogy in which cost and benefit are required to be equal, it was found that the incremental rate of increasing prevention effectiveness declines rapidly as probability reduction targets go from 0.001 to 0.0001 to 0.00001. Since the loss probability is decreasing on a logarithmic scale, the potential increment in marginal benefit drops comparably, resulting in ever smaller increments in the protection above the preceding base level. Conversely, delaying a prophylaxis programme for anthrax, a disease with a short incubation period and a high death rate, increases the risk for loss in a manner akin to a semilogarithmic scale. Arithmetic increases in response time buy disproportionate increases in benefit. The potential for reducing loss is great because an attack is assumed, thus increasing the actuarially fair premium available to prepare for and implement a rapid response.

Large differences between prophylaxis costs and the threshold costs for most scenarios, particularly if prophylaxis is early, suggest that the estimates of savings from prophylaxis programmes are robust. Even with large increases in prophylaxis cost, net savings would still be achieved. The ability to rapidly identify persons at risk would also have significant impact on costs. For example, the threshold costs for brucellosis prophylaxis are often lower than intervention costs when the ratio of unexposed to exposed persons in the prophylaxis programme is 15:1. This finding provides an economic rationale for preparedness to rapidly and accurately identify the population at risk and reduce unnecessary prophylaxis costs.

The narration provides an economic rationale for preparedness measures to both reduce the probability of an attack and increase the capability to rapidly respond in the event of an attack. The larger portion of this preparedness budget should be allocated to measures that enhance rapid response to an attack. These measures would include developing and maintaining laboratory capabilities for both clinical diagnostic testing and environmental sampling, developing and maintaining drug stockpiles, and developing and practising response plans at the local level. These measures should be developed with a value-added approach.

The US Agency for Toxic Substances and Disease Registry (ATSDR) study, "Industrial Chemicals and Terrorism: Human Health Threat Analysis", completed in 1999, reported that terrorist groups, domestic and international, have targeted industrial facilities and specifically chemical and food processing plants. According to the report, 43 per cent of all terrorist targets are businesses or industries. Food processing plants are an attractive target because of the presence of chemicals such as anhydrous ammonia and ammonium nitrate, and the possibility of infecting the food supply with biological agents. The threat of contamination of the food supply is a primary concern of the government agencies, including the Environmental Protection Agency, Bureau of Investigations, Emergency Management Agency, Food and Drug Administration, Department of Agriculture, Centres for Disease Control and Prevention, and the Public Health Service. These agencies have increased their activities and focused their resources to address this threat.

The ATSDR report outlined a Ten-Step procedure to analyse, mitigate and prevent public health hazards resulting from terrorism involving industrial sites which can be applied to many other manufacturing activities. The Ten Step procedure consists of the following:

i) Identify, assess and prioritise threats.
ii) Identify local sources of chemicals that may be used in [or as] improvised weapons.
iii) Evaluate potential exposure pathways.
iv) Identify potential acute and chronic health impacts.
v) Estimate potential impacts on infrastructure and the environment.

vi) Identify health risk communication needs.

vii) Identify methods to mitigate potential hazards.

viii) Identify specific steps to prevent the use of industrial chemicals as improvised weapons.

ix) Incorporate the threat assessment, mitigation and prevention information into emergency response plans.

xi) Conduct training exercises to prepare to prevent and mitigate the health threats.

In addition to the ten-step ATSDR approach outlined above, there are additional measures to consider in anticipating, detecting and preventing the potentially serious and costly effects of a bioterrorist attack.

It is important for facilities to have in place a comprehensive crisis management programme and procedure. Such a procedure and programme should include, at a minimum, the following:

i) Listing of the members of the crisis management team, including all telephone numbers

ii) Description of each member's role and responsibility

iii) Product recall plan

iv) Listing of emergency telephone numbers

v) Emergency evacuation plan

vi) Business continuation plan

vii) Public relations/press package and a designated spokesperson.

The United States Postal Service, through its website and at local post offices, provides a checklist of steps to be taken if one receives a suspicious letter or package. That checklist describes how to identify a suspicious piece of mail, such as unexpected mail or mail from an unknown sender, addressee no longer at the address, handwritten with no return address or suspect return address, excessive amounts of tape, irregular or lumpy appearance, restrictive endorsements such as personal or confidential and excessive postage. Suggestions for handling a suspicious piece of mail include:

i) avoid contact with the article;

ii) do not shake, bump or sniff;

iii) place the article in a plastic bag or some other container;

iv) leave the room, close the door and section off the area;

v) wash hands thoroughly with soap and water;

vi) notify local law enforcement authorities.

These actions are not all inclusive and, depending upon the circumstances, additional or different actions may be necessary. The facility should conduct a risk assessment to determine the necessary security measures that may have to be implemented or modified. This risk assessment would include the identification of the firm's assets, identification and assessment of the threat of attack and the specific types or areas of attack to the facility.

Regulatory requirements in the areas of food and environmental protection and safety require various facility-specific programmes and systems which may be used to effect some of the preventive measures necessary to counter threats of bioterrorism. The elements of such rules and plans can be effective templates from which a company can develop a system-based plan to counter and mitigate risks associated with bioterrorism.

REFERENCES

Abramova, F.A.N., Grinberg, L.M., Yampolskaya, O.V., Walker, D.H., "Pathology of inhalational anthrax in 42 cases from the Sverdlovsk outbreak of 1979", *Proc. Natl. Acad. Sci.,* 1993.

Ban, J., 2000, "Agricultural biological warfare: An overview", *The Arena,* Number 9, June 2000, Washington: Chemical and Biological Arms Control Institute, 8 pp.

Benenson, A.S., ed., *Control of communicable diseases manual*, 16th ed. Washington (DC): American Public Health Association, 1995.

Cole, L.A., "The specter of biological weapons", *Sci. Am.,* 1996.

Friedlander, A.M., Welkos, S.L., Pitt, M.L.M., Ezzell, J.W., Worsham, P.L., Rose, K.J., et al., Postexposure prophylaxis against experimental inhalation anthrax, *J. Infect. Dis.,* 1993.

Gordon, J. C., and S., Bech-Nielsen, 1986, "Biological terrorism: a direct threat to our livestock industry", *Military Medicine,* 151, 357-363.

Haddix, A.C., Teutsch, S.M., Shaffer, P.A., Dunet, D.O., eds., *Prevention Effectiveness: A Guide to Decision Analysis and Economic Evaluation*, New York: Oxford University Press, 1996.

Kaufmann, A.F, Fox, M.D., Boyce, J.M., Anderson, D.C., Potter, M.E., Martone, W.J., et al., "Airborne spread of brucellosis", *Ann. NY. Acad. Sci.,* 1980;335:105-14.

McCrumb, F.R., "Aerosol infection of man with Pasteurella tularensis", *Bacteriolical Reviews,* 1961;25:262-7.

Messelson, M., Guillemin, J., Hugh-Jones M., Langmuir, A., Popova, I., Shelokov A., et al., "The Sverdlosvsk anthrax outbreak of 1979", *Science,* 1994;266:1202-8.

Olle-Goig, J.E., Canela-Soler, J., "An outbreak of Brucella melitensis infection by airborne transmission among laboratory workers", *Am. J. Public. Health,* 1987;77:335-8.

Rogers, P. S., Whitby and M., Dando, "Biological warfare against crops", *Scientific American*, 1999, June, pp. 70-75.

Sawyer, W.D., Dangerfield, H.G., Hogge, A.L., Crozier, D., "Antibiotic prophylaxis and therapy of airborne tularemia", *Bacteriolical Reviews,* 1966;30:542-8.

Staszkiewicz, J., Lewis, C.M., Colville, J., Zervos, M., Band, J., "Outbreak of Brucella melitensis among microbiology laboratory workers in a community hospital", *J. Clin. Microbial,* 1991;29:287-90.

Wheelis, M., 1999, "Biological Sabotage in World War", pp. 35-62 in E. Geissler and J. E. V. C. Moon (eds.) *Biological and Toxin Weapons: Research, Development and Use from the Middle Ages to 1945*, Oxford: Oxford University Press.

Whitby, S., and Rogers, P., 1997, "Anti-crop biological warfare-implications of the Iraqi and US programmes", *Defense Analysis,* 13, 303-318.

7

Social and Psychological Consequences

The stressors associated with a biological terrorist attack could create high numbers of acute and potentially chronic psychiatric casualties who must be recognised, diagnosed, and treated to facilitate triage and medical care. The idea of infection caused by invisible agents is frightening. It touches a deep human concern about the risk of being destroyed by a powerful, evil, imperceptible force. These beliefs activate emotions that are extremely difficult to direct with the tools of reason.

The response of specialists in medicine, epidemiology, infectious disease, molecular biology, nursing, and emergency medical services can bring some discipline and rationality to this situation. To be effective, the response must be well organised and communication must be made in terms that the public understands. Multiple organisations with conflicting and overlapping goals and responsibilities may increase the confusion and anxiety for the individual and community.

The novelty of biological weapons in combination with the activation of deeply rooted fears predict that strong psychological and physiological responses will occur. The immediate stressors associated with a biological terrorist attack are the threat and the consequences of infection. The specific nature of these stressors will depend on the organism or toxin used. Characteristics such as the incubation period and the virulence and toxicity of the agent will contribute to the psychological impact. The process of seeking and receiving immunisation or treatment is potentially stressful.

There will be acute and chronic psychiatric casualties as in other disasters. While the majority of people do not develop long-term psychiatric sequelae following disasters, certain groups are at higher risk. Biological agents may cause mental disorders due to toxins or infectious conditions such as viral encephalitis or bacterial meningitis. Illness and injury secondary to the attack increase the risk of the development of acute stress disorder and post-traumatic stress disorder, as well as depression and bereavement in survivors.

The psychological responses following a biological terrorist attack include:

i) horror
ii) anger
iii) panic
iv) magical thinking about microbes and viruses
v) fear of invisible agents
vi) fear of contagion
vii) anger at terrorists, government, or both
viii) attribution of arousal symptoms to infection
ix) scapegoating
x) paranoia
xi) social isolation
xii) demoralisation
xiii) loss of faith in social institutions

Psychiatric disability is a likely chronic outcome of biological attack. The incidence and prevalence of such problems remain a matter of speculation, although past occurrences can be used to anticipate consequences. Experiences with chemical weapons used by terrorists have demonstrated that psychiatric casualties are likely. The psychiatric sequelae will depend on the nature of and the response to the assault.

In contrast to explosive or chemical weapons, biological weapons may not produce instantaneously horrifying results. As the attack is discovered and the media reports the news, exposed and unexposed individuals may experience acute autonomic arousal. Signs and symptoms of muscle tension, tachycardia, rapid breathing, sweating, tremor, and a sense of foreboding are likely to generate health concerns. These signs and symptoms may be misattributed to infection or intoxication.

The acutely stressed and symptomatic individuals will add complexity and additional patients for triage during the initial phase of the crisis. However, if initial triage and management are successful, the risk for the development of psychiatric problems can be minimised. Forensic issues involved in the medical response influence psychological responses and treatment options. Preservation of evidence maximises the passibility of the perpetrators' being punished. The perception that justice is ultimately served can have a very positive psychological impact on those exposed and society. Some survivors may be critical witnesses in future legal actions. This may have little consequence for immediate life-saving care, but it might prompt the selection of psychotropic drugs that minimally interfere with recall or discourage the use of a technique, like hypnosis.

Distinguishing symptoms of hyperarousal from those of intoxication and infectious disease prodromes will be crucial. The type of exposure and any lack of complete information about the agent will increase uncertainty and the risk of psychiatric morbidity. The risk for secondary psychological trauma will increase if actions by leaders or helpers fail to provide a quick, accurate diagnosis, a sensitive process for communicating the nature of the risk, and a supportive environment for those exposed and their families. An attitude of expectation that those with hyperarousal or demoralisation will soon return to normal activities should be conveyed. Patients should be moved out of the patient role as quickly as possible. Diazepam-like anxiolytics may be helpful in reducing anxiety for patients who do not respond to reassurance.

The assignment of simple work tasks that facilitate the care of other patients can help restore function to the psychological casualties. The recovery environment should be constructed to create a sense of safety and to counteract the helplessness induced by the terrorist act. An effective medical response contributes to the creation of a supportive environment and accurate data for the at-risk population. Individuals can assess their risk and determine the actions that they can take to reduce the risk. Ideally, risk information should involve dialogue. Dialogue lets the at-risk population define the information that they need, and it enables the community leaders to assess their effectiveness in communicating the appropriate data. Failure to provide a public forum for information exchanges may actually increase anxiety and misunderstanding and amplify health concerns since individuals will tend to attribute autonomic symptoms to catastrophic illness. One consequence of appraisal error may be disabling somatic complaints offered in a setting where failure to find a medical or surgical disease is experienced as stigmatising and sadistic by the patients.

After a biological warfare, physical injury, disruption of daily communal routine, and increased use of public health facilities could place overwhelming demands on the medical systems. Feelings of helplessness and hopelessness could be increased if the rescue and post-disaster medical efforts appear to be failing. Angry, intense competition for available but limited resources can generate even more societal disruption and casualties.

The belief that treatment will be provided to some but not to others will contribute to the possibility of social disruptions such as riot or panic. Panic will be a particular risk when biological agents are used to threaten or to attack a sizable civilian population.

Demoralisation can also be a response to the predicaments presented by a biological attack. Demoralised individuals often lose their sense of social and group responsibilities and roles. If major community institutions fail to provide protection, citizens can lose faith in the ideological metaphors that bind the community together. In this way, demoralisation can increase isolation and feelings of hopelessness.

In this complex setting, some are likely to manifest psychiatric symptoms. Given the stigma attached to psychiatric illness and the fact that the individuals who manifest them are more likely to have been injured and to have been exposed to multiple infectious, environmental, and toxicological risks, the diagnostic and therapeutic dilemmas will be quite difficult. Quarantine requires the development of a specialised environment that will limit exposure to secondary infections. The creation of such an environment may disrupt social supports that reduce the post exposure risk of stress induced disorders. It can create a situation characterised by separation from friends and family, isolation, and a sense of stigmatisation.

Prior planning can ensure that modern communication technology can be used to mitigate these untoward effects by providing ongoing contact with families and others in the community outside quarantine. The maintenance of contact between parents and children is particularly important for the children. This may result in putting unexposed adult caregivers in quarantine. Additional stressors may arise from the mundane logistical demands associated with managing mass contamination and infection. One of the difficulties in the Japanese sarin attack was undressing patients and disposing of their clothing. Obtaining the necessary shower facilities for a large number of exposed survivors may be problematic.

The provision of privacy and assurance of conventional modesty may have to be sacrificed. It should not be forgotten that privacy and modesty are important to maintaining an individual's sense of control and autonomy. The imposition of special requirements such as public bathing should be accompanied by an explanation that attributes this undesirable demand to the terrorist attacker. Disaster responders and medical personnel also will have to contend with their own psychological reactions. One of the terrorist's goals is to provoke intense emotions that interfere with the capacity of caregivers to react in a thoughtful, organised fashion.

A biological attack using a highly infectious and virulent organism, dispersed in a fine spray, poses special stressors. Medical responders may be required to work in protective clothing and masks. This barrier protection will make the care of patients more difficult and increase the risk of heat, fatigue, and isolation stress for medical personnel. Disaster plans for managing a biological attack must be developed and realistic training provided to ensure effective response to an actual terrorist event. These plans must assume that emotional and psychiatric problems will occur in the unexposed population as well as the exposed. The exercises should be carried out with sufficient realism, so that the process of disrobing and showering is practised in real time.

Medical responders will need training to recognise the symptoms of anxiety, depression, and dissociation. It is critical that psychological responses be managed in ways that facilitate the triage, diagnosis, and treatment of those exposed or infected. Such plans need to include strategies for prevention and mitigation of stress for survivors as well as for those responding to the crisis and its consequences.

Debriefing, commonly used by emergency personnel following trauma, has been used to mitigate the effects of severe stress and can be helpful in identifying individuals who may need further assistance. Results from controlled studies of debriefing are only now beginning to become available. These studies will help clarify the role of intervention in the alleviation of pain, prevention of disability, return to social involvement, and the prevention of disease. Ironically, should a highly infectious agent be used, bringing people together for a debriefing may be contradicted.

The psychiatric interventions include:

i) prevention of group panic
ii) careful, rapid medical evaluation and treatment
iii) avoidance of emotion-based responses
iv) effective risk communication
v) control of symptoms secondary to hyperarousal
vi) reassurance
vii) diazepamlike anxiolytics for acute relief, as indicated
viii) management of anger, fear, or both
ix) management of misattribution of somatic symptoms
x) provision of respite as required
xi) restoration of an effective, useful social role
xii) return to usual sources of social supports in the community

The media coverage and behaviour of public officials can contribute to the stress and precipitate panic or demoralisation, particularly if inaccurate, confusing, or contradictory information is provided to the public. Rumors must be anticipated, monitored, and corrected with accurate information. Any damage to public trust at the beginning of the crisis ensures that distrust will continue throughout the crisis.

Inattention to the phenomenon of terror and its consequences for individuals, institutions, and society jeopardise the efficacy of disaster mitigation efforts. Leaders, scientists, and the media should develop protocols covering a broad range of scenarios that communicate accurate information about risk and diminish rumors. Governmental and private agencies should develop detailed strategies for responding to a biological terrorist attack that include consideration of the psychological and social impact of such an attack. These primary prevention efforts will be critical in preventing panic and demoralisation in the attacked community.

Training for biological attacks should include the probability of large numbers of psychological casualties.

Training exercises should be designed to test cooperation and coordination between organisations as well as test first responders and hospital staff. Hospital accrediting bodies should encourage medical facilities to incorporate biological scenarios into their annual training. Planning and preparation for biological attacks and their attendant psychological consequences can diminish the terrorists' ability to achieve their overall goal—the induction of terror. Education of the public and institutional preparedness can mitigate the horror of terrorism.

REFERENCES

Baum A., "Stress, intrusive imagery, and chronic distress", *Health Psychol*, 1990;9:653-675.

Fullerton, C.S., Ursano, R.J., Kao, T., Bhartiya, V., "The chemical and biological warfare environment psychological responses and social support in a high-stress environment", *J. Appl. Soc. Psychol*, 1992;22: 1608-1623.

_______________, Ursano, R.J., "Health care delivery in the high-stress environment of chemical and biological warfare", *Mil. Med.* 1994;159:524-528.

Russell, P.K., "Biologic terrorism: responding to the threat", *Emerg Infect. Dis.* [serial online], 1997.

Ursano, R.J., Fullerton, C.S., Norwood, A.E., "Psychiatric dimensions of disaster: patient care, community consultation, and preventive medicine", *Harv. Rev. Psychiatry*, 1995;3:196-200.

Weisaeth, L., "War-related psychopathology in Kuwait: an assessment of war-related mental health problems", In Fullerton, C.S., Ursano, R.J., eds., *Posttraumatic Stress Disorder: Acute and Long-Term Responses to Trauma and Disaster*, Washington, DC: American Psychiatric Press; 1997:91- 122.

8

Biological Weapons Control: Implications for the Future

Biological warfare, one of the potential weapon of mass destruction has became a major threat to the international society. The global diffusion of dual-use biotechnology provides these outlaw regimes with the means to perpetrate such attacks. The cost of this technology is significantly less than that associated with the development of nuclear or even chemical weapons. Biologists are well aware of the impact of infectious disease on society and humankind. The eradication of smallpox, considered by some as the perfect biological weapons agent, and the control and prevention of other infectious diseases reflects modern medicine's great intellectual and technical advances. Despite these advances, the legal and moral standard against the intentional use of these organisms has eroded, not advanced.

Any future biological weapons arms control agreement may only be palliative against nations intent on pursuing a biological weapons capability. In terms of the potential effectiveness of arms control to prevent bioterrorism, it is important not to be lulled into a false sense of security. The Biological and Toxin Weapons Convention (BWC) which prohibits the acquisition of biological materials for hostile purposes and armed conflict, entered into force in 1975 and now has the participation of 140 nations. Officially known as the Convention on the Prohibition of the Development, Production and Stockpiling of Bacteriological (Biological) and Toxin

Weapons and on Their Destruction, this treaty was opened for signature on April 10, 1972.

When it first entered into force, the BWC was unique among existing weapons control treaties. It prohibited an entire class of weapons, yet lacked specific mandatory enforcement measures to ensure compliance by participants. Events in the last several years have acutely raised the awareness of the BWC's limitations and cast doubt about its current effectiveness to slow, stop, or reverse the current trends in biological warfare proliferation. The number of countries known or suspected of having biological weapons capability has doubled since the convention went into force in 1975.

Many of the signatory nations are negotiating a legally binding protocol to correct the deficiencies of the BWC and reinforce the existing global prohibition against biological warfare. These diplomatic efforts, directed by the BWC Special Conference in September 1994 and described in detail below, reflect ubiquitous concerns about biological weapons proliferation. At the United Nations (UN) General Assembly meeting in September 1996, the then US President Clinton announced that his government was committed to complete this drafting effort by 1998.

There is widespread international expectation that a protocol will be completed and possibly ratified by the end of the decade. Russia admitted that the former Soviet Union had violated the BWC. The former Soviet Union did so with near impunity because the BWC has no effective mechanisms to investigate concerns about suspicious activities. Iraq, on the other hand, has been subject to the UN Special Commission's (UNSCOM's) multiple intrusive inspections and monitoring since the Persian Gulf War. A detailed analysis of the UNSCOM inspections is published elsewhere in this issue. Even with unrestricted access and a broad range of on-site measures, inspectors failed to uncover any unambiguous evidence of illicit biological weapons activity. The UNSCOM's inspections occurred after Iraq's violations, so it is not possible to assess its deterrence value.

Global domestic legislation to prevent non-state or terrorist biological weapons proliferation has yet to be universally enacted. The recent use of chemical agents by the Aum Shinrikyo cult in Japan and the Aum's unsuccessful attempt to disseminate anthrax spores and botulinum toxin in Tokyo raise the spectre of biological weapons terrorism by non-state actors. It remains to be seen whether domestic legislation that criminalises biological weapons development or use can entirely deter domestic biological weapons terrorist events. Efforts to heighten public and professional awareness about this threat are necessary. Additionally, capabilities must be enhanced to respond to biological weapons incidents.

Currently, ongoing efforts to improve domestic and global surveillance of infectious diseases represent part of an initiative that can strengthen the BWC. Effective surveillance and prompt investigation of unusual or suspicious outbreaks of disease can potentially deter biological weapons use by identifying intentional or accidental releases of biological weapons agents, albeit imperfectly. These efforts coupled with further medical education and research to address the threat posed by both biological weapons proliferation, as well as emerging and re-emerging diseases, can provide a scientific foundation to develop capabilities to diagnose, treat, and mitigate such occurrences.

The measures to prevent biological weapons development are began well before the First World War. Declarations signed at the 1899 and 1907 Hague International Peace Conferences called for prohibition of the use of poison during war. The use of chlorine and mustard gases during World War I prompted the victorious Allies to formalise these prewar prohibitions to strengthen the international norm against this type of weapon.

The landmark Geneva Protocol of 1925 reaffirmed the prohibition of the use in war of asphyxiating, poisonous, or other gases and extended this ban to the use of bacteriological weapons. This protocol never truly entered into force as an international agreement before World War II since the United

States and Japan never ratified it. Its terms, however, were largely respected and may account for the virtual absence of use of both chemical warfare and biological weapons during conflicts in the mid twentieth century. One notable exception was the dispersal of various biological weapons agents by the Japanese during World War II.

The Geneva Protocol did not ban possession of chemical warfare or biological weapons, but rather prohibited the use of these materials as weapons of war. The impact of the Geneva Protocol was additionally weakened by the declarations of the UK, the former Soviet Union, and France. These three countries stated that they would not be bound to this agreement if their enemies or the allies of their enemies used chemical warfare or biological weapons. Thus, the Geneva Protocol became a "no-first-use" agreement with no legally binding restrictions on the research, development, or deployment of either chemical warfare or biological weapons.

During the Second World War, both Axis and Allied nations used varied levels of efforts to develop biological weapons. Japan's Unit 731 conducted human experimentation using anthrax, cholera, typhoid, plague, and typhus. Recent published accounts describe Japanese attacks on Chinese villages and cities with biological weapons. Japan, however, was not alone in the pursuit of biological weapons. The United States, in cooperation with Canada and the UK, developed and produced anthrax bombs to retaliate against possible German or Japanese first use of biological weapons. The US research and development effort was likened to a smaller version of the Manhattan Project, reflecting the high level of scientific expertise brought together to create an offensive biological weapons programme.

The end of World War II saw the dawn of the nuclear age, yet many of those involved in the US offensive biological weapons effort, including its head, George Merck, foresaw the potential proliferation of this threat as early as 1946. In the years immediately following World War II, the international community engaged in little, if any, dialogue to limit or prohibit the development or use of biological weapons. On the contrary, the United States continued to expand its offensive programme. The US programme included the development and limited production of several biological weapons agents and delivery systems.

Only in the late 1960s did President Nixon, shortly after taking office, direct a study of US policy, programmes, and operational concepts regarding both chemical and biological weapons. The National Security Council assessed in this study that biological weapons were not ideal for tactical battlefield use because of the latency between exposure and onset of symptoms and the difficulty of confining biological weapons' effects to a given target area. On November 25, 1969, Nixon announced the results of this review and the unconditional, unilateral renouncement of all methods of biological weapons. His executive order directed the US Department of Defence to dispose of all existing stocks of biological agents and weapons. This unilateral prohibition was further extended to include toxin agents in February 1970. The renouncement was subsequently endorsed by Canada, Sweden and UK. This series of unilateral announcements created an international political momentum within the UN Conference of the Committee on Disarmament for negotiating a legally binding treaty to prohibit biological weapons.

The UN Conference of the Committee on Disarmament initially envisioned a treaty to ban the acquisition of materials intended for both chemical warfare and biological weapons, but technical differences between these two classes of weapons, as well as political considerations, led to separate negotiations for the chemical warfare and biological weapons problems. These negotiations resulted in the BWC and the first agreement since World War II that prohibited an entire class of weapons.

The fundamental tenet of the BWC is contained in Article I. Specifically, Article I prohibits the development, production, and stockpiling of microbial or other biological agents or toxins of types and quantities that have no justification for prophylactic, protective, and other peaceful purposes, and weapons, equipment, or means of delivery designed to use such agents or toxins for hostile purposes or in armed conflict. This language implicitly prohibits the exploitation of current and all possible future scientific and technical developments for purposes inconsistent with peaceful use. This intent clause has been the cornerstone and genius of the BWC and remains the foundation for any future biological weapons control protocol.

The BWC has no implementation or verification provisions. Effective verification is an arms control concept in which determination of compliance can be made by using a series of measures such as declarations of activities, visits to facilities, or other information that would yield accurate and unambiguous data about the nature of activities of potential concern. A treaty with "effective verification" would have a high probability of identifying a signatory nation that was in violation of the treaty's prohibitions on one hand, while being able to determine, with equally high probability, whether a signatory nation was in compliance with the treaty on the other. The medical equivalent to this concept would be having a diagnostic test that is simultaneously both highly sensitive and highly specific. These diagnostic tests must possess the even more stringent characteristics of high positive and negative predictive value.

It is essentially impossible to separate the dual-use nature of biological processes and equipment used in legitimate and prohibited activities. Translated into Bayesian terms familiar to physicians, no measures or combination of measures, to date, have been found with the requisite sensitivity or specificity that were useful for detecting violations of the BWC. In these circumstances, a BWC member nation that has a concern about another member nation's activities or that has been the target of a biological weapons attack would submit its complaint before the UN Security Council for review and consideration. The UN Security Council would then determine what further action, if any, should be taken. An inherent limitation of this mechanism is the potential for any one of the five permanent members of the Security Council (the United States, the UK, France, China, or Russia) to veto or obstruct any further investigation or action against the suspected violator.

Currently, the BWC also provides that if the Security Council finds that a member nation was indeed endangered by a violation of the BWC, parties to the BWC would be obligated to provide assistance. One other important provision is that BWC member nations are not relieved of the obligations imposed by the Geneva Protocol. The BWC entered into force, during the pentennial review conferences, incremental progress has been made to increase the transparency of biological activities that could be perceived as being of concern.

Nations that have ratified the BWC are encouraged to make voluntary annual data exchanges about high-containment facilities, human vaccine production facilities, military biodefence programmes, and outbreaks of disease. These voluntary data exchanges were formalised into confidence building measures after the Second Review Conference (REVCON) in September 1991.

The Biological and Toxin Weapons Convention (BWC) Confidence-Building Measures include:

i) Exchange of data including name, location, scope, and general description of activities on research centres and laboratories that meet very high national or international safety standards established for handling, for permitted purposes, biological materials that pose a high individual and community risk or specialise in permitted biological activities directly related to the BWC. Signatory nations further agreed to provide annually detailed information on their biological defense research and development programmes, including summaries of the objectives and costs of effort performed by contractors and in other facilities.

ii) Exchange of information on outbreaks of infectious diseases and similar occurrences caused by biological agents and toxins and on all such events that seem to deviate from the normal pattern concerning type, development, place, or time of occurrence. The information provided on events that deviate from the norm will include, as soon as it is available, data on the type of disease, approximate area affected, and number of cases.

iii) Encouragement of publication of results of biological research directly related to the BWC in scientific journals generally available to signatory nations, as well as promotion of use for permitted purposes of knowledge gained in this research.

iv) Active promotion of contact between scientists in biological research directly related tc the BWC, including exchanges and visits for joint research on a mutually agreed basis.

v) Declaration of legislation whether signatory nations have legislation, regulations, or other measures to prohibit the development, production, stockpiling, acquisition, or retention of microbial or other biological agents or toxins, weapons, equipment, and means of delivery within their territory or anywhere under their jurisdiction or control and in relation to the export or import of pathogenic microorganisms and toxins to humans, animals, and plants.

vi) Declaration of past activities in offensive and/or defensive biological research and development programmes since January 1, 1946.

vii) Declaration of vaccine production facilities, both governmental and non-governmental, within a nation's territory or under its jurisdiction or control anywhere, producing vaccine licensed by the signatory nation for the protection of humans.

Despite being broadly supported at the time, only about half of the signatory nations have ever filed any voluntary confidence-building measure declarations. The Third Review Conference reaffirmed and extended the confidence-building measures of the Second Review Conference and agreed to create an Ad Hoc Group of Governmental Experts (verification experts or VEREX) whose mandate was to identify, examine, and evaluate from a scientific and technical standpoint potential verification measures with respect to the prohibitions of the BWC.

Table 8.1
The VEREX measures

Off-site measures	*On-site measures*
Information monitoring	Exchange visits
Surveillance of publications	International arrangements
Surveillance of legislation	Continuous monitoring
Data on transfers and transfer requests	By instruments
	By personnel
Information-sharing	Inspections
Remote sensing	Interviews
Surveillance by satellite	Visual inspections
Surveillance by aircraft	Identification of key equipment
Ground-based surveillance	
Data exchange	Auditing
Declarations	Sampling and identification
Notifications	Medical examination
Inspections	
Sampling and identification	
Observation	
Auditing	

The VEREX effort produced a consensus report that resulted in several principal conclusions:

i) Potential verification measures could be useful in varying degrees in enhancing confidence, through increased transparency, that member nations were fulfilling their BWC obligations.

i) Reliance could not be placed on any single measure to differentiate conclusively between prohibited and permitted activities and to resolve ambiguities about compliance, though such measures could provide information of varying utility in strengthening the BWC.

ii) Concern was expressed that the implementation of any measure should ensure that sensitive commercial proprietary information and national security needs were protected.

The VEREX process did not state that effective verification was possible, only that certain measures in combination could help increase transparency and enhance confidence that members of the BWC were fulfilling their obligations.

No combination of measures could be found with sufficient certainty or reliability to convince the VEREX participants that it was possible to uncover violations with a high degree of confidence, while at the same time avoiding false accusations. In technical terms, neither high positive or negative predictive values could be identified during VEREX. A BWC Special Conference convened in September 1994 and established the Ad Hoc Group (AHG) to consider appropriate VEREX measures and draft proposals for a legally binding protocol to strengthen the BWC.

An interim AHG report was submitted to the Fourth Review Conference in November 1996 that resulted in a call by all signatory nations to complete this work as soon as possible before the next review conference in 2001. The specific measures being discussed during the AHG negotiations are the following:

Declarations of military biodefence facilities and human and veterinarian vaccine facilities.

i) Investigations of alleged use.
ii) Investigations of suspicious outbreaks of disease.
iii) On-site visits to address concerns about compliance.

Although diplomatic arms control efforts to improve the effectiveness of the BWC has progressed, trends in biological weapons proliferation reinforce the harsh realities of the problem. In 1975, when the convention was signed, only a handful of countries were known or suspected of having an offensive biological weapons programme. Today, that number has doubled. More disturbing, however, is a series of events and admissions that occurred since the Third BWC Review Conference in 1991.

In 1992, Russian president Boris Yeltsin admitted that the former Soviet Union had violated the BWC by developing an offensive biological weapons programme. Before the fall of the Soviet Union, that suspicion had existed, but it was only after Yeltsin's admission that the world began to understand the size and scope of their programme. Furthermore, the true nature of the 1979 anthrax outbreak in Sverdlovsk was exposed as an accident at a military biological weapons facility that resulted in human and animal cases and fatalities.

In addition, unconfirmed published reports from Russian defectors formerly involved in the biological weapons programme suggest that they were researching and developing new classes of biological weapons agents. These defectors disclosed that they were developing viral haemorrhagic fevers and genetically engineered biological weapons agents. They specifically mentioned creating a strain of *Yersinia pestis* that was resistant to multiple antibiotics and engineered to overcome the protection of available vaccines. These disclosures raise two ominous points.

First, the Soviet Union, one of the three depositories or sponsors of the BWC, pursued an offensive programme in spite of established international legal and moral prohibitions.

Second, despite bilateral agreements between the United States and the Russian governments to resolve concerns about the biological weapons capabilities that the Russian government inherited, concerns still persist about the veracity and completeness of Russian assurances.

Before the start of the Persian Gulf War, the Western agencies were aware of the fact that Iraq had an offensive biological weapons programme. This fact was only confirmed, however, in 1995 after the defection of the late Lieutenant General Hussein Kamel Hassan. While the pre-war public intelligence determination was correct, the intelligence agencies underestimated the size and scope of the Iraqi programme. Iraq admitted that before the onset of the war, they produced, filled, and deployed aerial bombs, 122-mm rockets, aircraft spray tanks, and SCUD missile warheads containing botulinum toxin, aflatoxin, and anthrax spores. Iraq had also conducted research into other potential biological weapons agents including *Clostridium perfringens,* rotavirus, and echovirus 71 and camelpox viruses.

The US Army estimated that if Iraq had used these weapons, there would have been "enormous fatalities," and the US Army's medical treatment system would have been overtaxed. Iraq successfully deceived, denied, and hid from UNSCOM inspectors information concerning their biological weapons programme for four years after the Persian Gulf War. Despite comprehensive mandatory declarations, numerous intrusive routine and challenge inspections to 80 biocapable facilities, including breweries, food production plants, pharmaceutical plants, and medical laboratories, UNSCOM found no incriminating evidence that would identify any of the sites as linked to a proscribed biological weapons programme.

Yet, based on Kamel Hassan's detailed technical analysis of materials taken from the Al Hakam single-cell protein and biopesticide facility, Iraq developed and maintained a stand-by biological weapons capability under the constant scrutiny of UN routine and no-notice inspections. The UNSCOM first visited the Al Hakam facility in August 1991. Despite suspicions and constant monitoring, the facility remained operational, producing metric tons of the dry form of the biopesticide *Bacillus thuringiensis*. In December 1994 and June 1995, sampling and analysis of spray driers at that facility showed that the *B thuringiensis* produced there was in a small particle size. This small size was inconsistent with biopesticide applications but well suited for aerosolised biological weapons purposes. The fermentation process used at this facility also lent itself to rapid conversion from production of *Bthuringiensis* to *Bacillus anthracis*. As a result of this technical analysis and Kamel Hassan's information, UNSCOM razed the Al Hakam facility in the summer of 1996.

The US intelligence community estimates that Iraq could reconstitute its biological weapons programme in a matter of weeks once sanctions are removed. The UNSCOM experience with Iraq raises questions about the effectiveness of various measures, no matter how intrusive, to conclusively detect or verify the existence of prohibited activities.

Unlike the biological weapons programmes associated with the Soviet and Iraqi governments, the events in Japan point out the risk of chemical warfare and biological weapons terrorism by a terrorist group, other non-state actors like this cult, or even a deranged individual. While it is widely known that the Aum perpetrated a sarin nerve agent attack in the Tokyo subway system, less publicity was given to the biological weapons capabilities they reportedly developed as well. Unconfirmed reports suggest that this cult attempted to produce and disseminate both botulinum toxin and anthrax before they launched the sarin attack.

The local and federal authorities recognised the potential risk and interdicted these persons before any possible harm could occur. An international legally binding protocol between nations could be expected to have some measure of, but not complete deterrence of a terrorist biological weapons attack. Requiring nations to comply with mandatory enactment of domestic legislation that criminalises biological weapons possession or activity would be helpful but not foolproof. Implementing legislation associated with a BWC protocol may limit the access terrorists would have to certain materials such as cultures of pathogenic organisms. It would not, however, necessarily restrict their access to dual-use equipment and supplies.

Biological weapons terrorist attacks can only be reasonably deterred or prevented by the constant vigilance and focused efforts of domestic law enforcement agencies. These events underscore the inherent limits of any future protocol to effectively limit biological weapons proliferation. In this context, the BWC protocol currently being negotiated would provide greater transparency of certain but not all biological activities that could be used for offensive biological weapons purposes.

It is unlikely that all facilities capable of producing pathogenic organisms in a given country will be subject to declarations or inspections. The BWC negotiators have already narrowed the likely categories of declarable activities and facilities to biosafety level four laboratories, facilities that produce vaccines, and military and biodefence programmes. They have already excluded from consideration hospitals, medical laboratories and biosafety level three laboratories, academic and research institutions, breweries, and food processing plants. They have yet to determine whether all pharmaceutical manufacturers or biotechnology companies will be declared under a future protocol or whether some arbitrary production threshold will be agreed to limiting declarations to only certain scale producers. Another important issue being considered during the current AHG negotiations is the protection of intellectual, commercial proprietary, and national security information.

In September 1996, in the UN General Assembly President Clinton outlined two specific measures during his speech. First, head vocated a mechanism to rectify the current weaknesses associated with investigations of alleged use. The mechanism he proposed would not be held hostage by a single nation's veto, but would be weighed on the merit of the evidence presented to and deliberated on by all the signatory nations. Second, President Clinton endorsed a measure to investigate unusual or suspicious outbreaks of disease. This concept first surfaced during World War II, when US medical experts believed that an unusual outbreak of disease would probably be the first indication of biological weapons agents use. That assumption remains valid today. An unusual disease outbreak could represent the release of biological weapons agents or the occurrence of an emerging or re-emerging disease. In either case, an epidemiologic investigation could differentiate between the two possibilities. Indeed, recent experience in the investigation of hantavirus pulmonary syndrome and Ebola virus outbreaks strongly suggest that the international epidemiology community has developed a useful set of tools for rapidly assessing the source and nature of spread of novel diseases or disease syndromes. Such investigations cannot always conclusively identify the cause of an outbreak, but they do provide an internationally recognised method to investigate such occurrences.

A recent US Department of Defence exercise further reinforced this concept by outlining preliminary criteria for suspicious outbreaks of disease that could provide indications of a possible biological weapons event. Not all disease out-breaks would automatically be subject to investigation by a future BWC protocol. Similar to the situation of alleged biological weapons use, evidence concerning the outbreak would be reviewed and deliberated on by all BWC member nations to determine whether a formal investigation should be conducted.

In addition to epidemiologic data, other sources of information such as intelligence could be considered. If the weight of the information presented indicates a reason to be concerned about biological weapons or if the characteristics of the outbreak remain unclear or suspicious, a BWC treaty–related investigation could occur. This type of mechanism and process could significantly limit the possibility of false accusations. At that time, an impartial UN expert international team would respond to such events and be afforded the necessary access to conduct a thorough epidemiologic investigation.

The opportunity to collect data, perform hypothesis generation, and conduct statistical analysis could provide greater insight into these outbreaks. Scientific analysis derived from these investigations could offer a valid scientific foundation for later political consideration. These types of investigations would provide greater transparency of national biological events and could enhance confidence in nations' compliance with the BWC. At a minimum, these investigations would provide further support of international public health efforts to enhance surveillance for infectious disease and efforts to control outbreaks. It would also prompt nations to more openly share information concerning disease occurrences and help establish a global epidemiologic baseline.

In the future under such a protocol, biological weapons use or accidents resulting in unusual outbreaks of disease could not easily evade investigation. With this mechanism in place supported by the weight of the international community, occurrences like the accident at the military-biological weapons facility at Sverdlovsk could not easily denied or obstructed for 12 years. Any future BWC protocol that would at a minimum, include investigations of alleged use and suspicious outbreaks could significantly advance the cause of biological arms control. Beside reinforcing the existing global norm against these weapons, they could provide an important deterrent against biological weapons development and use.

Primary prevention of biological weapons proliferation requires education, specific protective measures, and environmental modification. For the medical community, further education stressing the recognition of this threat is both timely and necessary. Primary prevention of biological weapons also rests on creating a strong global norm that rejects biological weapons development or use. The medical and scientific communities play an important role in raising the awareness and reinforcing this norm during international professional exchanges and meetings.

Historically, offensive biological weapons development required the support of medical researchers. Each of us has a duty to voice our profession's revulsion to this form of warfare.

Focusing intense public scrutiny on those who continue to violate the BWC can be effective adjunct therapy.

Therefore, efforts to improve disease surveillance and continue research and development of improved diagnostic capabilities, therapeutic agents, and effective response plans capable of mitigating the effects of infectious disease occurrences remain paramount.

It is vital to reaffirm the global biological weapons prohibition with a strengthened the Biological and Toxin Weapons Convention (BWC). The principles of prevention that help clinicians conceptualise strategies against disease are relevant as the medical profession considers the problem of biological weapons proliferation.

Primary prevention of biological weapons proliferation requires education, specific protective measures, and environmental modification. For the medical community, further education stressing the recognition of this threat is both timely and necessary. Primary prevention of biological weapons also rests on creating a strong global norm that rejects biological weapons development or use. The medical and scientific communities play an important role in raising the awareness and reinforcing this norm during international professional exchanges and meetings.

Historically, offensive biological weapons development required the support of medical researchers. Each of us has a duty to voice our profession's revulsion to this form of warfare. Focusing intense public scrutiny on those who continue to violate the BWC can be effective adjunct therapy.

Secondary prevention implies early detection and prompt treatment of disease. A strengthened BWC can help ensure that biological weapons proliferators who develop or use these weapons will stand a greater likelihood of being exposed and caught. A future protocol that ensures an effective mechanism to permit investigation of occurrences such as suspicious outbreaks of disease or alleged use can simultaneously enhance global security and public health.

The medical community plays an integral role in secondary biological weapons prevention because they participate in the network of disease surveillance and reporting that may provide the first indication of biological weapons use. Additionally, the medical community will be at the "tip of the spear" when it comes to the treatment of survivors of biological weapons incidents. Therefore, efforts to improve disease surveillance and continue research and development of improved diagnostic capabilities, therapeutic agents, and effective response plans capable of mitigating the effects of infectious disease occurrences remain paramount.

REFERENCES

Ad Hoc Group of Governmental Experts to Identify and Examine Potential Verification Measures From a Scientific and Technical Standpoint, Report. Geneva, Switzerland: United Nations, 1993.

Blackwill, R.D., *Arms Control and the US-Russian Relationship: Problems, Prospects and Prescriptions.* New York, NY: Council on Foreign Relations, 1996:65-66.

Brophy L, Miles, W.D., Cochrane RC. *The Chemical Warfare Service: From Laboratory to Field.* Washington, DC: US Army, 1959.

Bryden, J., *Deadly Allies: Canada's Secret War, 1937-1947.* Toronto, Ontario: McClelland & Stewart Inc., 1989:256.

Defense Nuclear Agency (DNA) Biological Weapons Proliferation. *Global Proliferation: Dynamics, Acquisition Strategies and Response.* Alexandria, Va: Defense Nuclear Agency; 1994, 4:10.

Ekeus, R., *Memorandum to the Biological Weapons Convention Fourth Review Conference.* New York, NY: United Nations, November 20, 1996.

Gertz, B., "Defecting Russian scientist revealed biological arms effort". *Washington Times,* July 4, 1992:A4.

Harris, S.H., *Factories of Death: Japanese Biological Warfare, 1932-1934, and the American Cover up.* New York, NY: Routledge, 1994:59, 68.

Holum, J.D., *Remarks for the Fourth Review Conference of the Biological Weapons Convention.* Geneva, Switzerland: US Arms Control and Disarmament Agency, November 26, 1996.

Janofsky, M., "Looking for motives in plague case", *New York Times,* May 24, 1995:A12.

Kaplan, D.E., Marshall, A., *The Cult at the End of the World,* New York, NY: Crown Publishers Inc., 1996:55.

Merck, G.W., Fred, E.B., Baldwin, I.L., Sarles, W.B., *Implications of Biological Warfare: The US and UN Report Series No. 5.* Washington, DC: US Dept of State, 1946:65-71.

Meselson, M., Guillemin, J., Hugh-Jones, M., et al., The Sverdlovsk anthrax outbreak of 1979. *Science,* 1994;266:1202-1208.

National Security Study Memorandum 59. Washington, DC: National Security Council, May 28, 1969:1.

Morganthau, T., "A shadow over the Olympics", *Newsweek,* May 6,1996:34.

Office of the President, White House. Speech to the UNGeneral Assembly; September 24, 1996; Washington, DC. Press release.

Sciolino E., "Iraqis could pose a threat soon, CIA chief says", *New York Times International,* January 16, 1992:A9.

Spertzel R., *Sampling and Analysis as a Monitoring Tool,* New York, NY: UN Special Commission, October 3, 1996:7.

Star, B., Iraq reveals astartling rangeof toxin agents. *Jane's Defence, Weekly,* November, 11, 1995:4.

US Army Activity in the US Biological Warfare Programs, I. Washington, DC: US Army, 1977.

US Arms Control and Disarmament Agency. *Arms and Control Disarmament Agreements: Texts and Histories of the Negotiations.* Washington, DC: US Arms Control and Disarmament Agency, 1996.

_______________ , *Fact Sheet: The Biological Weapons Convention.* Washington, DC: US Arms Control and Disarmament Agency; August 18, 1993.

Urban, M., "The Cold War's deadliest secret", *The Spectator Magazine,* January 23, 1993:9-10.

US Dept of the Army, *Lessons Learned From Operation Desert Shield / Desert Storm,* Washington, DC: US Dept of the Army, July 19, 1991.

Williams P., Wallace, D., *Unit 731: Japan's Secret Biological Warfare in World War II,* New York, NY: Free Press, 1989:28.

Zilinskas, R.A., "Iraq's biological weapons: the past as future", *JAMA,* 1997, 278:418-424.

9

Combating Biological Terrorism

Biological warfare is a massive destructive one so that it now ranks as a strategic threat to the international society, one that represents such potential widespread and profound suffering as to cause significant political consequences. International as well as national organisations are deeply engaged to detect, defeat, prevent and proliferate Weapons of Mass Destruction (WMD), terrorism. Within WMD biological terrorism is of particular concern because of its unique combination of lethal effects, relative ease of manufacture, and possibility of covert deployment. Seen as a strategic threat, the potential for biological terrorism raises critical issues of the proper relation between civilian and military sectors; state and local authorities; and domestic and international affairs.

The threat of terrorists using biological warfare (BW) agents has received increased attention in recent years. Congressional hearings, research studies, government warnings, and commentaries have all pointed to a potentially more ominous terrorism future. Many factors account for this concern revelations—that Iraq, a state sponsor of terrorism, stockpiled anthrax, botulinum toxin, and other BW agents during the Persian Gulf War; the discovery that Aum Shinrikyo, the Japanese religious cult that released the chemical agent sarin in the Tokyo subway system in 1995, had a research and development programme for BW agents; the low cost and minimum scientific knowledge required for producing BW agents; and the tendency for terrorists to move into new areas of violence when current ones no longer achieve the intended effect— publicity, reaction, chaos.

Despite this growing concern, however, we still know very little about the nature of BW terrorism. There has never been a major BW terrorist attack. Therefore, there is no track record of incidents, groups, tactics, motives, and targets for analysis to determine the best strategies for combating this global threat. In this regard, we are today with respect to BW terrorism where we were nearly 30 years ago with respect to conventional terrorism.

A new international threat was emerging then, but it was unclear as to the direction it would take. It took several years after the first major international hijacking in 1968 for the diverse nature of conventional terrorism (hijackings, bombings, hostage situations) to become clear and for governments to take action against the threat.

Biological warfare terrorism will not allow governments, publics, and the international community the luxury of time to watch this threat unfold and then determine the proper responses. Since BW terrorist attacks could have catastrophic effects in terms of lives lost and create a medical, political, and social crisis unparalleled in our history, it is important to prepare now for this new age of terrorism we are today with respect to BW terrorism where we were nearly 30 years ago with respect to conventional terrorism.

To combat the threat of bioterrorism successfully we must address some important challenges.

The first challenge is to be aware that an act of bioterrorism could happen. We have seen terrorism emerge as one of the thorniest problems of the post-cold war era, and we have seen that terrorists are always searching for new weapons. Somewhere, sometime in the future, terrorists may well threaten to use, or attempt to use, a biological weapon and we may not be always aware of it.

We should accept the reality that we will not be able to prevent every act of BW terrorism. Governments have learned that painful lesson with respect to conventional terrorism. While preventive measures must continue to be pursued, the greatest payoff in fighting BW terrorism lies in improving our response to an incident. There will be more opportunity for saving lives in the emergency medical response to a BW terrorist attack than in response to a conventional terrorist attack. Whereas most of the fatalities in a conventional terrorist bombing occur immediately or shortly after the explosion, in BW terrorism the incubation period for the virus, bacterium, or toxin could be several days.

The second challenge is to be prepared. The US Department of Health and Human Services (HHS) is spending $158 million this fiscal year to prepare for bioterorrism and why the president has proposed increasing that investment by an additional $72 million in his Fiscal Year 2000 budget. This investment will fund our ongoing Anti-Bioterrorism Initiative. To increase our level of preparedness, the initiative is expanding its activities in a number of key areas: surveillance, medical and public health response, building a stockpile of drugs and supplies, and research and development.

The third challenge is for the public health and medical communities to take the lead in our fight against bioterrorism. In a conventional terrorist attack, local first responders, such as the police, firefighters, and paramedics, constitute the first line of defence. With bioterrorism, the public health and medical communities stand directly on the front lines. How well we respond to a threat or attack will depend on the prepared-ness of our public health and medical communities.

For example, if a bioterrorist threat is issued—perhaps someone claims to have released a deadly pathogen in a public place—physicians must be able to recognise and report cases that come to attention in emergency rooms and doctors' offices; public health officials must be able to conduct investigations to establish the likely site/time of exposure, the size and location of the exposed population, and the prospects for secondary transmission; and appropriately trained laboratory personnel must be available to identify the biological agent. Whether the release of a bioweapon is announced or surreptitious, affected persons may not have symptoms for days or even weeks, and by then they would be geographically dispersed.

Quarantine is not practical because only one of the major biological agents—smallpox—is communicable. Even with smallpox, it would be impossible to know whom to quarantine because of the spread of disease by secondary transmission and the difficulty in accurately identifying those who have been exposed. A strong electronic communications network would be needed to piece together early reports, as well as epidemiologic and laboratory data, to determine what had happened so that public health and law enforcement officials can take prompt action. The Centres for Disease Control and Prevention would play an important role in this process because of its particular expertise in surveillance, infectious disease, and public health. Everyone from the physicians who first see victims to the scientists who identify the infectious agents must coordinate their efforts.

The medical and health communities will therefore play the most significant role in combating BW terrorism, and they will have to carry out their duties at a time of unprecedented crisis and fear throughout the country. To the extent that we can reduce the uncertainty about how BW terrorist incidents are likely to unfold, the better the medical and health professions will be prepared to deal with the aftermath of this most dangerous form of global terrorism.

The most distinguishing feature separating BW terrorism from conventional terrorism is the extraordinarily larger number of casualties that could follow a major terrorist attack involving biological agents. Whereas bombings of airplanes or buildings with conventional explosives have occasionally resulted in a few hundred deaths, each act of BW terrorism could result in hundreds of thousands or even millions of casualties.

Adding to the death toll would be the fact that civilian populations are not immunised against most BW agents and do not have protective equipment, such as filtered respirators and gas masks, readily available. Some biological agents have been used in the past for selective attacks. For example, Bulgarian agents assassinated Georgi Markov, a Bulgarian emigre and writer for the British Broadcasting Company, by stabbing him in London with an umbrella-type weapon that contained ricin, which is a potent protein toxin derived from the bean of the castor plant *(Ricinus communis)*. However, a terrorist group that uses BW agents will likely be attracted to the mass killing potential of these weapons. It makes little sense for terrorists to experiment with dangerous biological agents— they could be killed handling and using them—if their goal is a limited attack that could have been achieved by using safer and more familiar conventional weapons.

Biological warfare terrorism will also encompass a narrower range of tactics than conventional terrorism. Although BW agents could be used during a hijacking or hostage situation, there would be little incentive for terrorists to do so. The projected death toll would be no higher than if conventional weapons were used. And while BW agents could be delivered against a target by means of a bomb or missile, the likelihood that the organisms will be destroyed in the explosion makes this an unattractive delivery method.

The most likely BW terrorist tactic will be to release BW agents—anthrax spores, botulinum toxin, ricin, or other deadly agents—into the air as a biological aerosol, astable cloud of suspended microscopic droplets of bacterial or virus particles.

Since BW agents are invisible, odourless, and tasteless, no one would know that a terrorist attack is under way. The aerosol release of BW agents could be accomplished in several ways, including using low-flying airplanes, crop dusters, or trucks equipped with spray tanks and releasing the BW agent upwind of populated areas; leaving aerosol canisters filled with the BW agent and timing devices in subways, airports, air-conditioning/heating systems in buildings, or other crowded places; or directly contaminating bulk food supplies in restaurants, supermarkets, or other places with a BW agent. However, large US water supplies such as a city water supply would not be an attractive target for contamination due to the large amount of BW agent required and water purification procedures used by most cities in the United States.

Since there are no reliable detection systems for BW agents, terrorists will be able to strike any target they desire. Whereas terrorists with conventional weapons have to be concerned about metal detectors, X-ray machines, and other physical security measures, terrorists with BW agents do not face those means of detection. With maximum casualties, the likely goal, metropolitan areas, are the most at risk.

Hearings held in 1995 and 1996, the US Senate Permanent Subcommittee on Investigations, for example, found that the United States did not have a plan that coordinated federal, state, and local agencies in managing the consequences of a terrorist attack with a weapon of mass destruction. The subcommittee also found that principal field officers with police, fire, and emergency service departments in major cities are inadequately trained and do not have basic equipment to deal with biological, chemical, or nuclear terrorism, including protective gear, breathing apparatus, decontaminants, and antidotes. The lack of preparedness is attributable to two factors mainly:

i) Since the casualties from a biological terrorist incident are so disturbing even to think about, many public officials cling to the hope that with the right mix of police, security measures, and intelligence gathering, BW terrorism can be prevented. Funding for emergency responses to BW terrorism therefore has not been given the high priority it deserves until very recently.

ii) the difficult task of planning for an event that has never occurred before. Emergency response teams are therefore left only with alternative scenarios to guide them in their plans.

An amendment to the 1997 Defence Authorisation Act addresses some of these issues by calling for better training, equipment, and coordination among emergency response personnel in the United States to deal with a terrorist incident involving a weapon of mass destruction. There is also a need for hospitals to have adequate supplies—or ways to quickly obtain these supplies—of antibiotics and antitoxins that could be used to treat those exposed to BW agents. Medical personnel also should be trained to recognise the different symptoms of various BW agents so that those exposed can be treated quickly.

Most physicians do not see cases of anthrax in their daily practices. Since BW agents are invisible, odourless, and tasteless, no one would know that a terrorist attack is under way. An important part of the response to BW terrorism will be dealing with the psychological reactions among survivors, emergency workers, and the public. Terrorism is a form of psychological warfare with terrorists often perpetrating their violence to cause fear among the public. In BW terrorism, that fear will understandably be great as people watch their fellow citizens fall ill and possibly die in large numbers due to anthrax, botulism, or other diseases.

Contingency plans for dealing with public hysteria and disruption of health care delivery systems—including the possibility of health care professionals' becoming ill from the BW attack, or fleeing the affected area if they are not confident that they have adequate equipment to protect themselves—should be established in every large city. The mental health of emergency workers and medical personnel will have to be monitored during a BW terrorism crisis. Research indicates that the most traumatic events for emergency nurses are the death of a child and the death of a co-worker.

During a BW terrorist incident, rescue workers will face the unique situation of dealing with large numbers of deaths in a setting that otherwise seems very normal. There will not be any collapsed or bombed-outbuildings, fires, plane crashes, and so forth. The psychological impact of that situation on first responders needs to be addressed in contingency plans. The Critical Incident Stress Debriefing (CISD) process could help in dealing with the psychological aspects of a BW terrorist attack. This process is part of a broad crisis intervention programme known as Critical Incident Stress Management (CISM), which is designed to prevent or mitigate the development of adverse psychological reactions among emergency service and public safety personnel, nurses, physicians, and disaster workers. The programme has been used during earthquakes, plane crashes, terrorist bombings, and other tragic events.

Through various psychological intervention techniques, a CISD team led by mental health professionals and including peer support personnel from the emergency services can help emergency workers and medical personnel recover as quickly as possible from the stress associated with the crisis. A potential problem, however, is that some CISD and CISM teams could become a hindrance to first-responders. They might interfere with the duties of emergency service personnel, or inadvertently aggravate the emotional trauma being experienced by making incorrect assessments of mental health needs. It is therefore crucial that CISD and CISM teams be properly trained for crisis intervention services. The military will also play an important role in the aftermath of a BW terrorist attack. They will be called on to assist federal and local authorities, just as they have helped local communities.

The fight against terrorism is a shared imperative for the democracies and must become one for all nations. It isn't someone else's war into which we are supposedly being dragged, it is a necessary and methodical offensive to which we shall freely devote all our efforts. It calls for solidarity and cooperation. As the objective of his country's response to the attack of September 11, 2001, the United States president has set the identification and punishment of the perpetrators and, going beyond this, the dismantling of the terrorist networks, thanks to the cooperation of the countries in which they are established. Keen to build an international coalition without excluding anyone, aware of the risks involved if they were to take reprisals which were not understood or provoked outrage, the Americans have adopted a long-term, many-sided strategy, of which the use of arms will be only one aspect.

Since 11 September, two United Nations Security Council Resolutions have specified the international legal framework within which nations' responses to terrorist acts must be carried out. UNSCR 1368, describing the attacks of 11 September—and any act of international terrorism—as a threat to peace and international security, has recognised the applicability to such acts of the right of individual or collective legitimate self-defence, thus providing a legal basis for resorting to force. The Security Council's call for all states to work together to combat terrorism and implement in full the relevant international conventions, forms a genuine international instrument, whose use is incumbent on states, for fighting terrorism. It demands from them full cooperation and their immediate implementation of an exhaustive set of drastic measures, designed in particular to end in transfers of funds to people or organisations involved in terrorist acts.

The danger that darkened the United States of America and the civilised world on September 11, 2001 did not pass with the atrocities committed that day. Today we seek to meet the challenge of terrorism within our borders and targeted at our friends and neighbours with the same careful regard for the constitutional rights of Americans and respect for all human beings. The deficiencies of our current laws on terrorism reflect two facts:

i) The laws fail to make defeating terrorism a national priority. Indeed, we have tougher laws against organised crime and drug trafficking than terrorism.

ii) Technology has dramatically outpaced our statutes.

Law enforcement tools created decades ago were crafted for rotary telephones—not e-mail, the internet, mobile communications and voice mail. Every day that passes with outdated statutes and the old rules of engagement is a day that terrorists have a competitive advantage.

Law enforcement needs a strengthened and streamlined ability for intelligence-gathering agencies to gather the information necessary to disrupt, weaken and eliminate the infrastructure of terrorist organisations. We also need the authority for law enforcement to share vital information with our national security agencies in order to prevent future terrorist attacks. Terrorist organisations have increasingly used technology to facilitate their criminal acts and hide their communications from law enforcement.

Intelligence-gathering laws that were written for the era of land-line telephone communications are ill-adapted for use in communications over multiple cell phones and computer networks—communications that are also carried by multiple telecommunications providers located in different jurisdictions. Terrorists are trained to change cell phones frequently and to route e-mail through different internet computers in order to defeat surveillance. We need speed in identifying and tracking down terrorists. The ability of law enforcement to trace communications into different jurisdictions without obtaining an additional court order can be the difference between life and death of the citizens.

In the fight against bioterrorism, there should be that participation of all countrymen. The government has a leadership role. Among other things, we need to support state and local planning efforts, provide training at every level, develop an infrastructure for delivering mass medical care, and offer expertise to our communities. This is a fight we certainly cannot win by ourselves. Across the board, we must forge new working partnerships among health, public safety, and intelligence agencies. We need unprecedented cooperation among the federal government, state and local health agencies, and the medical community. We must ensure that plans for managing the medical consequences of terrorist acts are well integrated and coordinated with other emergency response systems.

An act of bioterrorism cannot be contained by any national border or barrier. When it comes to microbes, we are not protected. Since these organisms recognise no boundaries, in our battle against them, neither can we. Since we share a common future, we must share a common resolve.

REFERENCES

Danzig, R., Berkowsky, P.B., "Why should we be concerned about biological warfare?", *J. Am. Med. Assoc.,* 1997; 278:431-443.

Defense Nuclear Agency (DNA) Biological Weapons Proliferation. *Global Proliferation: Dynamics, Acquisition Strategies and Response,* Alexandria, Va: Defense Nuclear Agency, 1994;4:10.

Ekeus, R., *Memorandum to the Biological Weapons Convention Fourth Review Conference,* New York, NY: United Nations; November 20, 1996.

Geissler E., *Biological and Toxin Weapons Today*, New York, NY: Oxford University Press Inc., 1986.

Merck, G.W., Fred, E.B., Baldwin, I.L., Sarles, W.B., *Implications of Biological Warfare: The US and UN Report Series No. 5.* Washington, DC: US Dept. of State, 1946:65-71.

US Army Activity in the US Biological Warfare Programs, I. Washington, DC: US Army, 1977.

Kupperman, R. H., Smith, D.M., "Coping with Biological Terrorism", In Roberts, B., ed. , *Biological Weapons: Weapons of the Future*? Washington, DC: Centre for Strategic and International Studies, 1993.

Simon, J.D., "Biological Terrorism: Preparing to Meet the Threat", *JAMA*, 1997; 278:428-430.

______________ , *The New Age of Terrorism*, Boston Globe, April 19,1996:19.

Sims N.A., *The Diplomacy of Biological Disarmament*, New York, NY: Plenum Press, 1983.

Stockholm International Peace Research Institute (SPIRI), *The Rise of CB Weapons: The Problem of Chemical and Biological Warfare*, New York, NY: Humanities Press, 1971;1.

WHO Group of Consultants, *Health Aspects of Chemical and Biological Weapons*, Geneva, Switzerland: World Health Organisation, 1970.

10

Biological Terrorism: Future Concerns

Biological weapons are used by terrorists to kill and sicken thousands of innocent citizens indiscriminately or to cause large-scale damage to agriculture by killing economically valuable animals or crops. It is fairly easy to mount a biological attack with foodborne pathogens, which are not difficult to procure and propagate. This type of attack can certainly cause many people to become ill but is not likely to kill them.

Special technical skill and knowledge are necessary to develop biological weapons capable of killing large numbers of people. The most effective way for terrorists to do so is to disperse virulent pathogens in an aerosol over the population they want to eliminate. Several pathogens lend themselves to this purpose, including the bacterial species that cause anthrax, tularemia, plague, and Q fever, as well as the viruses that cause Venezuelan equine encephalitis and haemorrhagic fevers.

Not many people possess the skill and knowledge to develop mass-casualty biological weapons and of those who do, most are not interested in doing work related to biological weapons. The person or group responsible for the letters containing *Bacillus anthracis* spores appears to possess a significant capability in microbiology, but perhaps a lesser capability in engineering.

There are solid evidences which prove that terrorists indeed used biological weapons against unsuspecting populations since the early centuries. The current history of bioterrorism begins with the event occurred in the small towns of USA, in 1984, attempted by the Rajneeshees cult to win a local election that would give it control of the county government. The cult tried to keep voters in the small town of Dallas, Oregon, away from the polls by sickening them with the foodborne pathogen salmonella. Its method of attack was to simultaneously contaminate salad bars in 10 restaurants and one supermarket with a solution containing this pathogen. The cult failed to reach its objective, but the cost of the attack to the community was high; although no one died, 751 of the town's inhabitants became sick with gastro-intestinal disease.

Between 1991 and 1993 the Japanese cult Aum Shinrikyo disseminated on at least nine occasions aerosol containing botulinum toxin or *Bacillus anthracis*, but not a single person became sick. The cult's scientists, highly trained biologists working in well-furnished laboratories, had made some basic mistakes that resulted in the creation of a foul-smelling, mud-like concoction with no pathogenic properties.

Representatives of the United States inteligence community have stated that between seven and nine countries have biological weapons or are trying to acquire them. Some of these countries, including Iran, Iraq, North Korea, and Syria, have also been named by the State Department as supporting terrorist groups. Article 3 of the 1972 Biological and Toxin Weapons Convention (BWC) specifies that signatory states cannot transfer biological weapons or relevant knowledge to any recipient whatsoever, directly or indirectly.

It is widely known that Iraq operated an extensive and fairly sophisticated biological warfare (BW) programme until its defeat in the Persian Gulf war in early 1991. Iraqi workers, under the supervision of the post-war United Nations Special Commission (UNSCOM), completely levelled the mail Iraqi BW production plant, Al Hakam, and parts of a subsidiary facility at the Foot and Mouth Disease Vaccine Production Plant during 1996. In addition, the Iraqis themselves destroyed their main

BW research facility at Salman Pak before the first UNSCOM inspector arrived in August 1991.

The workforce of Iraqi BW programme consisting of scientists and engineers who developed biological weapons based on *Bacillus anthracis*, botulinum toxin, and aflatoxin could return to this kind of work immediately. At least 80 facilities in Iraq possess varying degrees of biological capabilities, ranging from dairy production plants to sophisticated university laboratories where genetic engineering experiments are performed. Many of them could be used as a cover for a dedicated BW facility. All the types of equipment necessary for the development and large-scale production of pathogens and toxins can be found in one or more of the existing biological facilities and could easily be transferred. We do not know whether a biological attack to a new development capable of causing mass casualties is in the offing, and production plant dedicated to BW.

The Iraqis maintain seed cultures of the bacteria they weaponised, as well as fungi and viruses that were researched for this purpose but were not yet weaponised by the time of defeat in April 1991. A seed culture can quickly be reconstituted and used to propagate a large quantity of pathogens or toxin-producing bacteria. In possessing this combination of elements trained workers, adequate facilities, ample equipment, and appropriate seed cultures, Iraq could immediately resume the production of biological weapons, including pathogen and toxin-filled missiles, bombs, artillery shells, and sprayer-equipped unmanned aerial vehicles, should the command be given.

UNSCOM inspectors have uncovered information indicating that Iraq president Saddam Hussein ordered the establishment of the Iraqi BW programme in 1985. No Iraqi decisionmaker has explained why this was done, but it was probably related to equipping the Iraqi military with a weapon that would enable it to conduct operations against Iran more effectively. After the Iran-Iraq war (1980-1988) ended, Saddam

Hussein's motive for acquiring WMD was to gain the strategic military capability to dominate the Middle East.

The heart of Iraq's WMD programme was long-range missiles that could be fitted with nuclear, chemical, or biological warheads. Iraq's defeat in 1991 thus came at an opportune time for the international community because had Iraq's weapons scientists and engineers been given another two or three years to perfect their creations, they would have been able to supply the Iraqi military with medium-range missiles, effective biological and chemical weapons, and possibly a nuclear device.

Today, where Iraq's obvious military weakness precludes any possibility of it establishing regional hegemony the Iraqi leadership may be more interested in exacting retribution for perceived wrongs done in the past by the coalition, with the United States at the top of the list. The United States led the coalition forces that defeated Iraq and, in the process, caused a large number of Iraqi casualties. The United States was the major supporter of UNSCOM, supplying by far most of its inspectors and the equipment that enabled them to do their work.

It is imperative for nations to strengthen the Biological Weapons Convention. Although the strictures of the convention bind only its signatory nations, it is an appropriate starting point for controlling the global spread and deployment of biological weapons. But on July 25, 2001, USA decided that it would not support a protocol to the BWC that would have included legally binding provisions that specified measures to investigate alleged violations of the treaty and unusual outbreaks of disease, and to institute the transparency of certain microbiology and biotechnology activities. With the protocol now dead, the Bush administration must offer strong, practical ideas to strengthen the BWC.

The dangers posed by biological weapons did not disappear when the United States began to unilaterally dismantle its own offensive programme in 1969. The dangers did not vanish with the signing of the Biological and Toxin Weapons Convention of 1972, and they did not dissipate with the end of the Cold War or the threat of nuclear retaliation against Iraq during the Persian Gulf conflict. Only by planning and investing in the right training and defensive measures can we diminish the likelihood that biological weapons will be used and reduce the risks, disruption, and casualties in the event that such weapons are used.

Biological weapons are characterised by low visibility, high potency, substantial accessibility, and relatively easy delivery. The basic facts are well known: a millionth of a gram of anthrax constitutes a lethal inhalation dose. A kilogramme, depending on meteorological conditions and means of delivery, has the potential to kill hundreds of thousands of people in a metropolitan area. These small quantities make the concealment, transportation, and dissemination of biological agents relatively easy.

Many of these agents—bacteria, viruses, and toxins—occur naturally in the environment. Moreover, many are used for wholly legitimate medical purposes, and much of the technology required to produce and weaponise them is available for civilian or military use. Unlike nuclear weapons, missiles or other advanced systems are not required for the delivery of biological weapons.

Since aerosolisation is the predominant method of dissemination, extraordinarily low-technology methods, including agricultural crop dusters, back-pack sprayers, and even purse-size perfume atomizers will suffice. Small groups of people with modest finances and basic training in biology and engineering can develop an effective biological weapons capability. Recipes for making biological weapons are even available on the internet.

The delayed effects and vulnerability to weather make biological weapons ill-suited to military purposes such as seizing territory. But biological weapons can effectively impede the mobilisation and massing of troops that would be required to sustain our role in a conventional conflict. They can be used to threaten civilian populations and create mass panic. Used this way, biological weapons can achieve military goals by undercutting the civilian support necessary for military operations or by holding civilians hostage to prevent military operations. Since defence against a biological attack is both unfamiliar and difficult, there is a natural tendency to put it aside in favour of problems that are more comfortable.

The belief that because biological weapons have never been used they therefore never will be. And this is in turn buttressed by a sense that a regime can be deterred from using biological weaponry if we make it clear that this would invite nuclear retaliation. These modes of thought are dangerously inappropriate. If we address deterrence first, many argue that Saddam Hussein's unwillingness to unleash Iraq's biological arsenal, in the face of not so subtle threats of nuclear retaliation, validates the primacy of our deterrent. However, nations are not the only potential users of biological weapons. If one of the most likely scenarios entails their use by non-state actors, small groups, or even individuals, a nuclear deterrent may be ineffective. Of course, terrorists can often be associated with state sponsors, but the quantum of proof we would require before responding to such a perceived linkage with a nuclear attack would be awfully high.

That biological weapons will not be used in the future because they have not been used in the past is based on an error of fact. History is replete with examples in which biological weapons have been used, including the following in the Middle Ages infected cadavers were catapulted over the walls of European cities and castles under siege; in the French and Indian Wars, the British supplied Indians with smallpox-infected blankets; during World War II, Japanese Unit 731 experimented with biological weapons on prisoners of war in Manchuria, resulting in more than 1,000 deaths. There are also abundant examples that bring the threat much closer to home. In 1995, two members of a Minnesota militia group were convicted of possession of ricin, which they had produced themselves for use in retaliation against local government officials. In 1996, an Ohio man with connections to an extremist group was able to obtain bubonic plague cultures through the postal service. It has even come to light that Aum Shinrikyo, the Japanese cult organisation responsible for the sarin attacks on the Tokyo subway system, was working on anthrax and botulism as weapons. The group's biological capability, its production and testing and laboratory infrastructure, and its experimental delivery systems existed for years while escaping detection by Western intelligence.

World War I brought chemists and war fighters together; World War II brought physicists into the fold; and the cold war represented an era of the primacy of the computing, telecommunications, and electronics communities in the defense arena. What little connection the US government maintained with the biological community dissipated when, in 1969, we foreswore any offensive biological and toxin weapon capability. The United Nations' inspections of Iraq after the Persian Gulf conflict should be a wake-up call in this regard. Along with the information of a high-level defector who had responsibility for Iraq's unconventional weapons programme, these inspections revealed a large-scale biological production and weaponisation effort that had gone substantially undetected by the West.

The US Department of Defence has embarked on a challenging programme to enhance its capabilities to defend against biological warfare. The programme includes, among other things, the development and fielding of state-of-the-art biodetectors; the creation and designation of selected military units with expertise in medical prophylaxis, hazard mitigation, and decontamination; investments in vaccine and antibiotic research, development, and stockpiling; refinement and acquisition of masks and improvements in air filtration systems to preclude infection via inhalation; improved intelligence collection and analysis; enhanced training; and the development of doctrine regarding how to pre-empt and, when necessary, respond to a biological attack. An additional critical element of this programme, however, is the need for an enhanced relationship between the military and those agencies charged with protecting the civilian population of the United States.

In that regard, biological weapons necessarily alter our strategic thinking about national security and the nature of warfare. Wars may not always be fought on set-piece traditional battlefields, and it is time to throw away the anachronistic notion that the military's only role is to defend the United States against threats on foreign soil.

In the event of a domestic incident of biological weapons use, no matter who the perpetrator, it is unlikely that the response would be left to local law enforcement and health officials or even to the Federal Bureau of Investigation, the Federal Emergency Management Agency, or the US Public Health Service. The military would undoubtedly be called on because of its resources, capabilities, and expertise. At the same time, if a biological incident were to occur in a military context, the Department of Defence would look to and need the help of such civilian agencies as the Centres for Disease Control and Prevention (CDC). Although achieving it is one of our greatest challenges, an enhanced cooperation between military and civilian institutions is also likely to pay big dividends. To facilitate and enhance this civil-military cooperation, US Congress recently enacted the Defence Against Weapons of Mass Destruction Act of 1996, which seeks to enhance our domestic preparedness in several fundamental ways, including the following: by strengthening the federal government's ability to prevent and respond to terrorist incidents involving weapons of mass destruction; by enabling the Department of Defence and other federal supports to state and local prevention and response efforts; and by improving the capabilities of state and local emergency responders themselves. More than 100 cities in the United States have already been designated under the provisions of this legislation; their fire, police, rescue, and hospital emergency department personnel will receive training and equipment in an ambitious programme conducted by the Department of Defence that began this summer.

The good news wrapped inside the particular problems posed by biological weapons is that in this arena, public health is the best form of civil defence. Our everyday domestic investments to detect and diagnose disease can and should be strengthened because of our national security trends.

FUTURE OF BIOLOGICAL WEAPONS

The new scientific developments in microbiology were used both for the benefit of civil society and in preparation for use in warfare, continued throughout the twentieth century. A number of European countries, as well as Japan, developed bioweapons during the 1930s and 1940s, fuelled in part by inflated intelligence estimates of the biological warfare capabilities of others. Japan went on to use biological weapons extensively against China in the Second World War, causing substantial mortality.

In the post-war period at least three countries—the United States, the United Kingdom and the Soviet Union—are known to have had large, ambitious programmes of biological weapons development. The offensive programmes of the United States and the United Kingdom were discontinued in the 1960s; that of the Soviet Union lasted at least until its break-up.

More recently, Iraq is known to have had a small, but mature, biological weapons programme. The facilities and munitions were largely destroyed by UNSCOM, but concerns about its resurgence in the absence of UN monitoring remain. Intelligence analysts of many countries believe that several developing countries currently have covert biological weapons programmes.

The background papers produced by States Parties to the Biological and Toxin Weapons Convention (BTWC) for the Review Conferences every five years have shown an increasing sense of concern about the potential impact of the new revolution in biology. This revolution began in the 1970s with a set of techniques known as genetic engineering, or recombinant DNA technology, and has since been expanded by the development of rapid DNA sequencing technology that has led to the field of genomics —the extraction of information from complete DNA sequences of organisms, and the analysis and cataloguing of that information.

A second aspect of this revolution has been the increasingly precise understanding of the physical chemistry of protein folding and of the diversity and mutual interactions of the many thousands of different proteins in the living cell, a field generally known as proteomics. Thus a set of immensely powerful experimental and modelling techniques have become available in the last few decades that allow an unprecedented capability to modify living organisms and their products in precise and predictable ways, and to design small molecules to interact in specific ways with proteins in living organisms to alter their functioning in predictable ways.

Dangers that could arise from new scientific and technological developments in microbiology were well understood at the time that the BTWC was negotiated. As the revolution in genetic engineering got underway it is therefore not surprising that specific concerns began to be expressed at Review Conferences that the new technological developments might have applications to offensive biological weapons development. The first concern articulated was that they might allow the easier production of militarily significant quantities of toxins. Thus the final declaration of the Second Review Conference in 1986 noted that in regard to Article I, on the scope of the prohibition:

> The Conference reaffirms that the Convention unequivocally applies to all natural or artificially created microbial or other biological agents or toxins whatever their origin or method of production. Consequently, toxins (both proteinaceous and non-proteinaceous) of a microbial, animal or vegetable nature and their synthetically produced analogues are covered. (emphasis added).

The Final Declaration of the Third Review Conference in 1991 was much more wide-ranging in regard to its concerns about how scientific and technological developments might impact on Article I, stating:

> The Conference, conscious of apprehensions arising from relevant scientific and technological developments, *inter alia*, in the fields of microbiology, biotechnology, molecular biology, genetic engineering and any application resulting from genome studies, and the possibilities of their use for purposes inconsistent with the objectives and provisions of the Convention, reaffirms that the undertakings given by the States Parties in Article I applies to all such developments. The Conference also reaffirms that the Convention unequivocally covers all microbial or other biological agents or toxins, naturally or artificially created or altered, whatever their origin or method of production. (emphasis added).

By the time of the Fourth Conference of the BTWC in 1996 these concerns had been clearly extended to genomics, the Final Declaration stating:

> The Conference, conscious of apprehensions arising from relevant scientific and technological developments, *inter alia*, in the fields of microbiology, biotechnology, molecular biology, genetic engineering, and any application resulting from genome studies, and the possibilities of their use for purposes inconsistent with the objectives and the provisions of the Convention, reaffirms that the undertaking given by the States Parties in *Article I applies to all such developments*.

The States Parties to the BTWC see the potential impact of new scientific and technological developments as an increasingly serious problem.

A proliferator nowadays is likely to attempt initially to weaponise the agents which have been weaponised previously in major offensive programmes, or other unmodified organisms. Thus the classical agents developed in the middle of the twentieth century by the United States—anthrax, botulinal toxin, tularemia, etc.—would likely be the first agents of choice. Such agents, having already been proven to be effective, would require limited retesting by the proliferator.

However, after the development of a functional biological weapons programme along classical line, it seems probable that agents would be further developed through genetic engineering techniques. For example, an official American study in 1997 suggested that the following novel agents might be produced:

i) benign micro-organisms, genetically altered to produce a toxin, venom or bioregulator;
ii) microorganisms resistant to antibiotics, standard vaccines and therapies;
iii) microorganisms with enhanced aerosol and environmental stability;
iv) immunologically altered microorganisms able to defeat standard identification, detection and diagnostic methods; and
v) combinations of the above four types with improved delivery systems.

According to the study, it was difficult to predict what might happen as a result of further developments in biotechnology, but noted that there were clearly trends in current work which could affect biological weapon possibilities. Before we go on to review these trends, it is necessary to consider the use of biological weapons from a wider perspective than just the use of highly lethal agents against human beings. Biological agents were used to attack draft animals in the First World War. Anthrax bacteria were also weaponised for use against the German cattle industry by the British in the Second World War, although never used. The fungal agents *Puccinia graminis tritici* and *Pyricularia oryzae* were weaponised in the American biological weapons programme during and after the war. Strategic application leading to considerable food shortages was the intended use of these stockpiles.

In the current world, use of these and other agents to attack the agricultural sector of a target country would more likely be for economic reasons, and the consequences could include international trade sanctions whose economic impact could far exceed the direct costs of disease mortality and morbidity. In regard to the use of anti-personnel biological agents, it is of course true that highly lethal weapons such as anthrax, plague and smallpox have been weaponised, and that massive strategic attacks producing enormous casualties—essentially use of biological weapons of mass destruction—would be possible.

Yet lethal biological weapons could also be used on a smaller scale for tactical purposes. Non-military use of lethal agents could also be undertaken on a range of scales by terrorists. Furthermore, non-lethal biological agents could be used as incapacitants in different types of operations. While thinking about biological warfare and the potential impact of new technology, we have to keep in mind that we are not just dealing with one particular type of weapon and how it might be changed. We are dealing with many different kinds of potential weapon systems, many different ways they could be used, and, as we shall see, many different ways in which they could perhaps be modified.

The genomics revolution will open up many new civil technological possibilities and form the basis of major industrial investment and growth in the coming decades. It is at the heart of a linked set of developments which will transform human life. The biotech century brings with it a new resource base, a new set of transforming technologies, new forms of commercial protection to spur commerce, a global trading market, an emerging eugenics science, a new supporting sociology, a new communications tool and a new cosmological narrative to accompany the journey.

Massive reorganisations are taking place in the pharmaceutical and chemical industries to take advantage of the new opportunities for medical drug discovery and profit. In short, the economic opportunities opened up by the new science are likely to ensure that there is ample money available for new technological innovations to be exploited and developed in civil industry. Given the dual-use (civil and military) nature of such technology, there will necessarily be many ways in which biological agents and their products, resulting from civil developments, can be manipulated for military purposes.

For the biologist, understanding the structure of the genome, though useful and interesting, is but the beginning of the story. The real aim is to have a complete understanding of how the structure works—that is, to have an understanding of functional genomics. The Human Genome Project is best understood as the twentieth century version of the discovery and consolidation of the periodic table. The Project aims to produce biology's periodic table—not 100 elements, but 100,000 genes—a tree structure depicting ancestral and functional affinities among the human genes. There would be a range of new goals like:

i) systematic identification of all common variants in human genes;
ii) simultaneous monitoring of the expression of all genes;
iii) genetic tools for manipulating cell circuitry;
iv) monitoring the level and modification state of all proteins;
v) systematic catalogues of protein interactions; and
vi) identification of all basic protein shapes.

Functional genomics will follow on from structural genomics and will have the initial aim of understanding the mechanistic details of cellular functioning and how the information encoded in the DNA determines the properties of the organism. This understanding will then allow manipulation for particular human objectives. One aspect of this scientific and technological revolution very difficult for those of us living through it to grasp is the sheer rate of change. This results both from the opportunities that arise within genomics itself but also from its interaction in complex ways with other scientific and technological developments. Clearly, for example, the revolution in computing and information technology has provided tools essential to handle the vast amounts of information on DNA sequences and protein structures generated and used in the genomics revolution.

However, genomics also affects other scientific areas. Within neuroscience, for example, over the last decade there has been an explosion of knowledge about the receptor systems on nerve cells that are of critical importance in receiving the chemical transmitter substances released by other nerve cells. This level of structural information has only become available because of the application of genomic techniques in neurobiology.

Along with the advent of cloning and expression techniques has come the ability to manipulate gene expression *in vivo*, which represents perhaps the most powerful method to analyse (receptor) function to date. Once a gene has been cloned, it is thus possible to delete it from the genome, or from specific tissues, or to change the level of its expression and then study the consequences. By such means great strides are being made in our understanding, for instance, of learning and memory.

But of course these same receptors are potential targets of novel bioweapons, made possible by the same technologies and knowledge that support the rapid advances in biomedical sciences. The foregoing is the context against which we have to assess the possibilities for new biological and toxin weapons.

The United States report, to which reference was made earlier, suggested that the following trends could be of importance:

> Genetically engineered vectors in the form of modified infectious organisms will be increasingly employed as tools in medicine and the techniques will become more widely available.
>
> Strides will be made in understanding of infectious disease mechanisms and in microbial genetics that are responsible for disease processes.
>
> An increased understanding of the human immune system function and disease mechanisms will shed light on the circumstances that cause individual susceptibility to infectious disease.
>
> Vaccines and antidotes will be improved over the long term, perhaps to the point where classical biological warfare agents will offer less utility as a means of causing casualties.

It is not difficult to imagine how understanding of the immune system develops, and the ability to better redesign proteins comes about, highly specific weapons could become possible to attack the immune system in various ways. For instance, rather than deliberately infecting a target population with a single disease, a biological aggressor could use a toxin to cripple the immune system, and nature would insure that opportunistic infections of many different kinds ensued.

A novel toxin agent could derange the immune system so that it becomes directly pathogenic itself, causing debility or death through its malfunctioning. Should these strategies seem fanciful, it is worth remembering that one of the classical agents, staphylococcal enterotoxin B (SEB), exerts its incapacitating effects in part via specific effects on the immune system.

Physiological systems other than the immune system could equally well be targets for such specific attack. Novel toxins weapons could be normal proteins involved in immune system modulation, discovered through genomic studies, that are toxic due to their unnaturally high concentration, their presence in tissues from which they are normally absent, or the presence in adult tissues of regulatory proteins normally expressed in a specific developmental stage. Alternatively, such toxins could be genetically engineered by combining parts of different proteins, since it is now known that many proteins are composed of several functional domains.

The immunomodulatory domain of a normal regulatory protein could be combined with a domain that targets the protein to a specific tissue, thus leading to effects that would never be exerted by the normal protein. Development of novel protein toxins is not the only application of bioinformatics to bioweapon development. The ability to recognise the genes for different classes of protein in genomic sequences, and to then predict their three-dimensional shape and to infer their function from comparative genomics and proteomics, will shortly lead to a massive increase in our understanding of the ways that the physiology of cells is modulated by external signals. This will in turn allow the rational design of small molecules that bind to such surface receptors and alter their function in predictable ways. Such designer chemical weapons could be immensely potent, easy to manufacture and stable. And perhaps most worrisome, large numbers of such agents will be developed in the course of the peaceful study of cell functioning, and as therapeutic agents.

Thus the revolution in biology and medicine, on the brink of which we are now poised, will also open up an immense range of new technologies for novel biological, toxin and chemical weapons. Manipulation of toxins and bioregulatory chemicals was in fact the subject of a special report produced by the Canadian government for the States Parties to the 1991 Third Review Conference of the BTWC. This illustrates very clearly that even a decade ago there were considerable concerns about how such agents might be developed and used, particularly the possibility of new forms of non-lethal weaponry. It is also, unfortunately, possible to imagine new biological weapons with specificity for particular subpopulations of organisms.

These kinds of novel bioweapon developed from the application of genomics and proteomics only affect individuals with the particular target protein or structure against which they were designed. In many cases the target would be nearly universal within the species. However, in other cases there might be alternative structures, and only individuals with a particular form of the structure would be vulnerable to the toxic effects of the new weapon. This possibility has led to speculation about bethnic weapons—ones that would affect one ethnic or racial group while leaving others untouched.

However, among humans the amount of intragroup genetic variation is generally greater than the intergroup variation, making such weapons almost certainly highly non-specific. Absent a lucky accident, it is unlikely that an appropriate target for an effective ethnic weapon could be found. Unfortunately, the same is not true for most of the staple crops and domestic animals on which humans depend for food. Especially in the developed world, but increasingly in the developing world as well, agriculture relies on the monoculture of genetically identical plants, or the intensive husbandry of highly inbred animals. This makes crop plants and domestic food animals ideal targets for such genotype-specific weapons. This vulnerability is further enhanced by the high density and huge numbers of individual plants and animals often involved.

In the race between the defence and the offence, a race so often seen before in military history, the defence seems to be leading for the moment. This being the case, the international arms control community has a small window of opportunity to design and put into place mechanisms to meet the threat of advanced bioweaponry. It is essential that this opportunity be grasped and that a protocol designed to strengthen the BTWC be completed in time for the 2001 Review Conference. To fail in that endeavour is to leave the world open to some very frightening possibilities in the early decades of this new century. A fundamental step toward addressing the threat of bioterrorism is comprehensive planning that focuses first and foremost on local preparedness and response capacity—integrating the role of state, regional, and federal governments, as well as state, regional, and national assets. To plan effectively, we have to think through the different types of scenarios that may confront us, including the announced release of a biological agent, the silent release of a biological agent, or some kind of hybrid event, such as having a bomb go off, that is followed by the release of a biological or chemical agent.

PRECUATIONS FOR THE BIOWARFARE ERA

Bioterrorism covers a very broad spectrum of concerns, from catastrophic terrorism with mass casualties, to microevents using low technology but producing civil unrest, disruption, disease, disabilities, and death. All these scenarios must be considered. We need to identify the assets and capabilities at all different levels and identify the gaps, critical players, policy makers, and stakeholders, and we must forge working relationships within the public health and health-care community as well as with outside partners. We need to develop shared understandings and mechanisms of communication.

We need to strengthen the public health infrastructure. A strong and robust public health system requires effective working partnerships with the medical care community. For a host of reasons over many years, the worlds of public health and medicine have existed too far apart, even though they share a common set of goals and the mission of promoting health and preventing disease.

We need to build linkages and understanding. We also need to make sure that the public health community works with medical providers to give them the kind of information they need to respond to infectious disease threats in the community, understand emerging disease trends, and implement appropriate prevention and control strategies. Improvements to health can be achieved through more effective daily working relationships and even through a crisis. In addition, we have to link with other partners beyond the public health and medical community, particularly law enforcement and intelligence.

We must learn how to educate and communicate with policy makers. We should define policies to support our preparedness efforts, the true needs for new resources, and the places in which to invest. They must address the challenge of informing the public and educating them about the reality of bioterrorism.

We must develop the framework of understanding and support required to both put in place the systems to respond effectively in a crisis and to achieve a level of understanding that can form the foundation for sharing information and developing knowledge when a crisis occurs. Hoaxes, a growing problem, offer an opportunity to examine our coordination and response. Thinking through the different types of hoaxes helps us develop protocols and strategies that lead to recognition of a true event.

The conventional bomb—where something blows up, you come in, respond, take care of the injured, clean up, and then return, more or less, to life as it was before—is not going to be the case in a bioterrorist attack, particularly in a scenario with human-to-human transmission. Instead, cases will initially appear in a scattered, sporadic manner, but rapidly increasing and overwhelming the capacity of the health-care system and continuing in concentric circles of infection and disease. We cannot address consequence management in the way emergency plans traditionally have for earthquakes, fires, or bomb blasts.

We need to build a system that brings together local, state, and national capacities in an ongoing way. We also must recognise the need to supplement our health-care delivery capacity with non-medical support that may come in the form of police, National Guard, or possibly military support, both to assist in the provision of services and for crowd control and the maintenance of order.

The research and development agenda needs to be addressed both through governmental efforts, including the institutes of health, the centres for disease control and prevention, army medical research institutes of infectious diseases, and also through private industry and other research institutions. Improved and more rapid diagnostic methods, new and better drugs for treatment or prophylaxis, and new vaccines, especially against anthrax and smallpox, are needed. In addition to biomedical research, further research into such diverse concerns as defining appropriate personal protective gear or decontamination procedures is fundamental to our overall preparedness for a bioterrorist attack.

REFERENCES

Christopher, G.N., Cieslak, T.J., Pavlin, J.A., Eitzen, E.M., "Biological Warfare: a Historical Perspective", *JAMA,* 1997, 278:412-417.

Danzig, R., Berkowsky, P.B., "Why should we be concerned about Biological Warfare?" *JAMA,* 1997, 285:431-2.

Daplan, E., Marchell, A., *The Cult at the End of the World*, New York: Crown Publishing Group, 1996.

Ekeus, R., *Iraq's biological weapons programme: UNSCOM's experience*, Memorandum report to the United Nations Security Council, 20 Nov., 1996, New York.

Fenner, F., Henderson, D.A., Arita, I., Jezek, Z., Ladnyi, I., *Smallpox and its Eradication*, Geneva: World Health Organisation, 1988.

Horrock N., "The new terror fear: biological weapons: detecting an attack is just the first problem", *US News & World Report*, May 12, 1997:36

Olson, K.B., "Biological weapons and the terror in Japan", *Terrorism,* August 1997;1:1.

Roberts, B., "New Challenges and New Policy Priorities for the 1990s, In Biologic Weapons: Weapons of the Future", Washington: Center for Strategic and International Studies, 1993.

Tucker, J.B., *"National health and medical services response to incidents of chemical and biological terrorism"*, *JAMA*. 1997, 278:362-368.

Vorobyov, A., "Criterion rating as a measure of probable use of bio agents as biological weapons", *In Papers presented to the Working Group on Biological Weapons Control of the Committee on International Security and Arms Control*, US National Academy of Sciences, 1994 Apr; Washington.

Wehrle, P.F., Posch, J., Richter, K.H., Henderson, D.A., "An airborne outbreak of smallpox in a German hospital and its significance with respect to other recent outbreaks in Europe", *Bull. World Health Organ,* 1970, 4:669-79.

Zilinskas, R., "Iraq's Biological Weapons: The Past as Future?", *JAMA,* 1997, 278: 418-424.

Appendix - I

Convention on the Prohibition of the Development, Production and Stockpiling of Bacteriological (Biological) and Toxin Weapons and on Their Destruction

Opened for signature at London (L), Moscow (M) and Washington (W): 10 April 1972

Entered into force: 26 March 1975

Depositary Governments: Russian Federation, United Kingdom of Great Britain and Northern Ireland and United States of America

The States Parties to this Convention,

Determine to act with a view to achieving effective progress toward general and complete disarmament, including the prohibition and elimination of all types of weapons of mass destruction, and convinced that the prohibition of the development, production and stockpiling of chemical and bacteriological (biological) weapons and their elimination, through effective measures, will facilitate the achievement of general and complete disarmament under strict and effective control,

Recognising the important significance of the Protocol for the Prohibition of the Use in War of Asphyxiating, Poisonous or

Other Gases, and of Bacteriological Methods of Warfare, signed at Geneva on June 17, 1925, and conscious also of the contribution which the said Protocol has already made and continues to make, to mitigating the horrors of war,

Reaffirming their adherence to the principles and objectives of that Protocol and calling upon all States to comply strictly with them,

Recalling that the General Assembly of the United Nations has repeatedly condemned all actions contrary to the principles and objectives of the Geneva Protocol of June 17, 1925,

Desiring to contribute to the strengthening of confidence between peoples and the general improvement of the international atmosphere,

Desiring also to contribute to the realisation of the purposes and principles of the Charter of the United Nations,

Convinced of the importance and urgency of eliminating from the arsenals of States, through effective measures, such dangerous weapons of mass destruction as those using chemical or bacteriological (biological) agents,

Recognising that an agreement on the prohibition of bacteriological (biological) and toxin weapons represents a first possible step towards the achievement of agreement on effective measures also for the prohibition of the development, production and stockpiling of chemical weapons, and determined to continue negotiations to that end,

Determined, for the sake of all mankind, to exclude completely the possibility of bacteriological (biological) agents and toxins being used as weapons,

Convinced that such use would be repugnant to the conscience of mankind and that no effort should be spared to minimise this risk,

Have agreed as follows:

ARTICLE I

Each State Party to this Convention undertakes never in any circumstance to develop, produce, stockpile or otherwise acquire or retain:

Microbial or other biological agents, or toxins whatever their origin or method of production, of types and in quantities that have no justification for prophylactic, protective or other peaceful purposes;

Weapons, equipment or means of delivery designed to use such agents or toxins for hostile purposes or in armed conflict.

ARTICLE II

Each State Party to this Convention undertakes to destroy, or to divert to peaceful purposes, as soon as possible but not later than nine months after the entry into force of the Convention, all agents, toxins, weapons, equipment and means of delivery specified in Article I of the Convention, which are in its possession or under its jurisdiction or control. In implementing the provisions of this article all necessary safety precautions shall be observed to protect populations and the environment.

ARTICLE III

Each State Party to this Convention undertakes not to transfer to any recipient whatsoever, directly or indirectly, and not in any way to assist, encourage, or induce any State, group of States or international organisations to manufacture or otherwise acquire any of the agents, toxins, weapons, equipment or means of delivery specified in Article I of the Convention.

ARTICLE IV

Each State Party to this Convention shall, in accordance with its constitutional processes, takes any necessary measures to prohibit and prevent the development, production, stockpiling, acquisition or retention of the agents, toxins, weapons, equipment and means of delivery specified in Article I of the Convention, within the territory of such State, under its jurisdiction or under its control anywhere.

ARTICLE V

The States Parties to this Convention undertake to consult one another and to cooperate in solving any problems which may arise in relation to the objective of, or in the application of the provisions of the Convention. Consultation and cooperation pursuant to this article may also be undertaken through appropriate international procedures within the framework of the United Nations and in accordance with its Charter.

ARTICLE VI

1) Any State Party to this Convention which finds that any other State Party is acting in breach of obligations deriving from the provisions of the Convention may lodge a complaint with the Security Council of the United Nations. Such a complaint should include all possible evidence confirming its validity, as well as a request for its consideration by the Security Council.
2) Each State Party to this Convention undertakes to cooperate in carrying out any investigation which the Security Council may initiate, in accordance with the provisions of the Charter of the United Nations, on the basis of the complaint received by the Council. The Security Council shall inform the States Parties to the Convention of the results of the investigation.

ARTICLE VII

Each State Party to this Convention undertakes to provide or support assistance, in accordance with the United Nations Charter, to any Party to the Convention which so requests, if the Security Council decides that such Party has been exposed to danger as a result of violation of the Convention.

ARTICLE VIII

Nothing in this Convention shall be interpreted as in any way limiting or detracting from the obligations assumed by any State under the Protocol for the Prohibition of the Use in War of Asphyxiating, Poisonous or Other Gases, and of Bacteriological Methods of Warfare, signed at Geneva on June 17, 1925.

ARTICLE IX

Each State Party to this Convention affirms the recognised objective of effective prohibition of chemical weapons and, to this end, undertakes to continue negotiations in good faith with a view to reaching early agreement on effective measures for the prohibition of their development, production and stock-piling and for their destruction, and on appropriate measures concerning equipment and means of delivery specifically designed for the production or use of chemical agents for weapons purposes.

ARTICLE X

1) The States Parties to this Convention undertake to facilitate, and have the right to participate in the fullest possible exchange of equipment, materials and scientific and technological information for the use of bacteriological (biological) agents and toxins for peaceful purposes.

Parties to the Convention in a position to do so shall also cooperate in contributing individually or together with other States or international organisations to the further development and application of scientific discoveries in the field of bacteriology (biology) for prevention of disease, or for other peaceful purposes.

2) This Convention shall be implemented in a manner designed to avoid hampering the economic or technological development of States Parties to the Convention or international cooperation in the field of peaceful bacteriological (biological) activities, including the international exchange of bacteriological (biological) agents and toxins and equipment for the processing, use or production of bacteriological (biological) agents and toxins for peaceful purposes in accordance with the provisions of the Convention.

ARTICLE XI

Any State Party may propose amendments to this Convention. Amendments shall enter into force for each State Party accepting the amendments upon their acceptance by a majority of the States Parties to the Convention and thereafter for each remaining State Party on the date of acceptance by it.

ARTICLE XII

Five years after the entry into force of this Convention, or earlier if it is requested by a majority of the Parties to the Convention by submitting a proposal to this effect to the Depositary Governments, a conference of States Parties to the Convention shall be held at Geneva, Switzerland, to review the operation of the Convention, with a view to assuring that the purposes of the preamble and the provisions of the Convention, including the provisions concerning negotiations on chemical weapons, are being realised. Such review shall take into account any new scientific and technological developments relevant to the Convention.

ARTICLE XIII

1) This Convention shall be of unlimited duration.
2) Each State Party to this Convention shall in exercising its natural sovereignty have the right to withdraw from the Convention if it decides that extraordinary events, related to the subject matter of the Convention, have jeopardised the supreme interests of its country. It shall give notice of such withdrawal to all other States Parties to the Convention and to the United Nations Security Council three months in advance. Such notice shall include a statement of the extraordinary events it regards as having jeopardised its supreme interests.

ARTICLE XIV

1) This Convention shall be open to all States for signature. Any State which does not sign the Convention before its entry into force in accordance with paragraph (3) of this Article may accede to it at any time.
2) This Convention shall be subject to ratification by signatory States. Instruments of ratification and instruments of accession shall be deposited with the Governments of the United States of America, the United Kingdom of Great Britain and Northern Ireland and the Union of Soviet Socialist Republics, which are hereby designated the Depositary Governments.
3) This Convention shall enter into force after the deposit of instruments of ratification by twenty-two Governments, including the Governments designated as Depositaries of the Convention.

4) For States whose instruments of ratification or accession are deposited subsequent to the entry into force of this Convention, it shall enter into force on the date of the deposit of their instrument of ratification or accession.
5) The Depositary Governments shall promptly inform all signatory and acceding States of the date of each signature, the date of deposit of each instrument of ratification or of accession and the date of the entry into force of this Convention, and of the receipt of other notices.
6) This Convention shall be registered by the Depositary Governments pursuant to Article 102 of the Charter of the United Nations.

ARTICLE XV

This Convention, the English, Russian, French, Spanish and Chinese texts of which are equally authentic, shall be deposited in the archives of the Depositary Governments. Duly certified copies of the Convention shall be transmitted by the Depositary Governments of the signatory and acceding States.

Draft Final Declaration

December 7, 2001

The states parties to the Convention on the Prohibition of the Development, Production and Stockpiling of Bacteriological (Biological) and Toxin Weapons and on Their Destruction, which met in Geneva from November 19 to December 7, 2001, to review the operation of the Convention, solemnly declare:

The determination of the states parties to accomplish the total elimination of all weapons of mass destruction;

The determination of the states parties also to achieve general and complete disarmament under strict and effective international control, which is the ultimate objective of the efforts of states in the disarmament process;

Their reaffirmation that the Convention on the Prohibition of the Development, Production and Stockpiling of Bacteriological (Biological) and Toxin Weapons and on Their Destruction is essential for international and regional peace and security;

Their reaffirmation of their firm commitment to the purposes of the Preamble and the provisions of the Convention;

Their dissatisfaction at the fact that, after a quarter of a century since the entry into force of the Convention, universality has not yet been achieved;

Their reiteration that the effective contribution of the Convention to international peace and security would be enhanced through universal adherence to the Convention, and their call on signatories to ratify, and other non-states parties to accede to the Convention at the earliest;

Their reaffirmation that under any circumstances the use, development, production and stockpiling of bacteriological (biological) and toxin weapons is effectively prohibited under Article I of the Convention;

Their continued determination, for the sake of humankind, to exclude completely the possibility of the use of bacteriological (biological) agents and toxins as weapons, and their conviction that such use would be repugnant to the conscience of humankind;

Their renewed determination to ensure, through the full implementation of Article I prohibitions that biological and toxin weapons are never acquired, developed, produced, stockpiled or used;

Their conviction that terrorism in all its forms and manifestations and whatever its motivation, is abhorrent and unacceptable to the international community and that terrorists must be prevented from acquiring agents, toxins, biological weapons or associated knowledge;

Their conviction that the full implementation of the provisions of the Convention should facilitate economic and technological development and international cooperation in the field of peaceful biological activities;

Their recognition of the particular importance of responding to the threat posed by biological weapons by strengthening the Convention including through binding measures agreed by all states parties.

The states parties recognise that the important principles contained in this Solemn Declaration can also serve as a basis for further strengthening of the Convention.

PREAMBLE

The Conference reaffirms the importance of the elements in the review of the Preamble to the Convention contained in the Final

Declaration of the Second Review Conference of the States Parties to the Convention on the Prohibition of the Development, Production and Stockpiling of Bacteriological (Biological) and Toxin Weapons and on their Destruction.

ARTICLE I

[Each state party to this Convention undertakes never in any circumstances to develop, produce, stockpile or otherwise acquire or retain: (1) Microbial or other biological agents, or toxins whatever their origin or method of production, of types and in quantities that have no justification for prophylactic, protective or other peaceful purposes; (2) Weapons, equipment or means of delivery designed to use such agents or toxins for hostile purposes or in armed conflict.]

1. The Conference notes the importance of Article I as the provision which defines the scope of the Convention. The Conference reaffirms its support for the provisions of this Article.
2. The Conference reaffirms that the Convention prohibits the development, production, stockpiling, other acquisition or retention of microbial or other biological agents or toxins harmful to plants and animals, as well as humans, of types and in quantities that have no justification for prophylactic, protective or other peaceful purposes.
3. The Conference reaffirms that the use by the states parties, in any way and under any circumstances, including within their own territory, of microbial or other biological agents or toxins, as well as of weapons, equipment or means of delivery designed to use such agents or toxins for hostile purposes or in armed conflict, that is not consistent with prophylactic, protective or other peaceful purposes, is effectively a violation of Article I of the Convention.

4. The Conference reaffirms the undertaking in Article I never in any circumstances to develop, produce, stockpile or otherwise acquire or retain weapons, equipment or means of delivery designed to use such agents or toxins for hostile purposes or in armed conflict, including by transmission by means of vectors of biological origin, in order to exclude completely and forever the possibility of their use.
5. The Conference also reaffirms that the Convention unequivocally covers all microbial or other biological agents or toxins, naturally or artificially created or altered, as well as their components, whatever their origin or method of production, of types and in quantities that have no justification for prophylactic, protective or other peaceful purposes.
6. The Conference, conscious of apprehensions arising from relevant scientific and technological developments, *inter alia,* in the fields of microbiology, biotechnology, molecular biology, genetic engineering, and any applications resulting from genome studies, and the possibilities of their use for purposes inconsistent with the objectives and the provisions of the Convention, reaffirms that the undertaking given by the states parties in Article I applies to all such developments.
7. The Conference notes that experimentation involving open-air release of pathogens or toxins harmful to humans is inconsistent with the undertakings contained in Article I; experimentation involving open-air release of pathogens or toxins harmful to animals or plants that has no justification for prophylactic, protective or other peaceful purposes is inconsistent with the undertakings contained in Article I.
8. The Conference appeals through the states parties to their scientific communities to lend their support only to activities that have justification for prophylactic, protective and other peaceful purposes, and refrain from undertaking or supporting activities which are in breach of the obligations deriving from provisions of the Convention.

9. The Conference condemns the use of all biological agents or toxins, including anthrax, as tools of terrorism and finds such acts reprehensible.
10. The Conference emphasises, once more, the vital importance of full implementation by all states parties of all the provisions of the Convention, especially Article I. The Conference calls upon all states parties and signatories to comply fully with their obligations on the basis of the conviction that any non-compliance with its provisions could undermine confidence in, and achieving the basic provisions of, the Convention.

ARTICLE II

[Each state party to this Convention undertakes to destroy, or to divert to peaceful purposes, as soon as possible but not later than nine months after entry into force of the Convention, all agents, toxins, weapons, equipment and means of delivery specified in Article I of the Convention, which are in its possession or under its jurisdiction or control. In implementing the provisions of this article all necessary safety precautions shall be observed to protect populations and the environment.]

1. The Conference recognises that for any state acceding to the Convention after the entry into force of the Convention, the destruction or diversion to peaceful purposes specified in Article II would be completed upon accession to the Convention. The Conference emphasises that the destruction or diversion to peaceful purposes specified in Article II should be carried out completely and effectively.
2. The Conference stresses that states, which become parties to the Convention, in implementing the provisions of this Article, shall observe all necessary safety precautions to protect populations and the environment.

ARTICLE III

[Each state party to this Convention undertakes not to transfer to any recipient whatsoever, directly or indirectly, and not in any way to assist, encourage, or induce any state, group of states or international organisations to manufacture or otherwise acquire any of the agents, toxins, weapons, equipment or means of delivery specified in Article I of this Convention.]

1. The Conference recognises the continuing importance of Article III and affirms that its provisions are sufficiently comprehensive to cover transfer to any recipient whatsoever, directly or indirectly, at international, national and sub-national levels.
2. The Conference notes that a number of states parties stated that they have taken concrete measures to give effect to their undertakings under this Article, and in this context also notes statements by states parties at the Conference about the legislative and administrative measures they have taken since the Fourth Review Conference.
3. The Conference calls for appropriate measures by all states parties, within their constitutional and legislative procedures, to ensure effective implementation of this Article. The Conference underlines that transfers relevant to the Convention should be authorised only for purposes not prohibited under the Convention.
4. The Conference urges states parties to take appropriate measures to prevent and respond to any violation, including by individuals or sub-national groups, of transfer regulations or legislation, including the qualification of such a violation as a punishable offence, consistent with the provisions of the Convention.
5. The Conference stresses that any recipient, including a state not party, must be prevented from acquiring biological agents or toxins of types and in quantities that

have no justification for prophylactic, protective or other peaceful purposes; weapons, equipment or means of delivery, and information that would assist the development, production, stockpiling and means of delivery of biological and toxin weapons.

6. The Conference emphasises that terrorists and terrorist groups should be prohibited from receiving materials and capabilities relevant to the Convention.
7. The Conference reiterates that the provisions of this Article should not be used to impose restrictions and/or limitations on the transfers for purposes consistent with the objectives and purposes of the Convention of scientific knowledge, technology, equipment and materials under Article X.
8. The Conference encourages states parties to consider, within the framework of the Convention, ways to enhance the implementation of this Article, including elaboration of a set of common principles and guidelines in the field of export controls.
9. The Conference takes note with interest of the provisions of the Cartagena Protocol on Biosafety which addresses, *inter alia*, transboundary movements of living genetically modified organisms.

ARTICLE IV

[Each state party to this Convention shall, in accordance with its constitutional processes, take any necessary measures to prohibit and prevent the development, production, stockpiling, acquisition, or retention of the agents, toxins, weapons, equipment and means of delivery specified in Article I of the Convention, within the territory of such a state, under its jurisdiction or under its control anywhere.]

1. The Conference underlines the importance of Article IV. It reaffirms the commitment of states parties to take the

necessary national measures under this Article, in accordance with their constitutional processes. These measures are to ensure the prohibition and prevention of the development, production, stockpiling, acquisition or retention of the agents, toxins, weapons, equipment and means of delivery specified in Article I of the Convention anywhere within their territory, under their jurisdiction or under their control, in order to prevent their use for purposes contrary to the Convention. The states parties recognise the need to ensure, through the review and/or adoption of national measures, the effective fulfilment of their obligations under the Convention in order, *inter alia,* to exclude use of biological and toxin weapons in terrorist or criminal activity.

2. The Conference reaffirms that under all circumstances the use of bacteriological (biological) and toxin weapons is effectively prohibited by the Convention.

3. The Conference notes those measures taken by a number of states parties in this regard, for example the adoption of penal legislation, and reiterates its call to any state party that has not yet taken the necessary measures to do so immediately, in accordance with its constitutional processes. Such measures should apply within its territory, under its jurisdiction or under its control anywhere. The Conference invites each state party to consider, if constitutionally possible and in conformity with international law, the application of such measures also to actions taken anywhere by natural persons possessing its nationality.

4. The Conference encourages states parties to adopt promptly, in accordance with their constitutional processes, measures to prevent terrorists from acquiring biological agents or toxins, dual use equipment and information on the production, stockpiling, acquisition or retention of the agents, toxins, weapons, equipment and means of delivery specified in Article I of the Convention,

anywhere within their territory, under their jurisdiction or under their control. The Conference calls upon states to make all possible efforts to prevent all terrorist acts including bioterrorist acts in all their forms and manifestations.

5. The Conference stresses the importance of:
   — Legislative, administrative and other measures designed to enhance domestic compliance with the Convention;
   — Legislation, regulations and other measures regarding the physical protection of laboratories and facilities to prevent unauthorised access to and removal of microbial or other biological agents, or toxins;
   — Inclusion in textbooks and in medical, scientific and military education programmes of information dealing with the prohibitions and provisions contained in the Biological and Toxin Weapons Convention and the Geneva Protocol of 1925;
   — Efforts by industry and scientific community to develop codes of conduct and/or ethical standards for work relevant to the prohibitions of the Convention, without prejudice to the primary responsibility of states parties to adopt legislative, administrative and other measures to implement the provisions of the Convention. Such codes could include, inter alia, a statement that scientists will use their knowledge and skills for the advancement of human welfare and will not conduct any activities directed toward use of microorganisms or toxins or other biological agents for hostile purposes or in armed conflict.

6. The Conference believes that such measures which states parties might undertake in accordance with their constitutional processes would strengthen the effectiveness of the Convention, as requested by previous Review Conferences.

7. The Conference notes that some states parties, as requested by the Second Review Conference, have provided to the United Nations Department for Disarmament Affairs information on the texts of specific legislation enacted or other measures taken to assure domestic compliance with the Convention. The Conference invites these states parties, and encourages all states parties, to provide such information and texts in the future.

   The Conference further notes that some states parties have provided information in response to the confidence-building measure agreed to at the Third Review Conference entitled Declaration of legislation, regul-ations and other measures. The Conference encourages all states parties to provide such information in the future. In addition, the Conference encourages all states parties to provide any useful information on the implementation of such measures.

8. The Conference encourages cooperation and initiatives, including regional ones, towards the strengthening and implementation of the Biological and Toxin Weapons Convention regime.

9. The Conference calls upon each state party to consider to adopt and implement national regulations to establish and maintain the protection of biological agents and toxins considered to be dangerous and relevant to the objectives of the Convention, including regulations on who may possess or acquire them and where and how they may be handled as well as regulations governing domestic and international transfers, and to enforce all such regulations by legislative or administrative measures, including penal measures, as appropriate.

10. The Conference encourages each state party to consider adopting and implementing, if it is not yet the case, national guidelines for genetic engineering work consistent with the objectives and purposes of the Convention.

11. The Conference urges each state party to provide appropriate legal assistance, in accordance with their national

legislation and international agreements, in connection with criminal investigations or criminal proceedings relating to the development, production, acquisition, stockpiling or use by natural persons or legal entities of the agents, toxins, weapons, equipment and means of delivery specified in Article I of the Convention.

12. The Conference calls on each state party to enhance its ability to prosecute or, where appropriate, extradite individuals for biological weapons offences, in accordance with their national law and bilateral extradition agreements.
13. The Conference invites states parties to consider, as appropriate, the negotiation of legal agreements to prevent and eliminate crimes involving biological and toxin weapons.
14. The Conference notes also that some states parties have provided proposals and suggestions of further strengthening international law and relevant national legislation, and believe those proposals and suggestions are worthy of further exploration and consideration. The Conference also welcomes and encourages other states parties to provide relevant comments, suggestions and proposals in this regard.

ARTICLE V

[The states parties to this Convention undertake to consult one another and to cooperate in solving any problems which may arise in relation to the objective of, or in the application of the provisions of, the Convention. Consultation and cooperation pursuant to this Article may also be undertaken through appropriate international procedures within the framework of the United Nations and in accordance with its Charter.]

1. The Conference notes the importance of Article V and reaffirms the obligation assumed by states parties to consult and cooperate with one another in solving any problems which may arise in relation to the objective of, or

in the application of the provisions of, the Convention. The Conference reiterates its appeal to states parties made at the Third Review Conference to make all possible efforts to solve any problems which may arise in relation to the objective of, or in the application of the provisions of the Convention with a view towards encouraging strict observance of the provisions subscribed to. The Conference notes that this Article provides an appropriate framework for resolving any such problems, and reaffirms that any state party which identifies such a problem should, as a rule, use these procedures to address and resolve it.

2. The Conference also reviewed the operation of the procedures to strengthen the implementation of the provisions of Article V which were adopted in the Final Declaration of the Third Review Conference and which built on the agreements reached at the Second Review Conference. The Conference notes that the implementation provisions were invoked since the Fourth Review Conference and calls on any state party which identifies a problem arising in relation to the objective of, or in the application of the provisions of the Convention to use these procedures, if appropriate, to address and resolve it.

3. The Conference stresses the need for all state parties to deal effectively and promptly with compliance issues. In this connection, states parties reconfirm their agreement to provide specific, timely responses in solving any problems which may arise in the application of any provision of the Convention. Such responses should be submitted, if appropriate, in accordance with the procedures agreed upon by the Second Review Conference and further developed by the Third Review Conference. The Conference reiterates its request that information on such efforts be provided to the Review Conferences. The Conference reaffirms that consultation and cooperation pursuant to this Article may also be undertaken through

appropriate international procedures within the framework of the United Nations and in accordance with its Charter.

4. The Conference stresses its determination to strengthen effectiveness and improve the implementation of the Convention, and its recognition that effective verification could reinforce the Convention.

5. In accordance with the decision of the Fourth Review Conference, the Conference reviewed the effectiveness of the confidence building measures as agreed in the Final Declaration of the Third Review Conference and reaffirmed at the Fourth Review Conference. The Conference notes the continued importance of the confidence-building measures agreed upon at the Second and Third Review Conferences, as well as the modalities elaborated by the Ad Hoc Meeting of Scientific and Technical Experts from states parties to the Convention, held in 1987.

6. The Conference notes the background information document providing, in summary tabular form, data on the participation of states parties in the agreed confidence building measures since the last Review Conference.

7. The Conference recognises that participation with confidence building measures since last review conference has not been satisfactory nor universal and that not all responses have been prompt or complete. In this regard, the Conference urges all states parties to complete full and timely declarations in the future, noting the value of nil returns. The Conference further reminds all states parties of the importance of submitting their CBMs to the United Nations by April 15 each year. In this regard, the Conference also recognises the technical difficulties experienced by some states parties with respect to preparing CBM responses.

8. The conference invites states parties to consider setting up or designating a national entity responsible for the national implementation of the CBMs.

9. The Conference takes note of proposals to expand the scope of existing confidence-building measures, to improve existing measures and to create new measures, in order to provide a broader range of relevant information, consistent with the approach agreed upon in 1991. Therefore, the Conference invites states parties to further discuss modifications of CBMs.

ARTICLE VI

[(1) Any state party to this convention which finds that any other state party is acting in breach of obligations deriving from the provisions of the Convention may lodge a complaint with the Security Council of the United Nations. Such a complaint should include all possible evidence confirming its validity, as well as a request for its consideration by the Security Council. (2) Each state party to this Convention undertakes to cooperate in carrying out any investigation which the Security Council may initiate, in accordance with the provisions of the Charter of the United Nations, on the basis of the complaint received by the Council. The Security Council shall inform the states parties to the Convention of the results of the investigation.]

1. The Conference notes that the provisions of this Article have not been invoked.
2. The Conference reaffirms the importance of Article VI, which, in addition to the procedures contained in Article V, provides that any state party which finds that any other state party is acting in breach of its obligations under the Convention may lodge a complaint with the United Nations Security Council. The Conference emphasises the provision of Article VI that such a complaint should include all possible evidence and documents confirming its validity. It stresses that, as in the case of the implementation of all the provisions and procedures set forth in the Convention, the procedures foreseen in Article VI

should be implemented in good faith within the scope of the Convention.

3. The Conference invites the Security Council to consider immediately any complaint lodged under Article VI and to initiate any measures it considers necessary for the investigation of the complaint in accordance with the Charter. The Conference reaffirms the undertaking of each state party to cooperate in carrying out any investigations which the Security Council may initiate.

4. The Conference invites states parties to consider the development by all states parties of a compliance mechanism within the framework of the Convention to conduct investigations regarding alleged breaches of the Convention.

5. The Conference recalls, in this context, United Nations Security Council resolution 620 (1988), which at the time encouraged the United Nations Secretary-General to carry out prompt investigations, in response to allegations brought to its attention by any Member State concerning the possible use of chemical and bacteriological (biological) or toxin weapons that could entail a violation of the 1925 Geneva Protocol or of any other applicable rule of international treaty or customary law. The Conference also recalls the technical guidelines and procedures contained in Annex I of United Nations document A/44/561 to guide the United Nations Secretary-General on the timely and efficient investigation cf reports of the possible use of such weapons. The states parties reaffirm their agreement to consult, at the request of any state party, regarding allegations of use or threat of use of bacteriological (biological) or toxin weapons and to cooperate fully with the United Nations Secretary-General in carrying out such investigations. Pending the establishment of the mechanism described in the paragraph above, the Conference stresses that in the case of alleged use the United Nations is called upon to take appropriate measures expeditiously,

which could include a request to the Security Council to consider action in accordance with the Charter.

6. The Conference invites the Security Council to inform each state party of the results of any investigation initiated under Article VI and to consider promptly any appropriate further action which may be necessary.
7. The Conference notes that the procedure outlined in this Article is without prejudice to the prerogative of the states parties to the Convention to consider jointly the cases of alleged non-compliance with the provisions of the Convention and to make appropriate decisions in accordance with the Charter of the United Nations and applicable rules ofinternational law.

ARTICLE VII

[Each state party to this Convention undertakes to provide or support assistance, in accordance with the United Nations Charter, to any party to the Convention which so requests, if the Security Council decides that such party has been exposed to danger as a result of violation of the Convention.]

1. The Conference notes with satisfaction that these provisions have not been invoked.
2. The Conference underlines the importance of Article VII and reaffirms the undertaking made by each state party to provide or support assistance in accordance with the Charter of the United Nations to any Party to the Convention which so requests, if the Security Council decides that such party has been exposed to danger or damage as a result of a violation of the Convention.
3. The Conference affirms that, should a request for assistance be made, it should be promptly considered and an appropriate response provided. In this context, pending consideration of a decision by the United Nations Security Council, timely emergency assistance could be provided by

states parties or appropriate international organisations, if requested. The Conference takes note of the proposal that states parties might need to coordinate procedures for assistance in order to ensure that timely emergency assistance could be provided if requested.

4. The Conference invites each state party in a position to do so to identify possible types of medical, veterinary, or other assistance that might be made available. The Conference urges states parties to commit, to the extent that they are able to provide or contribute to the training and operation of national and/or international rapid response teams for emergency medical assistance, as well as necessary materials and equipment, especially for detection.
5. The Conference expresses concern at the possibility of biological weapons use or threat of use. The Conference underlines the value of promoting, as appropriate, access to medicines, medical prophylaxis and treatment as a crucial condition in the combat of outbreaks of diseases resulting from a violation of the Convention.
6. The Conference considers that in the event this Article might be invoked, the United Nations, with the help of appropriate intergovernmental organisations such as the World Health Organisation (WHO), Office International des Epizooties (OIE) and the Food and Agriculture Organisation (FAO), could play a coordinating role in providing assistance.

ARTICLE VIII

[Nothing in this Convention shall be interpreted as in any way limiting or detracting from the obligations assumed by any State under the Protocol for the Prohibition of the Use in War of Asphyxiating, Poisonous or Other Gases, and of Bacteriological Methods of Warfare, signed at Geneva on June 17, 1925.]

1. The Conference reaffirms the importance of Article VIII and stresses the significance of the Protocol for the Prohibition of the Use in War of Asphyxiating, Poisonous or Other Gases, and of Bacteriological Methods of Warfare, signed at Geneva on June 17, 1925.
2. The Conference acknowledges that the 1925 Geneva Protocol, by prohibiting the use of bacteriological methods of warfare, forms an essential complement to the Convention on the Prohibition of the Development, Production and Stockpiling of Bacteriological (Biological) and Toxin Weapons and on Their Destruction.
3. The Conference reaffirms that nothing contained in the Convention on the Prohibition of the Development, Production and Stockpiling of Bacteriological (Biological) and Toxin Weapons and on their Destruction shall be interpreted as in any way limiting or detracting from the obligations assumed by any State under the Protocol for the Prohibition of the Use in War of Asphyxiating, poisonous or Other Gases, and of Bacteriological Methods of Warfare.
4. Noting the actions in support of the Protocol taken by the Security Council and General Assembly of the United Nations, and recalling the solemn reaffirmation of the prohibition as established in the Protocol, issued by the Conference of states parties to the 1925 Geneva Protocol and other interested states held in Paris from 7 to 11 January 1989, the Conference appeals to all states parties to the Geneva Protocol to fulfil their obligations assumed under that Protocol and urges all states parties not yet parties to the 1925 Geneva Protocol to accede to it without delay.
5. The Conference stresses the importance of the withdrawal of all reservations to the 1925 Geneva Protocol related to the Biological and Toxin Weapons Convention.
6. The Conference welcomes the actions which states parties have taken to withdraw their reservations to the 1925

Geneva Protocol related to the Biological and Toxin Weapons convention, and calls upon those states parties that continue to maintain pertinent reservations to the 1925 Geneva Protocol to withdraw those reservations, and notify the Depositary of the Protocol of their withdrawals without delay.

7. The Conference notes that reservations concerning retaliation, implying the possible use of any of the objects prohibited by the Biological and Toxin Weapons Convention, even if conditional, are totally incompatible with the absolute and universal prohibition of the development, production, stockpiling, acquisition and retention of bacteriological (biological) and toxin weapons, with the aim to exclude completely and forever the possibility of their use.

ARTICLE IX

[Each state party to this Convention affirms the recognised objective of effective prohibition of chemical weapons and, to this end, undertakes to continue negotiations in good faith with a view to reaching early agreement on effective measures for the prohibition of their development, production and stockpiling and for their destruction, and on appropriate measures concerning equipment and means of delivery specifically designed for the production or use of chemical agents for weapons purposes.]

1. The Conference reaffirms that Article IX identifies the recognised objective of the effective prohibition of chemical weapons. The Conference welcomes the entry-into-force on April 29, 1997 of the Convention on the Prohibition of the Development, Production, Stockpiling and Use of Chemical Weapons and on Their Destruction, thus fulfilling the provisions of this Article.

2. The Conference also welcomes the fact that 143 countries have become states parties to the Convention and some others have declared their intention to adhere to the Convention. It strongly urges all those that have not yet ratified or acceded to do so, in order to achieve the early universalisation of the Convention and a world free of chemical weapons. In this connection, the Conference urges all states parties to persuade non-parties to the Chemical Weapons Convention to ratify or accede to the Convention to realise its universality.
3. The Conference also underlines the importance of effective and full implementation of the Convention in all its aspects.
4. The Conference takes note that the First Review Conference of the Chemical Weapons Convention will take place in 2003, and affirms the complementarity between the objectives of the two Conventions.

ARTICLE X

[(1) The states parties to this Convention undertake to facilitate, and have the right to participate in, the fullest possible exchange of equipment, materials and scientific and technological information for the use of bacteriological (biological) agents and toxins for peaceful purposes. Parties to the Convention in a position to do so shall also cooperate in contributing individually or together with other states or international organisations to the further development and application of scientific discoveries in the field of bacteriology (biology) for prevention of disease, or for other peaceful purposes. (2) This Convention shall be implemented in a manner designed to avoid hampering the economic or technological development of states parties to the Convention or international cooperation in the field of peaceful bacteriological (biological) activities, including the international exchange of bacteriological (biological) and toxins and equipment for the processing, use or production of bacteriological (biological) agents and toxins for peaceful purposes in accordance with the provisions of the Convention.]

1. The Conference once more emphasises the increasing importance of the provisions of Article X, especially in the light of recent scientific and technological developments—including innovative research on genome sequencing like the human genome project—in the field of biotechnology, bacteriological (biological) agents and toxins with peaceful applications, which have vastly increased the potential for cooperation between states to help promote economic and social development, and scientific and technological progress, particularly in developing countries with a specific focus on least developed countries, in conformity with their interests, needs and priorities.
2. The Conference notes that, since the Fourth Review Conference, states parties—both bilaterally and multilaterally, including through specialised international organisations such as WHO, UNDP, FAO, OIE and ICGEB and other relevant organisations have increased their contributions to facilitate international cooperation in the field of biotechnology, which focused on, *inter alia:*
   a) Research activities aimed at improving the capabilities of states parties to monitor emerging and re-emerging diseases and to treat them;
   b) International cooperation on disease outbreaks;
   c) International cooperation on vaccine research and production and on global vaccination programmes;
   d) Technology transfers;
   e) Training of national experts from developing countries on microbiology, molecular biology, immunology and pathology, plant biology, protein structure and function, virology, industrial biotechnology;
   f) Research activities on genome dynamics;
   g) Establishment of biological databases;

h) Publication, exchange and dissemination of relevant information.

3. The Conference, while acknowledging what has already been done towards this end, notes with concern the gap still existing between the developed and developing countries in the field of biotechnology, genetic engineering, microbiology and other related areas. The Conference urges all states parties to actively continue to promote international cooperation and exchange with states parties in the peaceful uses of biotechnology, and urges all states parties possessing advanced biotechnology to adopt positive measures to promote technology transfer and international cooperation on an equal and non-discriminatory basis, in particular with developing countries, for the benefit of all mankind. At the same time, the Conference stresses that measures to implement Article X need to be consistent with the objectives and provisions of the Convention.
4. The Conference welcomes the information provided by a number of states parties on the cooperative measures they have undertaken towards fulfilling their Article X obligations and encourages other states parties in a position to do so to provide such information.
5. The Conference underlines the importance, in the context of Article X implementation, of the Convention on Biological Diversity and of the Rio Declaration and the Agenda 21 adopted by the United Nations Conference on Environment and Development held in Rio de Janeiro Brazil, 1992. The Conference underlines the importance, in the context of Article X implementation, of the Convention on Biological Diversity and of the Rio Declaration and the Agenda 21 adopted by the United Nations Conference on Environment and Development held in Rio de Janeiro, Brazil, 1992. The Conference welcomes the adoption of the Protocol on Biosafety to the Convention on Biological Diversity in 2001 and looks

forward to further steps being taken during the World Summit on Sustainable Development, to be held in Johannesburg, in 2002.

6. The Conference urges states parties to continue to implement specific measures designed to enhance compliance with and ensure effective and full implementation of Article X of the Convention among the states parties. The implementation of such measures shall, *inter alia*, be aimed at:
   a) Promoting scientific and technological exchanges and fostering international co-operation, as appropriate, on a multilateral, regional or bilateral basis in the field of peaceful bacteriological (biological) and toxin activities;
   b) Facilitating free trade and the fullest possible exchange in biological agents, toxins, equipment and materials for peaceful purposes in order to enhance the economic and technological development of states parties, and ensuring the right of states parties to participate in such exchanges to the fullest extent possible;
   c) Avoiding hampering the economic and technological development of states parties through any restrictions incompatible with the obligations undertaken under the Convention or limitations on the transfer, for purposes consistent with the objectives and the provisions of the Convention, of scientific knowledge, technology, equipment and materials.

7. The Conference recalls that the states parties have a legal obligation to facilitate, and have the right to participate, in the fullest possible exchange of equipment, materials and scientific and technological information for the use of bacteriological (biological) agents, and toxins for peaceful purposes and not to hamper the economic and technological development of states parties.

8. The Conference reiterated the confirmation of the Forth Review Conference that the provisions of Article III should not be used to impose restrictions and/or limitations on the

transfers for purposes consistent with the objectives and the purposes of the Convention, of scientific knowledge, technology, equipment and materials under Article X.

9. The Conference urges states parties to undertake or continue to promote and support the following activities, in furtherance of any current endeavours relevant to and in accordance with the Convention, where appropriate, individually, jointly, through arrangements with relevant international organisations including, but not limited to, the Food and Agriculture Organisation, International Center for Genetic Engineering and Biotechnology, International Vaccine Institute, Office International des Epizooties, Organisation for the Prohibition of Chemical Weapons, United Nations Environment Program, United Nations Industrial Development Organisation or World Health Organisation and the Secretariat of the Convention on Biological Diversity:

   a) The publication, exchange and dissemination of information on research and development on the peaceful uses of microbial or other biological agents and toxins, on bio-safety, prophylactics and protection, biotechnology, Good Laboratory Practice and current Good Manufacturing Practice, and diagnosis, surveillance, detection, treatment and prevention of diseases caused by microbial or other biological agents and toxins;

   b) The improvement and development, as appropriate, of research capabilities, including research institutes, in relevant fields of biosciences and biotechnology for peaceful purposes, through collaborative research programmes and projects, upon the specific request of, and in cooperation with, the state party concerned, in particular in the use of microorganisms and other biological agents and toxins for medical, agricultural, veterinary and industrial purposes;

   c) International cooperation on the research, development and production of vaccines;

d) Transfer and exchange of information concerning research programs in biosciences and greater cooperation in international public health and disease control;

e) Technological exchange of information among states parties of technology for the peaceful uses of genetic engineering, the prevention, diagnosis and treatment of diseases caused by microbial and other biological agents or toxins, in particular infectious diseases, and for other relevant fields of biosciences and biotechnology for peaceful purposes;

f) Participation on a fair and equitable basis and as wide a geographic basis as possible at the bilateral, regional or multilateral levels in the application of biotechnology and scientific research and development, for the prevention, surveillance, detection, diagnosis and treatment of diseases caused by microbial and other biological agents or toxins, in particular infectious diseases;

g) The establishment or continuation of a framework for cooperation aimed at improving and strengthening the capabilities of states parties through research activities in the field of prophylaxis and protection against diseases caused by microbial and other biological agents or toxins, in particular infectious diseases;

h) Transfer and exchange of information concerning research programmes in biosciences and greater cooperation in international public health and disease control;

i) Increased technical cooperation and assistance including training programmes, workshops and scientific conferences for health workers and experts in developing countries through interaction with relevant international organisations such as WHO, FAO and OIE;

j) Cooperation in providing information on epidemiological and epizootical study of diseases and data reporting systems on bilateral, regional and international levels in conjunction with relevant United Nations agencies within their competencies with a view to improve identification and timely reporting of outbreak of human, animal and plant diseases;

k) Promotion of exchange of scientists and experts to enhance the capability of states parties in strengthening their disease surveillance programmes;

l) Increased coordination, operation and updating of existing databases on infectious diseases in states parties as well as easy access to such databases by all states parties;

m) Strengthening the existing global networks for disease surveillance and building up their capabilities to respond to disease outbreaks in a timely fashion particularly in humanitarian assistance to the states parties affected by disease outbreaks, utilising relevant international organisations and agencies including WHO, and its global outbreak alert and response network launched in 2000 as well as its centre on communicable diseases surveillance and response established in Lyon in 2000, with the participation of relevant institutions of the states parties;

n) Assisting the states parties through relevant international bodies within their competencies to strengthen national and local programmes of surveillance for infectious diseases and improving early notification, surveillance, control, protection and response capabilities.

10. The Conference invites WHO, FAO and OIE to enhance their coordination efforts on epidemiological surveillance and disease prevention by making use of existing international efforts for enhancing a system of global cooperation for surveillance of infectious diseases.

11. The Conference urges the use of existing institutional means within the United Nations system and the full utilisation of the possibilities provided by the specialised

agencies and other international organisations, and considers that the implementation of Article X could be enhanced through greater coordination among international cooperation programmes in the biological field for peaceful purposes conducted by states parties, specialised agencies and other international organisations.

12. The Conference reiterates its call upon the Secretary-General of the United Nations to propose for inclusion on the agenda of a relevant United Nations body, before the next Review Conference, a discussion and examination of the means of improving institutional mechanisms in order to facilitate the fullest possible exchange of equipment, materials and scientific and technological information regarding the use of bacteriological (biological) agents and toxins for peaceful purposes.

13. The Conference welcomes to elaborate an international programme of vaccine development for the prevention of diseases which would involve the scientific and technical personnel from developing countries that are states parties to the Convention. The Conference recognises that such a programme will not only enhance peaceful inter-national cooperation in biotechnology but also contribute to improve health care in developing countries, assist in establishing systems for surveillance of communicable diseases, and provide transparency in accordance with the Convention.

14. The Conference, recognising progress already achieved in this field, calls upon all states in a position to do so to enhance cooperation in promotion and financing the establishment of vaccine and prophylactic agents production facilities. The Conference recommends further that relevant multilateral organisations and world financial institutions continue to provide assistance for establishment and promotion of vaccine and prophylactic agents production projects in these countries.

15. The Conference welcomes the establishment, in 1997, of the International Vaccine Institute, an international

institution devoted to strengthening the capacity of developing countries in vaccine development, production and use in immunisation programs.

16. The Conference calls upon states parties to explore ways of implementing at a global level Good Laboratory Practices, including audit trails for the transfer of pathogens and toxins between, and within, laboratories, taking into account the views of the WHO, the OIE, the FAO, the ICGEB and other relevant organisations as appropriate.

17. The Conference considers that enhanced synergy among existing national and international data banks would facilitate the flow of information in the field of genetic engineering, biotechnology and other scientific developments. In this context, the Conference underlines the importance of monitoring all related developments in the field of frontiers science and high technology in the areas relevant to the Convention.

18. The Conference notes that existing institutional ways and means of ensuring cooperation between states parties would profit from continued development in order to promote international cooperation in peaceful activities in areas such as medicine, public health and agriculture as well as related advanced fields of biotechnology.

19. The Conference proposes that states parties consult bilaterally and/or multilaterally as appropriate on the creation of opportunities for cooperation on matters relevant to scientific and technological exchanges for peaceful purposes related to the implementation of the Convention.

20. The Conference calls for the establishment of a forum for consultation and creation of opportunities for cooperation on matters related to the promotion of scientific and technological exchange in the field of peaceful, bacteriological (biological) and toxin activities, and review of the implementation of Article X of the Convention among the states parties to the Protocol.

21. The Conference urges the states parties, the United Nations and its specialised agencies to take appropriate measures within their competence for the fullest possible exchange of equipment, materials, scientific and technological information and to promote technology transfer among themselves in particular to developing countries for surveillance and control of disease caused by biological agents and toxins in humans, animals and plants. Such measures should include, *inter alia;*

   a) Exchange of information concerning research programmes in biosciences and close cooperation in international public health and control of infectious diseases;
   b) Increased technical cooperation and assistance including training programmes, workshops and scientific conferences for health workers and experts in developing countries through interaction with relevant international organisations such as WHO, FAO and OIE;
   c) Cooperation in providing information on epidemiological and epizootological study of infectious diseases and data reporting systems on bilateral, regional and international levels in conjunction with relevant United Nations agencies with a view to improve identification and timely reporting of outbreak of human, animal and plant diseases;
   d) Promotion of exchange of scientists and experts to enhance the capability of states parties in promoting their disease surveillance programmes;
   e) Increased coordination, operation and updating of existing databases on infectious diseases in states parties as well as easy access to such databases by all states parties;
   f) Implementation of a coordinating mechanism by the WHO, the FAO and OIE for epidemiological surveillance and disease prevention by making use of existing international effort for enhancing a system of global cooperation for surveillance of infectious diseases;

g) Strengthening the existing global networks for disease surveillance and building up their capabilities to respond to disease outbreaks in a timely fashion particularly in humanitarian assistance to the states parties affected by disease outbreaks, utilising relevant international organisations and agencies including WHO, with the participation of relevant institutions of the states parties;

h) Assisting the states parties to strengthen national and local programmes of surveillance for infectious diseases and improving early notification, surveillance, control, protection and response capabilities.

22. The Conference considers that the WHO has made valuable contributions in the area of humanitarian assistance in cases of outbreak of diseases and recognises the WHO's mandate for global health, epidemiological alert and response to outbreaks of human disease.

ARTICLE XI

[Any state party may propose amendments to this Convention. Amendments shall enter into force for each state party accepting the amendments upon their acceptance by a majority of the states parties to the Convention and thereafter for each remaining state party on the date of acceptance by it.]

The Conference notes the importance of Article XI. In this context the Conference underlines that the provisions of Article XI should in principle be implemented in such a way as not to affect the universality of the Convention.

ARTICLE XII

[Five years after the entry into force of this Convention, or earlier if it is requested by a majority of parties to the Convention by submitting a proposal to this effect to the

Depositary Governments, a conference of states parties to the Convention shall be held at Geneva, Switzerland, to review the operation of the Convention, with a view to assuring that the purposes of the preamble and the provisions of the Convention, including the provisions concerning negotiations on chemical weapons, are being realised. Such review shall take into account any new scientific and technological developments relevant to the Convention.]

1. The Conference decides that a Sixth Review Conference shall be held in Geneva at the request of the majority of states parties, or in any case, not later than 2006.
2. The Conference decides that the Sixth Review Conference shall consider, *inter alia:*
   - The impact of scientific and technological developments relating to the Convention;
   - The relevance of the provisions of, and the implementation of the Chemical Weapons Convention on the effective implementation of the Biological and Toxin Weapons Convention, duly taking into account the degree of universality attained by such conventions at the time of the Fifth Review Conference;
   - The effectiveness of confidence-building measures as agreed at the Second and Third Review Conferences;
   - The requirement for, and the operation of, the requested allocation by the United Nations Secretary-General of staff resources and other requirements to assist the effective implementation of the relevant decisions of the Fourth Review Conference;
3. The Review Conference reaffirms that conferences of states parties to review the operation of the Convention should be held at least every five years.

ARTICLE XIII

[(1) This Convention shall be of unlimited duration. (2) Each state party to this Convention shall in exercising its national sovereignty have the right to withdraw from the Convention if it decides that extraordinary events, related to the subject matter of the Convention, have jeopardised the supreme interests of its country. It shall give notice of such withdrawal to all other states parties to the Convention and to the United Nations Security Council three months in advance. Such notice shall include a statement of the extraordinary events it regards as having jeopardised its supreme interests.] The Conference notes the provisions of Article XIII and emphasises that the Convention is of unlimited duration and applies at all times.

ARTICLE XIV

[Entry into force, accession and ratification procedures.]

1. The Conference notes that eight states have ratified or acceded to the Convention since the Fourth Review Conference.
2. The Conference calls upon states which have not yet ratified or acceded to the Convention to do so without delay, thus contributing to the achievement of universal adherence to the Convention. In this connection, the Conference requests states parties to encourage universality of the Convention.

ARTICLE XV

[Convention's official languages.]

The Conference notes the importance of this Article as well as the legal status of the languages of the Convention and the United Nations system, including the Arabic language, which is an official language of the United Nations system, in the conduct of business related to the Convention. (Language awaited from Facilitator on Follow-Up/AHG (President).)

Appendix - III

Fourth Review Conference of the Parties to the Convention on the Prohibition of the Development, Production and Stockpiling of Bacteriological (Biological) and Toxin Weapons and on Their Destruction

(Geneva, 25 November-6 December 1996)

The States parties to the convention on the prohibition of the Development, Production and Stockpiling of Bacteriological (Biological) and Toxin Weapons and on their Destruction, which meet in Geneva, from 25 November to 6 December 1996 to review the operation of the convetion, solemly declare:

- Their conviction that the Convention is essential to international peace and security;
- Their reaffirmation of their determination to act with a view to achieving effective progress towards general and complete disarmament, including the prohibition and elimination of all types of weapons of mass destruction, and their conviction that the prohibition of the development, production and stockpiling of chemical and bacteriological (biological) weapons and their elimination, through effective measures, will facilitate the

achievement of general and complete disarmament under strict and effective international control;

— Their reaffirmation that under any circumstances the use, development, production and stockpiling of bacteriological (biological) and toxin weapons is effectively prohibited under Article I of the Convention.

— Their continued determination, for the sake of mankind, to exclude completely the possibility of the use of bacteriological (biological) agents and toxins as weapons, and their conviction that such use would be repugnant to the conscience of mankind;

— Their reaffirmation of their firm commitment to the purposes of the Preamble and the provisions of the Convention, and of their belief that universal adherence to the Convention would enhance international peace and security;

— Their determination to enhance the implementation and effectiveness of the Convention and to further strengthen its authority, including through the confidence-building measures and agreed procedures for consultations agreed by the Second and Third Review Conferences, and through the fulfilment of the mandate entrusted to the Ad Hoc Group established by the Special Conference in 1994;

— Their recognition that effective verification could reinforce the Convention;

— Their conviction that the full implementation of the provisions of the Convention should facilitate economic and technological development and international cooperation in the field of peaceful biological activities;

— Their recognition that purposes of this Convention include the prohibition of the use of biological weapons as contrary to the purpose of the Convention.

The States Parties recognise that the important principles contained in this Solemn Declaration can also serve as a basis for further strengthening of the Convention.

PREAMBLE

The Conference reaffirms the importance of the elements in review of the Preamble to the Convention contained in the Final Declaration of the Second Review Conference of the States Parties to the Convention on the Prohibition of the Development, Production and Stockpiling of Bacteriological (Biological) and Toxin Weapons and on their Destruction.

ARTICLE I

1. The Conference notes the importance of Article I as the provision which defines the scope of the Convention. The Conference reaffirms its support for the provisions of this Article.
2. The Conference reaffirms that the Convention prohibits the development, production, stockpiling, other acquisition or retention of microbial or other biological agents or toxins harmful to plants and animals, as well as humans, of types and in quantities that have no justification for prophylactic, protective or other peaceful purposes.
3. The Conference reaffirms that the use by the States Parties, in any way and under any circumstances, of microbial or other biological agents or toxins, that is not consistent with prophylactic, protective or other peaceful purposes, is effectively a violation of Article I of the Convention.
4. The Conference reaffirms the undertaking in Article I never in any circumstances to develop, produce, stockpile or otherwise acquire or retain weapons, equipment or means of delivery designed to use such agents or toxins for hostile purposes or in armed conflict, in order to exclude completely and forever the possibility of their use.
5. The Conference also reaffirms that the Convention unequivocally covers all microbial or other biological

agents or toxins, naturally or artificially created or altered, as well as their components, whatever their origin or method of production, of types and in quantities that have no justification for prophylactic, protective or other peaceful purposes.

6. The Conference, conscious of apprehensions arising from relevant scientific and technological developments, *inter alia*, in the fields of microbiology, biotechnology, molecular biology, genetic engineering, and any applications resulting from genome studies, and the possibilities of their use for purposes inconsistent with the objectives and the provisions of the Convention, reaffirms that the undertaking given by the States Parties in Article I applies to all such developments.
7. The Conference notes that experimentation involving open-air release of pathogens or toxins harmful to man, animals or plants that have no justification for prophylactic, protective or other peaceful purposes is inconsistent with the undertakings contained in Article I.
8. The Conference appeals through the States Parties to their scientific communities to lend their support only to activities that have justification for prophylactic, protective and other peaceful purposes, and refrain from undertaking or supporting activities which are in breach of the obligations deriving from provisions of the Convention.
9. The Conference emphasizes, once more, the vital importance of full implementation by all States Parties of all the provisions of the Convention, especially Articles I, II and III. The Conference agrees that the application by States Parties of positive approaches in accordance with the provisions of the Convention is in the interest of all States Parties and that any non-compliance with its provisions could undermine confidence in the Convention. Non-compliance should be treated with determination in all cases, without selectivity or discrimination.

ARTICLE II

1. The Conference recognises that for any State acceding to the Convention after the entry into force of the Convention, the destruction or diversion to peaceful purposes specified in Article II would be completed upon accession to the Convention. The Conference emphasizes that the destruction or diversion to peaceful purposes specified in Article II should be carried out completely and effectively.
2. The Conference notes the importance of Article II and welcomes the statements made by States which have become Parties to the Convention since the Third Review Conference that they do not possess agents, toxins, weapons, equipment or means of delivery referred to in Article I of the Convention.
3. The Conference notes that the submission to the Centre for Disarmament Affairs of appropriate information on destruction by States Parties which had stockpiles and have destroyed them in fulfilment of their Article II obligations and which have not already made such submissions could enhance confidence in the Convention and its objectives.
4. The Conference stresses that States which become Parties to the Convention, implementing the provisions of this Article, shall observe all necessary safety precautions to protect populations and the environment.

ARTICLE III

1. The Conference notes the importance of Article III and welcomes the statements which States that have acceded to the Convention have made to the effect that they have not transferred agents, toxins, weapons, equipment or means of delivery as specified in Article I of the Convention, to any recipient whatsoever and have not

furnished assistance, encouragement or inducement to any State, group of States or international organisations to manufacture or otherwise acquire them. The Conference affirms that Article III is sufficiently comprehensive to cover any recipient whatsoever at international, national or subnational levels.

2. The Conference notes that a number of States Parties stated that they have already taken concrete measures to give effect to their undertakings under this Article and in this context also notes statements made by States Parties at the Conference about the legislative or administrative measures they have taken since the Third Review Conference. The Conference calls for appropriate measures by all States Parties. Transfers relevant to the Convention should be authorised only when the intended use is for purposes not prohibited under the Convention.

3. The Conference discussed the question whether multilaterally-agreed guidelines or multilateral guidelines negotiated by all States Parties to the Convention concerning the transfer of biological agents, materials and technology for peaceful purposes to any recipient whatsoever might strengthen the Convention. In the development of implementation of Article III, the Conference notes that States Parties should also consider ways and means to ensure that individuals or subnational groups are effectively prevented from acquiring, through transfers, biological agents and toxins for other than peaceful purposes. The Conference notes that these issues are being considered as part of the ongoing process of strengthening the Convention.

4. The Conference reiterates that the provisions of this Article should not be used to impose restrictions and/or limitations on the transfers for purposes consistent with the objectives and purposes of the Convention of scientific knowledge, technology, equipment and materials under Article X.

ARTICLE IV

1. The Conference underlines the importance of Article IV. It reaffirms the commitment of States Parties to take the necessary national measures under this Article, in accordance with their constitutional processes. These measures are to ensure the prohibition and prevention of the development, production, stockpiling, acquisition or retention of the agents, toxins, weapons, equipment and means of delivery specified in Article I of the Convention anywhere within their territory, under their jurisdiction or under their control, in order to prevent their use for purposes contrary to the Convention. The States Parties recognise the need to ensure, through the review and/or adoption of national measures, the effective fulfilment of their obligations under the Convention in order, *inter alia,* to exclude use of biological and toxin weapons in terrorist or criminal activity.
2. The Conference notes those measures already taken by a number of States Parties in this regard, for example, the adoption of penal legislation, and reiterates its call to any State Party that has not yet taken any necessary measures to do so immediately, in accordance with its constitutional processes. Such measures should apply within its territory, under its jurisdiction or under its control anywhere. The Conference invites each State Party to consider, if constitutionally possible and in conformity with international law, the application of such measures also to actions taken anywhere by natural persons possessing its nationality.
3. The Conference notes the importance of:
   - — Legislative, administrative and other measures designed to enhance domestic compliance with the Convention;
   - — Legislation regarding the physical protection of laboratories and facilities to prevent unauthorised

access to and removal of microbial or other biological agents, or toxins:

— Inclusion in textbooks and in medical, scientific and military education programmes of information dealing with the prohibitions and provisions contained in the Biological and Toxin Weapons Convention and the Geneva Protocol of 1925.

4. The Conference believes that such measures which States Parties might undertake in accordance with their constitutional processes would strengthen the effectiveness of the Convention, as requested by the Second and Third Review Conferences.
5. The Conference notes that some States Parties, as requested by the Second Review Conference, have provided to the United Nations Department for Disarmament Affairs information on the texts of specific legislation enacted or other measures taken to assure domestic compliance with the Convention. The Conference invites these States Parties, and encourages all States Parties, to provide such information and texts in the future. In this regard the Conference welcomes information provided by States Parties in response to the confidence-building measure agreed to at the Third Review Conference entitled Declaration of legislation, regulations and other measures. In addition, the Conference encourages all States Parties to provide any useful information on the implementation of such measures.
6. The Conference encourages cooperation and initiatives, including regional ones, towards the strengthening and implementation of the Biological and Toxin Weapons Convention regime.
7. The Conference reaffirms that under all circumstances the use of bacteriological (biological) and toxin weapons is effectively prohibited by the Convention.

ARTICLE V

1. The Conference notes the importance of Article V and reaffirms the obligation assumed by States Parties to consult and cooperate with one another in solving any problems which may arise in relation to the objective of, or in the application of the provisions of, the Convention. The Conference reiterates its appeal to States Parties made at the Third Review Conference to make all possible efforts to solve any problems which may arise in relation to the objective of, or in the application of the provisions of the Convention with a view towards encouraging strict observance of the provisions subscribed to. The Conference notes that this Article provides an appropriate framework for resolving any such problems, and reaffirms that any State Party which identifies such a problem should, as a rule, use these procedures to address and resolve it.
2. The Conference also reviewed the operation of the procedures to strengthen the implementation of the provisions of Article V which were adopted in the Final Declaration of the Third Review Conference and which built on the agreements reached at the Second Review Conference. While noting that these procedures have not yet been invoked, the Conference reaffirmed their present validity. The Conference calls on any State Party which identifies a problem arising in relation to the objective of, or in the application of the provisions of the Convention to use these procedures, if appropriate, to address and resolve it.
3. The Conference reaffirms that consultation and cooperation pursuant to this Article may also be undertaken through appropriate international procedures within the framework of the United Nations and in accordance with its Charter.
4. In accordance with the decision of the Third Review Conference, the Conference reviewed the effectiveness of

the confidence-building measures as agreed in the Final Declaration of the Third Review Conference. The Conference notes the continued importance of the confidence-building measures agreed upon at the Second and Third Review Conferences, as well as the modalities elaborated by the Ad Hoc Meeting of Scientific and Technical Experts from States Parties to the Convention, held in 1987.

5. The Conference notes the background information document prepared by the United Nations Secretary-General providing data on the participation of States Parties in the agreed confidence-building measures since the Third Review Conference. The Conference welcomes the exchange of information carried out under the confidence-building measures, and notes that this has contributed to enhancing transparency and building confidence. The Conference recognises that participation in the confidence-building measures since the last Review Conference has not been universal, and that not all responses have been prompt or complete. In this regard, the Conference also recognises the technical difficulties experienced by some States Parties with respect to preparing CBM responses. In this regard, the Conference urges all States Parties to complete full and timely declarations in the future. The Conference notes that the Ad Hoc Group of States Parties established by the Special Conference in 1994 is, as part of its continuing work, considering the incorporation of existing and further enhanced confidence-building and transparency measures, as appropriate, in a regime to strengthen the Convention.

6. The Conference stresses its determination to strengthen effectiveness and improve the implementation of the Convention, and its recognition that effective verification could reinforce the Convention.

7. In this regard, the Conference recalls that:

— The Third Review Conference established the Ad Hoc Group of Governmental Experts open to all States Parties to identify and examine potential verification measures from a scientific and technical standpoint.

— The Group held four sessions in 1992-1993 and circulated its report to all States Parties in September 1993.

— A Special Conference was held in September 1994 to consider the report, and decided to establish an Ad Hoc Group open to all States Parties. The Conference considered the work of the Ad Hoc Group under agenda item 12 and its conclusions are reflected in the section of this document entitled Consideration of the work of the Ad Hoc Group established by the Special Conference in 1994.

8. The Conference stresses the need for all States Parties to deal effectively with compliance issues. In this connection, the States Parties had agreed to provide a specific, timely response to any compliance concern alleging a breach of their obligations under the Convention. Such responses should be submitted in accordance with the procedures agreed upon by the Second Review Conference and further developed by the Third Review Conference. The Conference reiterates its request that information on such efforts be provided to the Review Conferences.

ARTICLE VI

1. The Conference notes that the provisions of this Article have not been invoked.

2. The Conference reaffirms the importance of Article VI, which, in addition to the procedures contained in Article V, provides that any State Party which finds that any other State Party is acting in breach of its obligations under the

Convention may lodge a complaint with the United Nations Security Council. The Conference notes that the provisions of Article VI will be taken into account, as appropriate, for any future verification regime resulting from the consideration by the Ad Hoc Group of a system of measures to promote compliance with the Convention. The Conference emphasizes the provision of Article VI that such a complaint should include all possible evidence confirming its validity. It stresses that, as in the case of the implementation of all the provisions and procedures set forth in the Convention, the procedures foreseen in Article VI should be implemented in good faith within the scope of the Convention.

3. The Conference invites the Security Council to consider immediately any complaint lodged under Article VI and to initiate any measures it considers necessary for the investigation of the complaint in accordance with the Charter. The Conference reaffirms the undertaking of each State Party to cooperate in carrying out any investigations which the Security Council may initiate.

4. The Conference recalls, in this context, United Nations Security Council resolution 620 (1988), which at the time encouraged the United Nations Secretary-General to carry out prompt investigations, in response to allegations brought to its attention by any Member State concerning the possible use of chemical and bacteriological (biological) or toxin weapons that could entail a violation of the 1925 Geneva Protocol or of any other applicable rule of international treaty or customary law. The Conference also recalls the technical guidelines and procedures contained in Annex I of United Nations Document A/44/561 to guide the United Nations Secretary-General on the timely and efficient investigation of reports of the possible use of such weapons. The States Parties reaffirm their agreement to consult, at the request of any State Party, regarding allegations of use or threat of use of bacteriological

(biological) or toxin weapons and to cooperate fully with the United Nations Secretary-General in carrying out such investigations. The Conference stresses that in the case of alleged use the United Nations is called upon to take appropriate measures expeditiously, which could include a request to the Security Council to consider action in accordance with the Charter.

5. The Conference invites the Security Council to inform each State Party of the results of any investigation initiated under Article VI and to consider promptly any appropriate further action which may be necessary.
6. The Conference notes that the procedure outlined in this Article is without prejudice to the prerogative of the States Parties to the Convention to consider jointly the cases of alleged non-compliance with the provisions of the Convention and to make appropriate decisions in accordance with the Charter of the United Nations and applicable rules of international law.
7. The Conference notes that provisions for investigating alleged breaches of the Convention, including measures for the investigation of alleged use of biological and toxin weapons, continue to be considered by the Ad Hoc Group of States Parties, in accordance with its mandate.

ARTICLE VII

1. The Conference notes with satisfaction that these provisions have not been invoked.
2. The Conference reaffirms the undertaking made by each State Party to provide or support assistance in accordance with the Charter of the United Nations to any Party to the Convention which so requests, if the Security Council decides that such Party has been exposed to danger as a result of violation of the Convention.

3. The Conference takes note of desires expressed that, should a request for assistance be made, it be promptly considered and an appropriate response provided. In this context, pending consideration of a decision by the Security Council, timely emergency assistance could be provided by States Parties if requested.
4. The Conference takes note of the proposal that the Ad Hoc Group might need to discuss the detailed procedure for assistance in order to ensure that timely emergency assistance would be provided by States Parties if requested.
5. The Conference considers that in the event that this Article might be invoked, the United Nations, with the help of appropriate intergovernmental organisations such as the World Health Organisation (WHO), could play a coordinating role.

ARTICLE VIII

1. The Conference reaffirms the importance of Article VIII and stresses the importance of the Protocol for the Prohibition of the Use in War of Asphyxiating, Poisonous or Other Gases, and of Bacteriological Methods of Warfare, signed at Geneva on 17 June 1925.
2. The Conference acknowledges that the 1925 Geneva Protocol, by prohibiting the use of bacteriological methods of warfare, and the Biological and Toxin Weapons Convention complement each other.
3. The Conference reaffirms that nothing contained in the Biological and Toxin Weapons Convention shall be interpreted as in any way limiting or detracting from the obligations assumed by any State under the Protocol for the Prohibition of the Use in War of Asphyxiating, Poisonous or Other Gases, and of Bacteriological Methods of Warfare.

4. Noting the actions in support of the Protocol taken by the Security Council and General Assembly of the United Nations, through Security Council resolution 620 (1988) and General Assembly resolutions 41/58 C, 42/37 C, 43/74 A, 44/115 B and 45/57 C and recalling the solemn reaffirmation of the prohibition as established in the Protocol, issued by the Conference of the States Parties to the 1925 Geneva Protocol and other interested States held in Paris from 7 to 11 January 1989, the Conference appeals to all States Parties to the Geneva Protocol to fulfil their obligations assumed under the Protocol and urges all States not yet Parties to the 1925 Geneva Protocol to accede to it without delay.

5. The Conference stresses the importance of the withdrawal of all reservations to the 1925 Geneva Protocol related to the Biological and Toxin Weapons Convention.

6. The Conference welcomes the actions which States Parties have taken to withdraw their reservations to the 1925 Geneva Protocol related to the Biological and Toxin Weapons Convention, and calls upon those States Parties that continue to maintain pertinent reservations to the 1925 Geneva Protocol to withdraw those reservations, and to notify the Depositary of the 1925 Geneva Protocol of their withdrawals without delay.

7. The Conference notes that reservations concerning retaliation, through the use of any of the objects prohibited by the Biological and Toxin Weapons Convention, even conditional, are totally incompatible with the absolute and universal prohibition of the development, production, stockpiling, acquisition and retention of bacteriological (biological) and toxin weapons, with the aim to exclude completely and forever the possibility of their use.

ARTICLE IX

1. The Conference reaffirms that Article IX identifies the recognized objective of effective prohibition of chemical weapons. The Conference welcomes conclusion of the Convention on the Prohibition of the Development, Production, Stockpiling and Use of Chemical Weapons and on Their Destruction, which was opened for signature on 13-15 January 1993 in Paris.
2. The Conference welcomes the fact that sixty-five instruments of ratification have now been deposited, and that the Convention will therefore enter into force on 29 April 1997.
3. The Conference stresses the importance to the Convention that all possessors of chemical weapons, chemical weapons production facilities or chemical weapons development facilities should be among the original parties to the Convention and, in this context, the importance of the United States of America and the Russian Federation, having declared possession of chemical weapons, being among the original States Parties to the Convention.
4. The Conference calls upon all States that have not yet done so to sign and/or ratify the Convention without delay.
5. The Conference notes that the Preparatory Commission for the Organisation for the Prohibition of Chemical Weapons, at its fourteenth session (22-26 July 1996) entrusted the Chairman of the Commission, in close consultation with its member States, with the task of convening, as necessitated by circumstances in connection with the occurrence of the trigger point, a meeting of the Commission to provide appropriate guidance.

ARTICLE X

1. The Conference once more emphasizes the increasing

importance of the provisions of Article X, especially in the light of recent scientific and technological developments in the field of biotechnology, bacteriological (biological) agents and toxins with peaceful applications, which have vastly increased the potential for cooperation between States to help promote economic and social development, and scientific and technological progress, particularly in the developing countries, in conformity with their interests, needs and priorities.

2. The Conference, while acknowledging what has already been done towards this end, notes with concern the increasing gap between the developed and the developing countries in the field of biotechnology, genetic engineering, microbiology and other related areas. The Conference urges all States Parties actively to continue to promote international cooperation and exchange with States Parties in the peaceful uses of biotechnology, and urges all States Parties possessing advanced biotechnology to adopt positive measures to promote technology transfer and international cooperation on an equal and non-discriminatory basis, in particular with the developing countries, for the benefit of all mankind. At the same time, the Conference stresses that measures to implement Article X need to be consistent with the objectives and provisions of the Convention.

3. The Conference recalls that the States Parties have a legal obligation to facilitate and have the right to participate in the fullest possible exchange of equipment, materials and scientific and technological information for the use of bacteriological (biological) agents and toxins for peaceful purposes and not to hamper the economic and technological development of States Parties.

4. The Conference emphasizes that States Parties should not use the provisions of the Convention to impose restrictions and/or limitations on transfers for purposes consistent with the objectives and provisions of the Convention of

scientific knowledge, technology, equipment and materials.

5. The Conference notes that existing institutional ways and means of ensuring multilateral cooperation between the developed and developing countries would need to be developed further in order to promote international cooperation in peaceful activities in such areas as medicine, public health and agriculture.
6. The Conference reiterates its call upon the Secretary-General of the United Nations to propose for inclusion on the agenda of a relevant United Nations body, before the next Review Conference, a discussion and examination of the means of improving institutional mechanisms in order to facilitate the fullest possible exchange of equipment, materials and scientific and technological information regarding the use of bacteriological (biological) agents and toxins for peaceful purposes.
7. The Conference recommends that invitations to participate in this discussion and examination should be extended to all States Parties, whether or not they are members of the United Nations or concerned specialised agencies.
8. The Conference, at the same time, notes that the Ad Hoc Group of States Parties was mandated by the Special Conference in September 1994 to consider specific measures designed to ensure effective and full implementation of Article X, which also avoid any restrictions incompatible with the obligations undertaken under the Convention, emphasizing that the provisions of the Convention should not be used to impose restrictions and/or limitations on the transfer for purposes consistent with the objectives and the provisions of the Convention of scientific knowledge, technology, equipment and materials.
9. The Conference takes note of the significant steps forward in promoting cooperation in the biological field taken by

the United Nations Conference on Environment and Development held in Rio de Janeiro, Brazil, in 1992, including the adoption of Agenda 21 and the Rio Declaration, and by the Convention on Biological Diversity, and underlines their importance in the context of Article X implementation.

10. The Conference shares the worldwide concern about new, emerging and re-emerging infectious diseases and considers that the international response to them offers opportunities for increased cooperation in the context of Article X application and of strengthening the Convention. The Conference welcomes the efforts to establish a system of global monitoring of disease and encourages States Parties to support the World Health Organization, including its relevant newly established division, the FAO and the OIE, in these efforts directed at assisting Member States to strengthen national and local programmes of surveillance for infectious diseases and improve early notification, surveillance, control and response capabilities.

11. The Conference urges the use of existing institutional means within the United Nations system and the full utilization of the possibilities provided by the specialised agencies and other international organisations, and considers that the implementation of Article X could be enhanced through greater coordination among international cooperation programmes in the biological field for peaceful purposes conducted by States Parties, specialised agencies and other international organisations.

12. The Conference urges States Parties, the United Nations and its specialised agencies to take further specific measures within their competence for the promotion of the fullest possible exchange of equipment, materials and scientific and technological information for the use of bacteriological (biological) agents and toxins for peaceful purposes and of international cooperation in this field.

Such measures could include, *inter alia:*

— Transfer and exchange of information concerning research programmes in biosciences and greater cooperation in international public health and disease control;

— Wider transfer and exchange of information, materials and equipment among States on a systematic and long-term basis;

— Active promotion of contacts between scientists and technical personnel on a reciprocal basis, in relevant fields;

— Increased technical cooperation and assistance, including training programmes to developing countries in the use of biosciences and genetic engineering for peaceful purposes through active association with United Nations institutions, including the International Centre for Genetic Engineering and Biotechnology (ICGEB);

— Facilitating the conclusion of bilateral, regional and multiregional agreements providing, on a mutually advantageous, equal and non-discriminatory basis, for their participation in the development and application of biotechnology;

— Encouraging the coordination of national and regional programmes and working out in an appropriate manner the ways and means of cooperation in this field;

— Cooperation in providing information on their national epidemiological surveillance and data reporting systems, and in providing assistance, on a bilateral level and/or in conjunction with WHO, FAO and OIE regarding epidemiological and epizootical surveillance, with a view to improvements in the identification and timely reporting of significant outbreaks of human and animal diseases;

— The promotion of programmes for the exchange and training of scientists and experts, and the exchange of scientific and technical information in the biological field between developed and developing countries.

13. The Conference considers that a worldwide data bank might be a suitable way of facilitating the flow of information in the field of genetic engineering, biotechnology and other scientific developments. In this context, the Conference underlines the importance of monitoring all related developments in the field of frontier science and high technology in the areas relevant to the Convention.

14. The Conference requests the Secretary-General to collate on an annual basis, and for the information of States Parties, reports on how this article is being implemented.

15. The Conference welcomes the information provided by a number of States Parties on the cooperative measures they have undertaken towards fulfilling their Article X obligations and encourages States Parties in a position to do so to provide such information.

16. The Conference welcomes efforts to elaborate an international programme of vaccine development for the prevention of diseases which would involve the scientific and technical personnel from developing countries that are States Parties to the Convention. The Conference recognises that such a programme will not only enhance peaceful international cooperation in biotechnology but also contribute to improving health care in developing countries, assist in establishing systems for worldwide monitoring of communicable diseases, and provide transparency in accordance with the Convention.

17. The Conference calls upon all States Parties in a position to do so to fully cooperate with the developing States Parties to the Convention in the area of promotion and financing the establishment of vaccine production facilities. The Conference recommends further that the relevant multilateral organisations and world financial institutions provide assistance for establishment and promotion of vaccine production projects in these countries.

ARTICLE XI

1. The Conference notes that the Islamic Republic of Iran has formally presented a proposal to amend Article I and the title of the Convention to include explicitly the prohibition of use of biological weapons.
2. The Conference notes that the Depositaries are notifying all States Parties of the proposal. The Conference encourages all States Parties to convey their views to the Depositaries on whether the Convention needs to be amended to make clear explicitly that the use of biological weapons is effectively prohibited.
3. The Conference requests the Depositaries to take such measures as may be requested by a majority of States Parties, including the option of convening a conference open to all States Parties to the Convention at the earliest appropriate opportunity to take a decision on the proposal, should a majority of the States Parties so decide.
4. The Conference meanwhile reaffirms the importance of Article XI. In this context the Conference underlines that the provisions of Article XI should in principle be implemented in such a way as not to affect the universality of the Convention.

ARTICLE XII

1. The Conference decides that a Fifth Review Conference shall be held in Geneva at the request of the majority of States Parties, or in any case, not later than 2001.
2. The Conference decides that the Fifth Review Conference shall consider, *inter alia*,

— The impact of scientific and technological developments relating to the Convention;

— The relevance of the provisions of, and the implementation of the Chemical Weapons Convention on the effective implementation of the Biological and Toxin Weapons Convention, duly taking into account the degree of universality attained by such conventions at the time of the Fifth Review Conference;

— The effectiveness of confidence-building measures as agreed at the Second and Third Review Conferences;

— The conclusions of a Special Conference, to which the Ad Hoc Group shall submit its report, including a legally-binding instrument to strengthen the Biological and Toxin Weapons Convention, which shall be adopted by consensus, to be held as soon as possible before the commencement of the Fifth Review Conference; and further action as appropriate;

— The requirement for, and the operation of, the requested allocation by the United Nations Secretary-General of staff resources and other requirements to assist the effective implementation of the relevant decisions of the Fourth Review Conference;

3. The Review Conference recommends that conferences of States Parties to review the operation of the Convention should be held at least every five years.

ARTICLE XIII

1. The Conference notes the provisions of Article XIII and, while emphasizing that the Convention is of unlimited duration and applies at all times, expresses its satisfaction that no State Party to the Convention has exercised its right to withdraw from the Convention.

ARTICLE XIV

1. The Conference notes with satisfaction that a number of States have acceded to the Convention since the Third Review Conference.

2. The Convention calls upon States which have not yet ratified or acceded to the Convention to do so without delay and upon those States which have not signed the Convention to join the States Parties thereto, thus contributing to the achievement of universal adherence to the Convention.
3. In this connection, the Conference requests States Parties to encourage wider adherence to the Convention.
4. The Conference particularly welcomes regional initiatives that would lead to wider accession to the Convention.
5. The Fourth Review Conference appeals to those States Parties to the Biological and Toxin Weapons Convention which have taken part in the Conference to participate in the implementation of provisions contained in the Final Declaration of this Conference. The Conference also appeals to all States Parties to participate actively in the Ad Hoc Group of States Parties, with a view to the early completion of its work to strengthen the Convention.

ARTICLE XV

The Conference notes the importance of this Article as well as the importance of the legal status of the languages of the Convention and United Nations system in the work of the Ad Hoc Group established by the Special Conference in 1994.

Consideration of the Work of the Ad Hoc Group Established by the Special Conference in 1994

The Conference welcomes the report on the progress of the Ad Hoc Group as contained in BWC/AD HOC GROUP/32 and notes in particular the following:

— The Special Conference of the States Parties to the Convention on the Prohibition of the Development,

Production and Stockpiling of Bacteriological (Biological) and Toxin Weapons and on Their Destruction (September 1994) agreed to establish an Ad Hoc Group open to all States Parties to consider appropriate measures, including possible verification measures, and draft proposals to strengthen the Convention.

— Since its establishment, the Ad Hoc Group has held one short organizational session and four substantive sessions of a duration of two weeks each.

— In accordance with its mandate, as contained in the Final Report of the Special Conference (BBC/SPCONF/1), the Ad Hoc Group has been considering appropriate measures, including possible verification measures, to strengthen the Convention. Where relevant, consideration of issues has sought to build on the considerable body of technical work connected with strengthening the Biological and Toxin Weapons Convention regime undertaken by the Ad Hoc Group of Technical Experts to Identify and Examine Potential Verification Measures from a Scientific and Technical Standpoint (VEREX) in 1992 and 1993.

— The Ad Hoc Group has made significant progress towards fulfilling the mandate given by the Special Conference, including by identifying a preliminary framework and elaborating potential basic elements of a legally-binding instrument to strengthen the Convention.

— Nevertheless, the Ad Hoc Group was not able to complete its work and submit its report including a draft of the future legally-binding instrument to the States Parties for consideration at the Fourth Review Conference. In this context it is noted that the cumulative period allocated to substantive negotiations in the Ad Hoc Group has been eight weeks.

The Conference welcomes the decision of the Ad Hoc Group, in order to fulfil its mandate, to intensify its work with a view to completing it as soon as possible before the commencement of the Fifth Review Conference and submit its report, which shall be adopted by consensus, to the States Parties, to be considered at a Special Conference. The Conference encourages the Ad Hoc Group to review its method of work and to move to a negotiating format in order to fulfil its mandate.

The Conference notes that the Ad Hoc Group is considering, as part of its continuing work, definitions of terms and objective criteria, such as lists of bacteriological (biological) agents and toxins, their threshold quantities, as well as equipment and types of activities, where relevant for specific measures designed to strengthen the Convention.

Bibliography

Abramova, F.A.N., Grinberg, L.M., Yampolskaya, O.V., Walker, D.H., "Pathology of inhalational anthrax in 42 cases from the Sverdlovsk outbreak of 1979", *Proc. Natl. Acad. Sci.,* 1993.

Acklund, J. R., Worswick, D. A., Marmion, B. P., Vaccine prophylaxis of Q fever, *Med., J. Aust,* 1994.

Ad Hoc Group of Governmental Experts to Identify and Examine Potential Verification Measures From a Scientific and Technical Standpoint, Report. Geneva, Switzerland: United Nations, 1993.

Arita, I., "Virological evidence for the success of the smallpox eradication programme", *Nature*, 1979.

Arms Control and Disarmament Agency, *Signatories and Ratifications of the Biological and Toxin Weapons Convention,* Available at: http://www.stimson.org/ cwc/bwcsigs.htm. Accessed February 24, 1997.

Ban, J., 2000, "Agricultural biological warfare: An overview", *The Arena,* Number 9, June 2000, Washington: Chemical and Biological Arms Control Institute, 8 pp.

Bamburg, J.R., Marasas WFO, Riggs, N.V., Smalley, E.B., Strong, F.M., "Toxic spiroepoxy compounds from fusaria and other hyphomycetes", *Biotechnol, Bioeng.*, 1968.

Bauer, D.J., St. Vincent L., Kempe C.H., Downie, A.W., "Prophylactic treatment of smallpox contacts with N-methylisatin-thiosemicarbazone" (compound 33T57, Marboran), *Lancet*, 1963.

____________, Prophylaxis of smallpox with methisazone, *Am. J. Epidemiol*, 1969.

Baum A., "Stress, intrusive imagery, and chronic distress", *Health Psychol*, 1990;9:653-675.

Baxby, D., "Poxviruses", In Belshe RB, ed., *Textbook of Human Virology*, Littleton, Mass: PSG Publishing, Co; 1984.

Bell, J.F., Lackman, D.B., Meis A., Hadlow W.J., Recurrent Reaction at Site of Q Fever Vaccination in a Sensitized *Person*, *Mil.Med.* 1964.

Becket, B., *Weapons of Tomorrow*, New York, NY: Plenum Press, 1983.

Benenson, A.S., *Q Fever Vaccine*, In Smadel, J.E., ed., *Symposium on Q Fever by the Committee on Rickettsial Diseases*, Washington, DC: Armed Forces Epidemiology Board; 1959.

Blackwill, R.D., *Arms Control and the US-Russian Relationship: Problems, Prospects and Prescriptions.* New York, NY: Council on Foreign Relations, 1996:65-66.

Brachman, P.S., "Inhalation anthrax", *Ann NY Acad. Sci.*, 1980.

Brophy L, Miles, W.D., Cochrane RC. *The Chemical Warfare Service: From Laboratory to Field.* Washington, DC: US Army, 1959.

Brouqui, P.B., Dupont, H.T., Drancourt, M., et al., Chronic Q Fever, *Arch. Intern. Med.*, 1993.

Bryden, J., *Deadly Allies: Canada's Secret War, 1937-1947.* Toronto, Ontario: McClelland & Stewart Inc., 1989:256.

Butler, T., *Plague and Other Yersinia Infections*, New York, NY: Plenum Press; 1983.

Cavanaugh, D.C., Cadigan, F.C., Williams, J.E., Marshall, J.D., *General Medicine and Infectious Diseases*, In: Ognibene A.J., Barrett, O.N., eds., *Internal Medicine in Vietnam.* Washington, DC: Office of the Surgeon General and Centre of Military History; 1982.

Centers for Disease Control, "Management of patients with suspected viral hemorrhagic fever", *MMWR Morb. Mortal. Wkly. Rep.*, 1988;37 (suppl): 1-16.

Chan, R., Hardiman, R.P., "Endocarditis caused by Brucella melitensis", *Med. J.Aust.*, 1993.

Chaowagul, W., "Melioidosis: a treatment challenge", *Scand. J. Infect. Dis.Suppl.* 1996;101:14-16.

Christopher, G.N., Cieslak, T.J., Pavlin, J.A., Eitzen, E.M., "Biological Warfare: a Historical Perspective", *JAMA,* 1997, 278:412-417.

Cochrane, R.C., *Biological warfare research in the United States*, In: *History of the Chemical Warfare Service in World War II*, Vol II. Frederick, Md: Historical Section, Plans, Training and Intelligence Division, Office of Chief, Chemical Corps, US Dept of the Army; 1947.

Cole, L.A., "The specter of biological weapons", *Sci. Am.*, 1996.

Crosby, E., Llosa, L., Miro, Q.M., Carrillo C., Gotuzzo E., "Hematologic changes in Brucellosis", *J.Infect. Dis.*, 1984.

Danzig, R., Berkowsky, P.B., "Why should we be concerned about biological warfare?", *J. Am. Med. Assoc.*, 1997; 278:431-443.

Daplan, D.E., Marshall A., *The Cult at the End of the World*, New York, NY: Crown Publishing Group, 1996.

Defense Nuclear Agency (DNA) Biological Weapons Proliferation. *Global Proliferation: Dynamics, Acquisition Strategies and Response.* Alexandria, Va: Defense Nuclear Agency; 1994, 4:10.

Derbes, V.J., *De Mussis and the Great Plague of 1348: A Forgotten Episode of Bacteriological War*, JAMA, 1966.

Derrick, E.H., "The Course of Infection with Coxiella burnetii", *Med J.Aust.*, 1973.

Downie, A.W., Meiklejohn, M., St .Vincent, L., Rao, A.R., Sundara Babu, B.V., Kempe, C.H., "The recovery of smallpox from patients and their environment in a smallpox hospital", *Bull. World Health Organ*, 1965.

Dupuis, G., Petite J., Olivier, P., Vouilloz, M., "An important outbreak of human Q fever in a Swiss alpine valley", *Int J.Epidemiol*, 1987.

Eitzen, E.M., *Use of biological weapons*, In Sidell, F.R., Takafuji, E.T., Franz, D.R., eds., *Medical Aspects of Chemical and Biological Warfare*, Falls Church, Va: Office of the Surgeon General, US Dept of the Army; 1997.

Ekeus, R., *Memorandum to the Biological Weapons Convention Fourth Review Conference.* New York, NY: United Nations, November 20, 1996.

Enria, D., Maiztegui, J.I., "Antiviral treatment of Argentine Hemorrhagic Fever", *Antiviral Res.*, 1994.

Evans, A.C., "Comments on the early history of human brucellosis", In Larson CH, Soule MH, eds., *Brucellosis*, Baltimore, Md: Waverly Press; 1950.

Evans, M.E., Friedlander, A.M., *Tularemia*, In Zajtchuk R, ed., *Textbook of Military Medicine: Medical Aspects of Chemical and Biological Warfare*, Washington, DC: US Dept of the Army, The Surgeon General, and the Borden Institute; 1997.

Fenner, F., Henderson, D.A., Arita, I., Jezek, Z., Ladnyi, I.D., *Smallpox and Its Eradication*, Geneva, Switzerland: World Health Organisation; 1988.

Ferrante, M. A, and Dolan M.J., "Q fever meningo Encephalitis in a soldier returning from the Persian Gulf War", *Clin. Infect. Dis.*, 1993.

Franck, P.T., Johnson, K.M., "An outbreak of Venezuelan encephalitis in man in the Panama Canal Zone", *Am. J.Trop. Med. Hyg.*, 1970.

Franz, D.R., Pitt, L.M., Clayton, M.A., Hanes, M.A., Rose, K.J., "Efficacy of prophylactic and therapeutic administration of antitoxin for inhalation botulism", In Das Gupta B, ed., *Botulinum and Tetanus Neurotoxins and Biomedical Aspects.* New York, NY: Plenum Press, 1993.

Fraser, J.D., "High-affinity binding of staphylococcal enterotoxins A and B to HLA-DR", *Nature*, 1989.

Friedlander, A.M., "Anthrax", In Zajtchuk R., ed., *Textbook of Military Medicine: Medical Aspects of Chemical and Biological Warfare.* Washington, DC: US Dept. of the Army, Surgeon General, and the Borden Institute, 1997.

Fullerton, C.S., Ursano, R.J., Kao, T., Bhartiya, V., "The chemical and biological warfare environment psychological responses and social support in a high-stress environment", *J. Appl. Soc. Psychol*, 1992;22: 1608-1623.

Geissler E., *Biological and Toxin Weapons Today*, New York, NY: Oxford University Press Inc., 1986.

Gertz, B., "Defecting Russian scientist revealed biological arms effort". *Washington Times,* July 4, 1992:A4.

Goldfield, M., Welsh, J.N., Taylor, B.F., "The 1959 outbreak of eastern encephalitis in New Jersey", *Am.. J. Epidemiol,* 1968.

Goldstein, L., "Saddam's Biological Warfare Card" *Washington Post*, October 11, 1996.

Gotuzzo, E., Carrillo, C., Guerra, J., Llosa, L., "An evaluation of diagnostic methods for brucellosis", *J.Infect. Dis.*, 1986.

Gordon, J. C., and S., Bech-Nielsen, 1986, "Biological terrorism: a direct threat to our livestock industry", *Military Medicine,* 151, 357-363.

Grimont, F., Verger, J.M., Cornelis, P., et al., "Molecular typing of Brucella with cloned DNA probes", *Res Microbiol.*, 1992.

Haddix, A.C., Teutsch, S.M., Shaffer, P.A., Dunet, D.O., eds., *Prevention Effectiveness: A Guide to Decision Analysis and Economic Evaluation*, New York: Oxford University Press, 1996.

Harris, S.H., *Factories of Death*, New York, NY: Routledge, 1994.

Harris, S., *Japanese Biological Warfare Research on Humans: A Case Study of Microbiology and Ethics*, Ann NY Acad Sci., 1992.

Hayes, R.O., *Eastern and western encephalitis*, In Beran, G.W,, ed., *Handbook Series in Zoonoses: Viral Zoonoses*, I. Boca Raton, Fla: CRC Press, 1981.

Health Aspects of Chemical and Biological Weapons: Report of a WHO Group of Consultants, Geneva, Switzerland: World Health Organisation, 1970.

Hinman, A.R., McGowan, J.E., Henderson, B.E., "Venezuelan equine encephalomyelitis", *Am. J.Epidemiol*, 1971.

Holum, J.D., *Remarks for the Fourth Review Conference of the Biological Weapons Convention.* Geneva, Switzerland: US Arms Control and Disarmament Agency, November 26, 1996.

Horgan, E.S., Ali Haseeb, M., "Cross immunity experiments in monkey between variola, alastrim, and vaccinia", *J.Hyg.,* 1939.

Horrock N., "The new terror fear: biological weapons: detecting an attack is just the first problem", *US News & World Report,* May 12, 1997:36

Huggins, J.W., "Prospects for treatment of viral hemorrhagic fevers with ribavirin, a broad-spectrum antiviral drug", *Rev Infect. Dis.,* 1989; 11:S750- S761.

Huxsoll, D.L., Patrick, W.C., Parrott, C.D., Veterinary services in biological disasters, *J.Am.Vet Med Assoc.*, 1987.

Ibrahim, A.I.A., Shetty, S.D., Saad, M, Bilal, N.E., "Genitourinary complications of brucellosis", *Br. Journal*, 1988.

Ibrahim, M.S., Esposito, J.J., Jarhling, P.B., Lofts. R.S., "The potential of 5 nuclease PCR for detecting a single-base polymorphism in orthopoxvirus", Mol. Cell Probes, 1997.

Jahrling, P.B., Frame, J.D., Rhoderick, J.B., MoNson, M.H., "Endemic Lassa fever in Liberia", *Trans R. Soc. Trop. Med. Hyg.*, 1985.

______________ , J., Swearengen, J.R., et al., "Passive immunisation of Ebola virus-infected cynomolgus monkeys with immunoglobulin from hyper-immunehorses", *Arch.Virol.* 1996; (suppl 11):135-140.

Janofsky, M., "Looking for motives in plague case", *New York Times,* May 24, 1995:A12.

______________ , "Filoviruses and arena viruses". In: Murray, P.R., Baron, E.J., Pfaller M.A., Tenover, F.C., Yolken, R.H., eds., *Manual of Clinical Microbiology,* 6th ed., Washington, DC: ASM Press; 1995.

Johnson, K.M., Martin, D.H., "Venezuelan equine encephalitis", *Adv. Vet. Sci. Comp. Med.,* 1974.

______________ , Wiebenga, N.H., Mackenzie, R.B., et al., "Virusisolations from human cases of hemorrhagic fever in Bolivia", *Proc Soc Exp Biol Med.*, 1965.

Kaplan, D.E., Marshall, A., *The Cult at the End of the World,* New York, NY: Crown Publishers Inc., 1996:55.

Kaufmann, A.F, Fox, M.D., Boyce, J.M., Anderson, D.C., Potter, M.E., Martone, W.J., et al., "Airborne spread of brucellosis", *Ann. NY. Acad. Sci.,* 1980;335:105-14.

Kupperman, R. H., Smith, D.M., "Coping with Biological Terrorism", In Roberts, B., ed. , *Biological Weapons: Weapons of the Future?* Washington, DC: Centre for Strategic and International Studies, 1993.

Lackman, D.B., Bell, E.J., Bell, J.F., Pickens, E.G., "Intradermal sensitivity testing in man with a purified vaccine for Q fever", *Am. J.Public Health*, 1962.

Lee, H.W., "Hemorrhagic fever with renal syndrome in Korea", *Rev. Infect. Dis.*, 1989.

Leon, C.A., Jaramillo, R., Martinez, S., et al., "Sequelae of Venezuelan equine encephalitis in humans: a four-year follow-up", *Int. J.Epidemiol.,* 1975.

Luzzi, G.A., Brindle, R., Sockett, P.N., Solera, J., Klenerman, P., Warrell, D.A., "Brucellosis", *Trans R. Soc. Trop. Med. Hyg.*, 1993.

Maiztegui, J., Feuillade, M., Briggiler, A., "Progressive extension of the endemic area and changing incidence of Argentine hemorrhagic fever", *Med. Microbiol Immunol.,* 1986.

Marmion, B.P., Ormsbee, R.A., Kyrkor, M., "Vaccine prophylaxis of abattoir-associated Q fever", *Epidemiol Infect.,* 1990.

Marrie, T.J., Langille, D., Papukna, V., Yates, L., "Truckin' pneumonia: an outbreak of Q fever in a truck repair plant", *Epidemiol Infect.*, 1989.

Martin, D.H., Eddy, G.A., Sudia, W.D., Reeves, W.C., Newhouse, V.F., Johnson, K.M., "An epidemiologic study of Venezuelan equine encephalomyelitis in Costa Rica, 1970, *Am. J.Epidemiol*, 1972.

McClain, D.J., Harrison, S., Yeager, C.L., et al., "Immunologic responses to vaccinia vaccines administered by different parenteral routes", *J.Infect. Dis.,* 1997.

McCormick, J.B., King, I.J., Webb, P.A., et al., Lassa fever: effective therapy with ribavirin", *N.Eng.l J. Med.*, 1986.

_______________ , Webb, P.A., Krebs, J.W., Johnson, K.M., Smith E., "A prospective study of epidemiology and ecology of Lassa fever", *J.Infect Dis.*, 1987.

McCrumb, F.R. Jr., "Aerosol infection of man with Pasteurella tularensis", *Bacteriol Rev.*, 1961.

McGovern, T.W., Friedlander, A.M., *Plague*, In Zajtchuk R, ed., *Textbook of Military Medicine: Medical Aspects of Chemical and Biological Warfare*, Washington, DC: US Dept. of the Army, Surgeon General, and the Borden Institute, 1997.

McKendrick, G.D.W.,Velayudhan, L., Kamalakshi, K., "Assessment of an isothiazole thiosemIcarbazone in the prophylaxis of contacts of variola major", *Lancet*, 1966.

McKinney, R.W., Berge, T.O., Sawyer, W.D., Tigertt, W.D., Crozier, D., "Use of an attenuated strain of Venezuelan equine encephalomyelitis virus for immunisation in man", *Am. J.Trop. Med. Hyg.*, 1963.

Merck, G.W., Fred, E.B., Baldwin, I.L., Sarles, W.B., *Implications of Biological Warfare: The US and UN Report Series No. 5.* Washington, DC: US Dept of State, 1946:65-71.

Meikeljohn, G., Kempe, C.H., Downie, A.W., Berge, T.O., St. Vincent, L., Rao, A.R., "Air sampling to recover variola virus in the environment of a smallpox hospital", *Bull. World Health Organ*, 1961.

Meyer, K.F., Cavanaugh, D.C., Bartelloni, P.J., Marshall, J.D. Jr., "Plague immunization: Past and present trends", *J. Infect. Dis.*, 1974;129(suppl):S13-S18.

Messelson, M., Guillemin, J., Hugh-Jones M., Langmuir, A., Popova, I., Shelokov A., et al., "The Sverdlosvsk anthrax outbreak of 1979", *Science,* 1994;266:1202-8.

Miller, R.P., Bates, J.H., "Pleuropulmonary tularemia", *Am. Rev. Respir. Dis.*, 1969.

Mitra, A.C., Sarkar, J.K., Mukherjee, M.K, "Virus content of smallpox scabs", *Bull. World Health Organ*, 1974.

Mollick, J. A., Cook, R.G., Rich, R.R., "Class II MHC molecules are specific receptors for staphylococcal enterotoxin A", *Science*, 1989.

Neff, J.M., "Vaccinia virus" (cowpox), In Mandell, G.L., Bennett, J.E., Dolin, R., eds., *Principles and Practice of Infectious Diseases*, New York, NY: Churchill Living-stone Inc; 1995.

Olle-Goig, J.E., Canela-Soler, J., "An outbreak of Brucella melitensis infection by airborne transmission among laboratory workers", *Am. J. Public. Health,* 1987;77:335-8.

Olson, K.B., "Biological weapons and the terror in Japan", *Terrorism*, August 1997;1:1.

Parkman, F., *The Conspiracy of Pontiac and the Indian War after the Conquest of Canada*, Boston, Mass: Little Brown & Co Inc., 1901.

Penn, R.L., *Francisella tularensis (tularemia)*, In Mandell, G.A., Bennett, J.E., Dolen, R., eds., *Principles and Practice of Infectious Diseases*, New York, NY: Churchill Livingstone Inc; 1995.

Perry, R.D., Fetherston, J.D., "Yersinia pestis:etiologic agent of plague", *Clin.Microbiol. Rev.*, 1997;10:35-66.

Pile, J.C., Malone, J.D., Eitzen, E.M., Jr, Friedlander, A.M., "Anthrax as a potential biological warfare agent", *Ann. Intern. Med.*, 1998;158:429-434.

Report of the Investigation Into the Cause of the 1978 Birmingham Smallpox Occurrence, London, England: Her Majesty's Stationery Office, 1980.

Richmond, J.Y., McKinney, R.W., *Biosafety in Microbiological and Biomedical Laboratories*, Washington, DC: US Dept of Health and Human Services; 1993, HHS publication CDC 93-8395.

Ricketts, T.F., *The Diagnosis of Smallpox*, London, England: Cassell; 1908.

Robertson, A. G., Robertson, L. J., *From Asps to Allegations: Biological Warfare in History*, Mil Med., 1995.

Roberts, B., "New Challenges and New Policy Priorities for the 1990s, In Biologic Weapons: Weapons of the Future", Washington: Center for Strategic and International Studies, 1993.

Rogers, P. S., Whitby and M., Dando, "Biological warfare against crops", *Scientific American*, 1999, June, pp. 70-75.

Rolicka, M., *New Studies Disputing Allegations of Bacteriological Warfare during the Korean War*, Mil Med., 1995.

Russell, P.K., "Biologic terrorism: responding to the threat", *Emerg Infect. Dis.* [serial online], 1997.

Salas, R., De Manzione, N., Tesh, R. B., et al., "Venezuelan haemorrhagic fever", *Lancet*, 1991

Sarkar, J.K., Mitra, A.C., Mukherjee, M.K., De, S.K., Mazumdar, D.G., "Virus excretion in smallpox", *Bull. World Health Organ,* 1973.

Sawyer, W.D., Dangerfield, H.G., Hogge, A.L., Crozier, D., "Antibiotic prophylaxis and therapy of airborne tularemia", *Bacteriolical Reviews,* 1966;30:542-8.

Schaap, B., *US Biological Warfare: The 1981 Cuban Dengue Epidemic, Covert Action*, 1982.

Sciolino E., "Iraqis could pose a threat soon, CIA chief says", *New York Times International,* January 16, 1992:A9.

Simon, J.D., "Biological Terrorism: Preparing to Meet the Threat", *JAMA*, 1997; 278:428-430.

Sims, N.A., *The Diplomacy of Biological Disarmament*, New York, NY: Plenum Press, 1983.

Spertzel R., *Sampling and Analysis as a Monitoring Tool,* New York, NY: UN Special Commission, October 3, 1996:7.

Star, B., Iraq reveals astartling rangeof toxin agents. *Jane's Defence, Weekly,* November, 11, 1995:4.

Staszkiewicz, J., Lewis, C.M., Colville, J., Zervos, M., Band, J., "Outbreak of Brucella melitensis among microbiology laboratory workers in a community hospital", *J. Clin. Microbial,* 1991, 29:287-90.

Stearn, E.W., Stearn, A.E., *The Effect of Smallpox on the Destiny of the Amerindian*, Boston, Mass: Bruce Humphries, 1945.

Stockholm International Peace Research Institute (SPIRI), *The Rise of CB Weapons: The Problem of Chemical and Biological Warfare*, New York, NY: Humanities Press, 1971, 1.

Stubbs, M., *Has the West an Achilles Heel: Possibilities of Biological Weapons*, NATO's Fifteen Nations, June/July 1962.

Tigertt, W.D., Benenson, A.S., "Studies on Q fever in man", *Trans. Assoc. Am. Physcians*, 1956.

Tomlin, V.V., Berezhnai R.V., *Exposure of Criminal Activity of the Japanese Military Authorities Regarding Preparation for Biological Warfare*, Voen Med Zh., 1985.

Tucker, J.B., *"National health and medical services response to incidents of chemical and biological terrorism"*, *JAMA*. 1997, 278:362-368.

Uhaa, I.J., Fishbein, D.B., Olson, J.G., et al., "Evaluation of specificity of indirect enzyme-linked immunosorbent assay for diagnosis of human Q fever", *J. Clin, Microbiol,* 1994.

Ulrich, R.G., Sidell, S., Taylor, T.J., Wilhelmsen, C.L., Franz, D.R., *Staphylococcal enterotoxin B and related pyrogenic toxins,* In Zajtchuk, R, ed., *Textbook of Military Medicine: Medical Aspects of Chemical and Biological Warfare*, Washington, DC: USDept of the Army, The Surgeon General, and the Borden Institute, 1997.

Urban, M., "The Cold War's deadliest secret", *The Spectator Magazine,* January 23, 1993:9-10.

Ursano, R.J., Fullerton, C.S., Norwood, A.E., "Psychiatric dimensions of disaster: patient care, community consultation, and preventive medicine", *Harv. Rev. Psychiatry*, 1995;3:196-200.

US Arms Control and Disarmament Agency. *Arms and Control Disarmament Agreements: Texts and Histories of the Negotiations.* Washington, DC: US Arms Control and Disarmament Agency, 1996.

US Congress, *Biological Testing Involving Human Subjects by the Department of Defense*, 1977.

US Dept of the Army, *US Army Activity in the US Biological Warfare Programs*, Washington DC: US Dept of the Army, February 24, 1977.

Vorobyov, A., "Criterion rating as a measure of probable use of bio agents as biological weapons", *In Papers presented to the Working Group on Biological Weapons Control of the Committee on International Security and Arms Control*, US National Academy of Sciences, 1994 Apr; Washington.

Waag, D., Chulay, J., Marrie, T., England, M., Willaims, J., "Validation of an enzyme immunoassay for serodiagnosis of acute Q fever", *Eur J.Clin. Microbiol. Infect. Dis.,* 1995.

Weisaeth, L., "War-related psychopathology in Kuwait: an assessment of war-related mental health problems", In Fullerton, C.S., Ursano, R.J., eds.,*Posttraumatic Stress Disorder: Acute and Long-Term Responses to Trauma and Disaster*, Washington, DC: American Psychiatric Press; 1997:91- 122.

Wehrle, P.F., Posch, J., Richter, K.H., et al., "An airborne outbreak of smallpox in a German hospital and its significance with respect to other recent outbreaks in Europe", *Bull. World Health Organ*, 1970.

Wheelis, M., 1999, "Biological Sabotage in World War", pp. 35-62 in E. Geissler and J. E. V. C. Moon (eds.) *Biological and Toxin Weapons: Research, Development and Use from the Middle Ages to 1945*, Oxford: Oxford University Press.

Whitby, S., and Rogers, P., 1997, "Anti-crop biological warfare-implications of the Iraqi and US programmes", *Defense Analysis,* 13, 303-318.

Williams P., Wallace, D., *Unit 731: Japan's Secret Biological Warfare in World War II,* New York, NY: Free Press, 1989:28.

World Health Organisation/International Study Team, Ebola haemorrhagic fever in Zaire, 1976, *Bull. World Health Organ*, 1978.

WHO Group of Consultants, *Health Aspects of Chemical and Biological Weapons*, Geneva, Switzerland: World Health Organisation, 1970.

Yu, V.L., *Serratia marcescens: Historical Perspective and Clinical Review*, N Engl J Med., 1979.

Zilinskas, R.A., *Iraq's Biological Weapons: The Past as Future*?, JAMA, 1997, 278:418-424.

Index